UNRAVELED:

A Story of
Heartache and Hope

by

ANN TAYLOR LAVERTY

All the events and incidents in this book are true. Some names have been changed at the request of the individuals or facilities. Otherwise all names are real and have been used with the permission of those individuals.

For Matt
I will never give up on you.

Foreword

When Ann Taylor Laverty asked me to read the rough draft of *Unraveled: A Story of Heartache and Hope*, I accepted, as I had a strong interest in the story and optimism that my input would be somewhat productive. After all, Ann is my sister, and Matt is my nephew. Although Ann and I e-mail or talk on the phone several times a week, the distance between our homes prevented me from being intimately involved and aware of the depth of this situation. As a result, when I read *Unraveled*, I was staggered and heartbroken by what their family was going through; their struggles went far beyond what I'd imagined. I was also astounded by the dynamics of how someone addicted to heroin impacts our society.

The story of Matt needs to be told. More important it needs to be heard—by addicts, families of addicts, parents, children, teachers, and all other members of a community. Ask yourself the questions I have asked myself. "If you knew heroin and other drugs were in the school where your seven-year-old, who had some social challenges, would be attending in four years, what would you do?" "What if your child is going to school there now?" "Do you even know the extent of drug usage in your schools? Do you know how to find out?" In trying to grasp the availability of these drugs, the strength of addiction, and how devastating addiction is to so many people, one can lay the foundation of hope that, with some proactivity, a person with an at-risk personality just won't cross that line.

Our leaders also need to read this book: local leaders, state leaders, and national leaders. Leaders in government, law enforcement, health care, education, religion, and other civic areas all have a role in how to create a system to deal with the wide array of problems and costs associated with the use of—and addiction to—illegal drugs. These include law-enforcement costs aimed at the prevention of smuggling drugs into the country, the distribution at the street level, and the investigation of crimes committed by users in order to procure more drugs. Costs to the victims of the crimes. Costs to the legal system. Costs realized by the medical community, including local emergency rooms and rehab facilities. Costs to the families. Clearly the various groups could work together in a much more efficient manner. Clearly the end goal of rehabilitating an addict is not being achieved with any rational degree of success. Clearly tax revenue is not being well spent, and we keep doing it over and over again. Clearly the leaders we elect are facing a huge challenge that we need them to fix. And clearly we as citizens must be involved directly if our skills are needed or indirectly as volunteers.

This book is a must read for everyone; it is truly one of those books "you can't put down." At times it will make you smile; at times it will make you cry; and at times it will make you shake your head. Most of all it will educate anyone who reads it and provide an angle no textbook can provide.

Steve Taylor
January 21, 2012

Introduction

This book started as a journal that I used to put my thoughts on paper and as a way to help me cope with the horror that our lives had become. I used it to keep myself somewhat sane, as well as to keep track of everything that was happening. I started this book in the midst of the story, in May 2010, when my son Matt entered rehab for the second time. I didn't know about his drug problem until he had been using heroin for about a year, and the way I found out left me numb. I couldn't process any of it for about another six months; during that time my husband Mike and I moved on autopilot. As I was ready to deal with the heartaches, and as I became aware of the lies, as they and Matt began to unravel, I worked backward, chronicling the history of his drug use and the beginning of his addiction. When *was* the beginning anyway?

I remember hearing Eric Clapton speak while he accepted an award for his song "Tears in Heaven," which he wrote after the death of his four-year-old son, Conor. He said, "I wrote this song to heal myself. It never occurred to me that people might like it." So, because of that statement, it does occur to me that people might want to hear my story—even need to hear it—although they may not particularly like it. I want others to know what my family and I are going through and help others feel they aren't alone. I don't have the answers, nor am I a doctor or a therapist. But maybe my story will offer some coping methods that others in my shoes hadn't considered. Maybe some addicts will read it, or people who are tempted and ready to give in to drug use, and they will see what addiction does to families. And maybe those families will understand a little better that this is an illness, a disease, and not something their child is doing to be rebellious.

Some things took longer for me to talk about, even if I was only "talking" on paper. Doing so put everything in perspective, as I looked back at events several months later, because I wasn't as emotionally wrecked as I was when everything happened. However, it also made me see how blind we were and are as parents, how easily we believed the lies and grasped at any excuse. There were so many times when Mike and I both said, "No, it's not drugs. We really believe it is… whatever." Because, as devastating as the "whatever" was, we thought it seemed more "fixable." But Matt is my child, and I can never love him conditionally; the horrid memories kept getting interrupted by happy memories of Matt's earlier days. I needed to remember the Matt before the addiction so that I didn't see just the addiction. These memories are what have given me hope throughout this journey, and I've interjected them throughout the story. Additionally I hope they will paint a picture for the reader of what a sweet kid Matt was and what a genuinely nice young man he is.

This is my healing process. There were so many times when my husband and I heard over the years, "You have so much on your plate" or "I don't know how you do it!" or "I don't understand why you've been dealt these cards." Well, those were the cards we were dealt, and all we can do is make the best of what we have. As I look around at friends, relatives, coworkers, and acquaintances, I see that almost all of them have some sort of tragic story in their lives. Right now I can't name anyone who seemingly has it all, who has everything they touch turn to gold. I've learned that money can buy creature comforts in life, but it can't buy good health. In some cases, such as having a drug addict in the family, money makes matters worse, as the family has money saved, invested, etc, and is there to be accessed. The criminal mind of an addict can certainly figure out how to access it. Certainly, all the money in the world can't "fix" the medical issues of my two disabled children, and although all the money in the world could help us afford the best rehabs in the world for my heroin-addicted son, only *he* can fix his problem. Can anyone even tell me which rehab facility is "the best" and why? What makes it "the best"? The fact that it's located on a tropical island? The fact that it serves gourmet meals? The fact that it has all the comforts of a resort spa? Ultimately none of these things will help. Our disabled children will never "get better." Their lives are in God's hands. The fate of my drug-addicted son is in God's hands too, but also in his own.

This book is for everyone: the addict, the parent, any relative or friend of an addict, anyone who wonders how a "good kid from a good family" can become a drug addict. Its message is hope; the goal is for people to see that one can live through the heartache and look toward a positive future. I also hope the reader will feel my emotions: the pain, the astonishment, the anger, the humor at times, the frustration, the heartache, and the hope.

Research has shown that teens have started to use drugs earlier and earlier and are experimenting with harder and harder drugs. Every parent should know that no child is immune to drug use. No parent should think that their child is "a really good kid" and that he or she never would do drugs.

It's so frustrating to watch what Matt is doing to himself and to know that we cannot stop it. I punish myself for falling for his lies, for being so naive, and for letting it all happen practically right in front of me. At the same time, I'm amazed at what an accomplished actor and liar he has become. He tells his counselors that he has a good relationship with me. I hope he really thinks that, although I'm sure part of that is the fact that he knows he can play me better than he can his dad. I'm in counseling myself, currently working on how to say no to Matt and stop enabling him. This addiction has been a struggle for us as a family and for everyone with whom we have come in contact since the beginning of 2009.

We have learned so much through all of this, and there is still so much that we don't know about our son, about drug abuse, about the mind of an addict, and about how to protect ourselves from him.

We can't get inside Matt's head, and so far neither can his counselors. Some get close, but something is buried deep inside him that no one can reach as of yet. Maybe it's a deep-seated fear or thought—something—that is locked inside of Matt. Maybe it's just his genetic and chemical makeup. I know there is no cure; he will be an addict for the rest of his life, though hopefully a *recovering* addict.

I hope we can say we are recovering parents as well.

For now, though, I know what I was born to do—why I was put here. I was meant to be the voice of my children. For my two physically and mentally disabled children, I was meant to be their voice, asking questions and talking to doctors, teachers, and other professionals, because my children can't express their needs and really don't know what their needs are. I was meant to be Matt's voice of reason, his conscience at times, his voice of hope, as well as the voice of hope for all families of addicts who also must endure this painful journey. I've been chronicling our journey in the hopes that I can share with others the knowledge that they are not alone.

This is a story that needs to be told.

Serenity Prayer

God grant me the serenity
to accept the things I cannot change;
courage to change the things I can;
and wisdom to know the difference.

*Although known most widely in its abbreviated form above,
the entire prayer reads as follows.*

Living one day at a time;
Enjoying one moment at a time;
Accepting hardships as the pathway to peace;
Taking, as He did, this sinful world
as it is, not as I would have it;
Trusting that He will make all things right
if I surrender to His Will;
That I may be reasonably happy in this life
and supremely happy with Him
Forever in the next.
Amen.

Twelve Steps of Narcotics Anonymous

1. We admitted that we were powerless over our addiction, that our lives had become unmanageable.
2. We came to believe that a Power greater than ourselves could restore us to sanity.
3. We made a decision to turn our will and our lives over to the care of God as we understood Him.
4. We made a searching and fearless moral inventory of ourselves.
5. We admitted to God, to ourselves, and to another human being the exact nature of our wrongs.
6. We were entirely ready to have God remove all these defects of character.
7. We humbly asked Him to remove our shortcomings.
8. We made a list of all persons we had harmed, and became willing to make amends to them all.
9. We made direct amends to such people wherever possible, except when to do so would injure them or others.
10. We continued to take personal inventory and when we were wrong promptly admitted it.
11. We sought through prayer and meditation to improve our conscious contact with God as we understood Him, praying only for knowledge of His will for us and the power to carry that out.
12. Having had a spiritual awakening as a result of these steps, we tried to carry this message to addicts, and to practice these principles in all our affairs.

("Twelve Steps" reprinted by permission of AA World Services, Inc.)

un·rav·el
to separate and clarify the elements of (something mysterious or baffling)

CHAPTER ONE
May, 2012

Our son Matt is a compulsive gambler. No, wait. That's not true. He's a heroin addict. Or maybe he's also a compulsive gambler. I know he's a compulsive liar. I'm so confused. But let me back up a bit.

We went through eleven months of lies—probably more like ten years of lies. But the *big lie* started in January 2009, when Matt announced to us that he had a gambling debt. One lie followed another: his secrecy, his avoiding us, his disappearing, the money he needed and the stories about why he needed the money. He admitted to being a compulsive gambler. He said he gambled online, at the casinos, through a bookie—wherever and however. He finally agreed to see a counselor for his problem and started going to Gamblers Anonymous meetings. Mike and I went to GamAnon meetings at the same time. I never felt completely comfortable in the meetings, didn't feel like I could connect with the other attendees. Most were spouses of gamblers. I had some sort of panic attack during the first meeting: palpitations, hot flashes, and dizziness. I had suffered from them a few times before, almost ten years prior to this, but they had subsided once I'd started working. Once they had started up again during that meeting, they've continued on and off since then. They seem to happen more in the evening, because this is the time when I finally start to slow down and have time to think.

Matt got away with so many things until November 11, 2009, when everything started to unravel.

When did all the lies start? Ninth grade? Probably earlier, but that's when he started getting caught in them.

Maybe the lies started from the time he was old enough (and young enough) to know the difference. When Matt was born, he had a five-year-old mentally retarded and physically challenged brother. To him that's what a "normal family" was. Tim and Matt were joined by a sister when Matt was twenty-two months old. Once again we were blessed with a special child—a mentally retarded and physically challenged child with multiple medical struggles. Going to doctor appointments at major hospitals was our way of life. They were just part of the daily errands. At what age did Matt start to realize that not all families were like this? And at what age did he start to feel uncomfortable about our family's life? Or is that a cop-out—*my* cop-out?

Maybe we overindulged him, overcompensated to make sure he didn't feel he had to "do without" because Tim and Laura held him—held us—back. He got the family vacations, and not just a week at the nearest beach. He got Disney World, Aruba, the Bahamas, Mexico. He went to major sporting events, sat in the suites. Hell, he got to go into the locker rooms and on the team planes. He got to meet the players, run on the fields, and get their autographs.

As I start this journal, this tracking of events to help keep me sane, Matt has asked to return to inpatient treatment for the second time (aka round two). All I can do is think about the past and the present, try to unravel all the lies, and hope for a happy ending to this nightmare.

CHAPTER TWO

I know two single white men from similar backgrounds. The difference between them is astounding.

One is twenty-four years old, slightly in need of a haircut and a shave, but not unkempt. He's nice looking, with white and straight teeth from years of wearing braces and getting annual dental check-ups. He has a really pleasant personality. His parents' friends always say how polite he is, that he can easily hold a conversation with adults. He loves dogs. He is patient, affectionate, and playful with babies.

He loves almost any sport but currently is most interested in skateboarding or bodyboarding. He's a college graduate and maintained a 3.0 average throughout his college years. He doesn't have a job yet, but he's looking; he's dragging his feet a bit maybe, because there are certain jobs that he must think are beneath him. He wants to get a job that will take him right to the top in the music industry.

He likes junk food, fast food, and takeout food but also has a few favorite meals that Mom makes, and he enjoys an occasional semi-formal meal as a family, when schedules permit. He is also happy to have a meal out at an upscale restaurant and seems comfortable in that setting. He usually wears T-shirts and shorts in the summer and sweaters and corduroys in colder weather; of course they sit at his hips, rather than his waist. He likes to wear hooded sweatshirts, mostly with the names and logos of surfing or skateboard companies.

This other young man is also twenty-four years old. He lies, steals, cheats, forges checks, helps himself to family members' credit cards, and disappears periodically for days at a time, when he will not return calls or text messages. He has frequent periods of insomnia, restlessness, lethargy, confusion, mood swings, loss of appetite, intestinal problems, and sinus infections. He can't hold down a job and isn't very interested in looking for one.

He often lies on the porch at all hours of the day and night, chain-smoking. He looks unkempt and goes for days without bathing or changing his clothes. He wears ratty dungarees and a hoodie, both with cigarette burns in them, the hood pulled up, hiding his face.

His teeth are brown and rotted, because he doesn't care about brushing them or getting regular dental checkups, and because all he eats is candy—the more sugar in it, the better. He's about twenty pounds underweight. The lies flow from his mouth readily, even when there's no reason to lie. (When asked if he brought in the newspaper, he'll say he did and we'll see the paper still sitting in the driveway.)

Both of these young men are versions of my son Matt. He is a heroin addict.

CHAPTER THREE

Right from the start of our marriage, my husband and I moved around a lot. New Orleans and Memphis were first. It was probably good for us to start our life together on our own, without family nearby. It gave us an opportunity to make our own routines and traditions. Our first child, Timmy, was born in Memphis. Mike already had been transferred to upstate New York, and we had sold the house in Memphis, so everyone was just waiting for the baby's arrival. Once Timmy arrived, things did not go smoothly for him. He needed immediate surgery to prevent further damage from the already destructive and previously undiagnosed hydrocephalus. After the doctors cleared him for travel, we headed north, staying at my mother's outside of Philadelphia while house hunting in Owego, New York. Timmy had his neurosurgery checkup at the Children's Hospital of Philadelphia (CHOP), which turned into more surgery, and so began a long and ongoing relationship with CHOP. Mike and I are so grateful to Dr. Leslie Sutton and the neurosurgery team for their excellent care. We stayed in Owego for a few years, then moved a bit farther north to Syracuse. Tim had early-intervention therapies right away, then started preschool in Syracuse. This is when it finally began to sink in that our routines would not be like those of most parents with young children.

Another transfer, this time to Little Silver, New Jersey, where Matt was born. He was born jaundiced and with "wet lungs", also called hyaline membrane disease, which occurs in infants whose lungs have not yet fully developed, such as premature infants, so he was transferred to another hospital (one with a better NICU) and spent an extra week there. Otherwise he was a very healthy, happy and active baby. He did everything early. Started solid food early because he drank too much formula. Crawled early, walked early. Hard to compare any of his milestones to Timmy's, because Timmy was so delayed and Matt seemed to do things earlier than normal (as I mentally compared with friend's' children). Timmy walked at age six, Matt walked at 8 months old. Tim had hip surgery at that time, and had a special wheelchair to move him around; Matt used the chair as a walker and just got himself walking. We made friends through a playgroup for Matt, and my sister and her family lived nearby, so with Timmy in school all day, we got a little taste of a less cumbersome routine. Matt and I could easily do errands, go to the beach, visit family and friends. At the same time, though, it was an expensive place to live, and it was frustrating to listen to our friends talk about their trips, their interior decorators and country club memberships, when we were just making ends meet. Not that Matt knew or cared. He was a precocious toddler having fun.

Then we made another move, this time to West Chester, Pennsylvania. I had a lot more family living near there, and moving there proved to be a godsend. Laura was born there, and again Mike and I renewed our intimate relationship with CHOP when she was just four months old. Before she was even born, I had enrolled Matt in a preschool/day-care center. There weren't many children on our busy street for him to play with, and even though he was barely two years old, he needed stimulation. He was into *everything*. We had been in the house for about two days when inquisitive Matt grabbed the car keys and stuck them in an electrical outlet. He walked into the kitchen rubbing his finger from the burn, and we had no phone service or power for the rest of the day. A few weeks later, he walked out to the garage to get a juice box out of the refrigerator and walked back in with my car's back windshield wiper. Yup, he needed to be with other kids his own age. After Laura was born, Mike and I soon realized that she needed physical and occupational therapy, as well as blood pressure checks and testing her stool for blood. We also had to give her daily injections of a steroid to control her seizures and she was fed through a gastrostomy, tube placed for her nutritional needs, and the doctors actually told us to expect that she wouldn't live to see her first birthday. Matt needed an outlet for all of his energy and creativity, and we didn't want his preschool years to be filled with his siblings' medical issues.

When Matt was about four years old, he wanted to get his hair cut in a style that he called a "California short cut," which I guess was also called a "California flattop." That same summer, we had planted sunflower seeds in our enormous garden. We took pictures of it weekly to document its growth. I vividly remember one picture of Matt standing next to it, in his muscle shirt and plaid blue shorts that came down past his knees. He has his "California short cut" in that picture; his face is sunburned, and he's grinning from ear to ear.

While we were in West Chester, when Laura was at her most fragile, I spoke to an extremely kind and caring person in the neurology department at CHOP, Claire Chee, a neurology nurse specialist, who gave me some sage advice. I had asked her what I should say to Matt, who was only two and a half, about Laura's illness and the predicted outcome, should that come to be, How should I handle the inevitable questions? Claire was always so kind and comforting during that horrible time, and she continues to be a great support to me throughout Laura's medical issues. I've never forgotten her advice, for that particular situation, as well as other times. She said I should start the conversation but let Matt take it wherever he wanted it to go. She said I should answer his questions truthfully but simply and not elaborate unless Matt wanted more information. She said he would ask what he wanted to know, when he wanted to know it. That was such a comfort to me, knowing that the burden of that conversation only had to be as big or as small as Matt made it.

Mike and I thank God for the support of our family. We thank God for the doctors at CHOP and Seashore House, the rehabilitation facility located on the campus of Children's Hospital, especially Laura's neurologist, Dr. Donald Younkin, at Children's Hospital; her feeding specialist, Dr. Peggy Eicher, formerly at Children's Hospital, and now the director at the Center for Pediatric Feeding and Swallowing; and Dr. Christopher Lam, formerly of the Behavioral Health Department at Children's Hospital. And we thank God for sparing Laura. She is our miracle from God, but the doctors at CHOP and Seashore House gave us hope.

CHAPTER FOUR

We moved back to Little Silver, New Jersey, when Matt was about three and a half years old and stayed there for more than twenty years. We finally felt like this was the place where we would put down our roots. We had a house built to our specifications. We still had friends there from the first time we had lived there, and our new neighborhood was perfect for Matt. He quickly made friends there, where there were about fifteen other children around his age on our street alone. We were close enough to CHOP for Timmy and Laura to continue their care there, especially Laura, whose seizures and feeding disorder were still unstable.

Up until now all our birthday parties for the kids had been comprised of just family and celebrated at our house or that of a relative, and sometimes just involved our own little family with a cake and a few presents. When Matt turned four years old, we had been in the new house for just a couple of months. I'd never had to organize kiddy birthday parties before, as Tim and Laura didn't understand them; they were just happy with people being there and singing "Happy Birthday." I didn't want to be a party planner, didn't want to organize games of Pin the Tail on the Donkey. But Matt deserved a real party. He shouldn't have to do without just because I wasn't the kind of mother who got into that sort of thing and also because the day-to-day routines of Timmy and Laura were sometimes difficult and tiresome.

Some of my family came from Pennsylvania. My sister, who lived nearby, also came, and a lot of Matt's friends showed up—friends he knew from his little playgroup there when he was a baby, as well as the children on the street where we lived. Matt was in his glory. At the party we had—on I think the hottest day of the summer—a Batman impersonator and cotton candy machine. I had Matt dressed in khaki shorts and a polo shirt, but even then he was a rebel and managed to get his clothes dirty so he could change into a mismatched outfit just before the guests arrived. When I saw him, I cringed, but he was so "Matthew" that I had to hug him. He liked tank tops ("muscle shirts," he called them), so he had on a bright-orange one, along with a bathing suit with squares and rectangles in turquoise, yellow, and gray. He looked like a street urchin, with dust streaked all over his face, but he was so adorable. He had a fantastic day. And I still love that picture.

CHAPTER FIVE

Our home in Little Silver was a perfect house for our family. It had so much room, and Mike's dream was to finish the basement by himself, to turn it into a combination game room and Irish pub—a man cave, they call it now. We envisioned a big TV, a pool table, a dartboard, and a bar. It would be a perfect place for Matt and all his twelve-year-old friends to congregate. But they never really came to our house as it was. They'd run around outside, all over the neighborhood, and stop in for something to eat or drink, but our house was never their gathering place. I think Matt felt awkward watching TV with friends with Tim and Laura in the room; surely he could see the furtive glances from his friends. One day he had a schoolmate over, and they were in the front yard, kicking a soccer ball around. When they came in for snacks, the kid said to Matt,"Ha ha. Timmy wears braces. He can't play soccer." That was pretty much the end of their friendship until high school, when they became pals again—drinking and drugging pals.

Surely the finished basement would change that. Friends could come over, run around, play pool, and watch movies and wouldn't have to feel so awkward because Tim and Laura wouldn't be down in the basement. There were always delays, however—money reasons mostly. So the basement didn't get finished until Matt was around fifteen. It was made with love and so beautiful, with dark-green plush carpet and deep-brown stained wainscoting (each piece stained by Mike), and a bar he'd made by hand. His brothers helped him add a bathroom down there. There was also a refrigerator with snacks. The basement had everything a teenager would want.

Even so, Matt and his friends still didn't use it. By then we had started to keep a closer eye on him and his friends, as there were a couple of drinking incidents, and they had found other places where they could get away with their forbidden activities. One night Matt did want to have a few people over to watch a football game. Mike and I were so happy that he was finally going to take advantage of this great rec room. We were out doing errands and stopped on the way home to pick up sodas and pizzas for them. Mike got out a big trashcan and put it downstairs for the recycling. That's when he saw the case of beer hiding there. So much for an innocent evening. Only later did we realize there wasn't even a football game on TV that night!

CHAPTER SIX

Matt was always a night owl, even as a baby. At first he resisted that last bottle, as he knew meant bedtime was just around the corner; later he verbalized excuses to put off bedtime. One of his frequent ploys, when he was around eight or nine, after I had started working, was to make me a "surprise." He'd come into my office bearing a snack for two—soda in champagne glasses and a dish of M&Ms or cookies, and we'd have our snack together. I knew the whole goal of the ritual, to Matt at least, was to stay up later and get that last bit of late-night goodies. To me it was so much more than that. I want to think it was also his way of acknowledging that Mom was working hard and deserved a little pampering. Although his visits may have interrupted my train of thought, those evenings were very special to me. I wish I could have some of them back.

CHAPTER SEVEN

High school brought the biggest changes in Matt—maybe because he was coming from small-town Little Silver, who's elementary and middle schools just had Little Silver kids in them. He rarely had left Little Silver or gotten together with anyone outside our town. He didn't have to. There was enough to do in Little Silver. Red Bank Regional High School (RBRHS), however, had kids from four surrounding towns filtering in. Additionally several other towns sent students to his high school, due to the performing arts program RBRHS offered.

Always the socialite, and while not exactly a follower, Matt was a willing participant in just about anything. He had several groups of friends—one he played sports with, one he played music with, one he bodyboarded with, and one he skateboarded with. I didn't know the names or faces of most of them. There were a few more drinking incidents—nights when we could tell he had been drinking because he slurred his words and wasn't quite steady on his feet. There were a couple of times that he was a pretty ugly drunk, and it took a lot of my attempts at amateur psychology to calm him down and just get him to pass out. He tended to drink too much, too fast. He later explained to me that if he didn't seem to feel a buzz right away, he would do a few more shots. By the time the initial rounds kicked in, he'd already had several more so the buzz he was looking for became a mess.

One day I got a call from Matt's high school to come get him because he had arrived at school reeking of marijuana. It was September 2001, just a couple of weeks after he'd started ninth grade, and he was fourteen years old. I was livid. I worked just a few miles from the school, so it wasn't a big deal to go get him, but it did scramble my schedule for the rest of the day. You know, you get the calls to come get your kid because he has a fever, or he's throwing up, or he fell and his arm is at an odd angle. You're not supposed to get a call saying that your son smoked pot on his way to school. From school I had to take him to a clinic for a urine drug screen, and then a physician would examine him to determine whether he could return to school. As Matt tried to walk a straight line, I saw him trying not to giggle but failing. Of course he was grounded. Among other things, he was forbidden to get a ride to school with the boy he had been with that day.

So Matt started ninth grade with the marijuana incident and ended ninth grade, the day before his last exam, by getting into a fight during a basketball game in the gym. It started with a few guys who had finished their exams and were killing time. Some elbowing got a little rough, which led to punches being thrown. I heard that Matt swung first but missed. The other kid connected solidly with Matt's face.

I received a call from the school nurse, who really said little, except that there was a bit of a fight and that Matt's lip was bleeding. My first thought was, *you're kidding, right? I have to stop everything, again, to go the high school because my almost fifteen-year-old son's lip is bleeding?* I nearly fainted, though, when I saw Matt's swollen, bloody, and bruised face. I took him directly to the dentist. All of his bottom teeth were loose and would have gone right down his throat if not for the permanent retainer he wore on his lower teeth. All the dentist could do was load him up with Novocain, to make him a little more comfortable, and send us off to an oral surgeon. He had lots of stitches, lots of dental work, some broken bones in his jaw and face, and two black eyes.

Both Matt and the other student were suspended. But how do you suspend someone with just one day of school left and that day being final-exam day? Their punishment was that, instead of taking their exams with the rest of their class, they had to sit in the principal's office together to take their exams.

Matt was due to start his summer job the next day, at the office where I work. What a way to start.

He told me just recently that the oral surgeon had given him painkillers. I wonder whether that led to his experimenting with other drugs. At that point I knew he was experimenting with marijuana and alcohol, but it never occurred to me that a legally prescribed medication would be added to the mix.

For a long time Matt used the topic of marijuana against me in arguments, saying, "You told me you used it in college." True, I did, and true, I admitted it to him when he asked me point blank once. I wasn't going to lie. He said, "I found your old pipe." God, how he must have picked through the boxes in the basement to find it. The pipe was packed in a carton with stuff from my premarriage days—a china animal collection and a small cedar box (all high school seniors were given one) that had in it, besides the pipe, the tassel from my graduation cap, an empty bottle of perfume I'd bought in Spain, a letter a good friend had written to me before that trip to Spain (my first time on an airplane), the translation of my college diploma from Latin into English, and a few Spanish coins. What would make him even want to dig through all of the boxes? But he found it and probably used it. And what could I say when he had proof that I experimented as a teenager? "I was older?" "It was different then?" "Everyone did it in the seventies?" Of course not. I made no excuses and told him it was something I did then and wish now that I hadn't.

Later he told me that the earlier pot incident was due to the stress he'd felt on 9/11. For most of us, for a long time, even now, a lot of things could be traced to 9/11. Maybe it was true—he did have several peers who lost parents in the tragedy at the World Trade Center. Maybe Matt started thinking, *What if?* What if Mike or I had lost our life that day? Or maybe, for him, it was just a damn good excuse. For so many people, 9/11 became the root of all things bad.

CHAPTER EIGHT

Months before 9/11, I'd realized that I was depressed. I cried a lot and slept a lot. I didn't care about anything. I used to really enjoy my job as a coding manager for a medical billing company, but over time I stopped caring.

I would drive to work and sit at a red light, waiting to turn left. Suddenly I'd think, *what if I just turned left when the light was still red and let the oncoming cars hit my car?*

It sounds like a commercial for antidepressants, but it's true. What was so wrong with my life? I had a job I used to love. It wasn't the kind I'd just forget about when 5:00 p.m. came; I had responsibilities, and it seemed like I worked all the time. Or maybe I worked to escape. My marriage was going through a rough patch; again I can't say why, but I just wasn't happy. Tim and Laura had continual medical issues, and Mike and I were raising a teenager who was suddenly not the sweet boy we once new. Finally I made an appointment to see my doctor, and the first thing the receptionist asked was whether I had lost someone on 9/11 or if I thought the events of 9/11 had brought about my depression.

I remember 9/11 vividly. The area where we lived lost more people on 9/11 than any other county in New Jersey. My nephew, John, worked in the Financial District, and I frantically called relatives until I knew *for sure* that he was all right. I got some basic information, and the following was all I could process in my apathetic state. John had just gotten off the ferry and was walking up the street to his office. When the planes hit the Twin Towers, he dove under a parked truck to protect himself for a while until he felt safe; afterward he was able to get back on the ferry and go home. That was pretty much all I needed to hear at the time—that John was fine. After that I walked around my office building thinking (but of course not saying) that everyone should get back to work and stop scouring the Internet and listening to the radio. So a couple of planes had hit a couple of buildings. Tall buildings, big planes. It was bound to happen. To this day I can't absorb the impact of that day, because I was so deep in my ennui of depression.

And now, as I check my information for this book, I've found out the real story, in John's words, of what he saw and did that day and I am appalled and ashamed at my own insensitivity

> *I was on a later ferry that day at 7:55 a.m., from Connor's Hotel (and bar). I was about sixty seconds from walking into the WTC, on the way through to my building (I would walk under the WTC towers as a shortcut) when the first plane hit. I tried walking around the south side of the WTC to get to my office. (I still thought it was an accident at this point.) That's when I saw the really tough part—everything that was going on at the WTC. When the second plane hit, the debris was landing where I was. That's when I got behind a mail truck to avoid the big pieces that were landing—and they were big.*
>
> *I stayed there for about five minutes and then made it down to my building, which was directly next to the WTC. I tried to walk through Battery Park on my way to the ferry dock when the first building came down, so I was in middle of the dust*

cloud. I made it over to the ferry dock and was there when the second building came down. At that point I decided to get out of downtown altogether, especially since people were panicking on the ferry dock, and it was starting to get dangerous. I started walking up the East Side, with a few other guys, to another ferry dock. I got there just in time to catch a ferry that was about to pull out and went straight to Connor's in Highlands.

After I read John's account, I told him I was horrified that I only now realized that he had been in more danger than I'd thought, and I was struck by how determined he had been to try to get work, even after he'd seen the devastation in the Financial District. I was also struck by how deep my depression ran and how indifferent I had been about that day—and pretty much everything—at that point in my life.

CHAPTER NINE

Matt was the kind of kid who's portrayed in commercials with his dad. He followed Mike around, always wanting to be "Daddy's really big helper." He had his own toy tool kit, lawnmower, tractor, and fishing rod. He loved to watch TV—especially sporting events—with Dad. He wanted to stay up and celebrate New Year's Eve with us. I remember all the years when we were invited to Super Bowl parties. I didn't care about going, but Mike was a big sports fan, and that was the highlight of sports season. Plus, Mike was much more of a socialite than I was, and was always up for a party or some sort of get-together. It always made me sad, and it still does, when young Matt would ask if we could have our own Super Bowl party, just the five of us, with snacks and drinks, and chili or pizza for dinner. We'd always say no, because we were going to a party. So Matt would stay home with a sitter, always so disappointed,

It was like the Harry Chapin song "Cat's in the Cradle." It wasn't that dramatic, of course. Mike was always one of the team coaches for whatever sport Matt was playing, and they did a lot of things together. Soon we started to stay home to celebrate the Super Bowl with him, but it was already too late. Matt would be invited to watch the game with friends, or he'd watch with us for a bit but then get on the computer and chat with his friends. We missed that small window of time when he wanted to do things with us and us with him.

CHAPTER TEN

My sister Beth passed away suddenly on December 8, 2001. I had been out for my early-morning walk that Sunday (walking was a means for me to work through my depression) and had a kind of premonition during my walk that I was going to get a call I wouldn't like. Shortly after I returned from my walk, my brother Johnny called to tell me that Beth had had an accident and didn't make it. She had hemorrhaged, fainted, and hit her head. In shock I called my other sister and her daughter, who lived a few miles away. Then Susan, Liz, and I made the awful trip to the West Chester, Pennsylvania, area to face Beth's husband and daughter, and my mother. Even now I don't know all of the details about Beth's death. Her heart stopped. A tumor had wrapped itself around her heart—What kind of tumor? It didn't matter. My sister, my best friend, was gone.

Then we made the long, sad drive home to normalcy. Soon after our return, my husband told me he had done the laundry and found rolling papers in Matt's pants pocket. I don't even know what Matt said—he was holding them for a friend, maybe? It didn't matter. I was in shock, numb from losing Beth, and just couldn't address it.

Matt didn't attend the funeral, something I'll always regret. But he was in the middle of final exams of his first semester of high school, and I felt it was important for him to take the exams with the rest of his class. I wonder why I didn't think it would be more prudent to keep him close to us, under our watchful eye, for the few days that the babysitter was in charge of things at home.

CHAPTER ELEVEN

Matt did everything ahead of schedule—or at least he tried to. He hit the ground running and never looked back. He really had no older sibling to emulate, with Timmy being so far behind developmentally, so he (and we) didn't know what he was "supposed" to do. He just did it. His younger sister pretty much just sat in a stroller or infant seat. When Mike took the training wheels off Matt's bike, he was four years old. Mike held the bike steady as Matt got on it, then waited with happy anticipation to jog down the street next to him, holding onto the bike until Matt said he was ready for Mike to let go. No way. Before Mike had time to stand up, Matt was off like a shot, riding down the street as if he had been doing it forever. Where did he learn to ride a two-wheeler? Who stole that milestone from us?

Soon after Matt's fifth birthday, he started asking if he could walk to the 7-Eleven with friends—no grown-ups. It was less than a mile from our house, and there were no streets for him to cross, but are you kidding me? Five years old? We managed to put that off for a couple of years. Then he wanted to ride his bike into town with friends. Again, it was only a couple of miles at most, but this time he would have to cross the two main roads in Little Silver. Again we were able to stall that activity for a while. Then he wanted to ride his bike to school—alone again, less than two miles, again crossing the two main roads. We were able to make him wait until he was about nine years old for that. When he went to Yankee games with his dad, he wanted to run around the entire concession area (alone) and explore the stadium by walking up to the top row of seats.

When Matt was in first or second grade, his teacher and I talked frequently, because he was occasionally disruptive in class. He wasn't naughty, and not exactly the class clown, just easily distracted and therefore distracting to others. One time he dropped a pencil or something, and it fell under his desk. Instead of quietly leaning down to pick it up, he crawled under the desk, completely on his stomach, to get it, and then proceeded to stand up, while still under the desk, of course completely upending the desk. Needless to say, it also upended the attention of the class for the remainder of the morning.

After hearing about that incident, I wondered whether Matt might be hyperactive. I talked to his pediatrician, who reassured me that as long as he slept well at night and had periods of quiet playtime, by his own choice, we shouldn't worry about him. Maybe he was a little immature in managing his behavior, but not hyperactive.

I also consulted with the school counselor both with and without Matt present. I wondered, of course, if having two multiply handicapped siblings might have anything to do with his occasional disruptive behavior in class, his schoolwork, the way he played, or the way he talked. The counselor and Matt's teachers felt he was very well adjusted; they felt he understood about Tim and Laura's limitations, as much as any seven-year-old could understand, and that he was sensitive to their needs but wasn't overly obsessed about them. In short they pretty much told me the same thing his pediatrician did— that he was just a bit on the immature side socially and would soon grow into himself.

I suppose he did, although he did have a bit of a disruptive moment in eighth grade, when for some unknown reason, he decided to drop his shorts and "moon" his gym class. The teacher never saw it happen; later that day a couple of kids were passing notes about it. A teacher intercepted one of the notes and brought Matt and the note to see the principal. As the principal relayed this information to me over the phone, I was trying hard not to laugh, and I think the principal was as well. Matt did have to serve detention for a few weeks, and his recreational basketball coach (his father!) benched him for several weeks.

So apparently it did take Matt a while to "grow into himself." Meanwhile he constantly told me I was the strictest mom of all of his friends.

Was he born to be a daredevil, or was he just really independent? He was never in a rush to get his permit for a driver's license, though. I wondered, even then, why not. He'd already had a couple of run-ins with the law. Did he not want to have a license, only to have it taken away if he got into any more trouble? Did he not want the responsibility of being the designated driver? Or was it something much simpler than that? Was he slightly embarrassed that he did not have a car of his own and didn't want to drive our family car? I preferred to think he was just timid about taking that responsibility, but he never said. As per usual, any feelings he had about it were kept locked inside of him.

CHAPTER TWELVE

Babysitters weren't easy to come by, and they weren't cheap. I also was pretty uneasy about leaving Laura alone, as her seizures and eating disorder weren't under control. So we were home at night most of the time. Matt's solution? He didn't often bring friends to our house at night anyway; he went to friends' houses, watching TV, playing video games, and later on, playing poker. He was always home by his curfew. I think he had friends over after school, while Mike and I were still at work and a babysitter was at the house. Matt's drum set was in the basement, so the band that he and some of his friends had formed practiced at our house.

On one of our rare nights out, Mike, a huge Rolling Stones fan, had eight tickets to see the band in concert at the Meadowlands. He and I, along with three other couples, planned to head to the stadium for an elaborate tailgate party followed by the concert. A reliable sitter, who worked at the kids' special ed program, was home with Tim and Laura. Matt would do his own thing with his friends. He pretty much rode his bike everywhere. That night was his first night of freedom after having been grounded for the pot-smoking incident.

It was a fun evening for us, very relaxing—delicious food, close friends, amazing concert. We got back to the car around eleven thirty.

I checked the messages on my cell phone; I had one message from the Little Silver police saying that Matt was in the hospital, along with many messages from the babysitter, telling us that the police had said he was in bad shape. Frantically Mike and I tried to get out of the parking lot, which took more than an hour. Finally we headed home, on the phone the whole time. I thank our friends, Janet and Scott, for offering to go back to our house, relieve the sitter, and stay overnight with Tim and Laura while we went to the hospital.

The story we finally got from the police was that they had received a 911 call from a motorist about a kid on a bike riding erratically down the middle of a fairly well-traveled road, frequently falling off. The motorist stayed behind him until the police arrived to help protect him from other cars. It was Matt, drunk, arrested for a DUI on a bike! The police took him to the hospital because of the cuts on his hands and legs, as well as his intoxicated state. He was swearing like a sailor and calling the police and nurses all kinds of horrible names. At one point he told the police, "I wish I were dead." In came the crisis unit at the hospital, and he couldn't be discharged until he was cleared by psych and until his blood alcohol level came down. Mike and I finally got him home around 8:00 a.m. We immediately set him up with a counselor, whose name we had received from his high school guidance department. Mike and I really didn't think too much about Matt's comment about wishing he was dead We thought it was just typical, if a bit overly dramatic, of a teenager commenting about knowing he was destined to get in trouble.

He was at an informal party at a friend's house and planned to be home and in bed by the time we got home. This was the night when he had done multiple shots of whiskey, feeling frustrated because he wasn't "catching a buzz." Thanks to the IV fluids he received in the ER, I don't think he even felt the effects of what should have been a nasty hangover.

CHAPTER THIRTEEN

Matt had a lot of opportunities to do some special things, part of the perks that came with Mike's job as a sales manager for a large food corporation. He often received tickets to concerts and sporting events.

Mike and Matt frequently went to watch the Philadelphia Eagles practice, as Mike was responsible for presenting an award to the "special teams player of the week." One weekend, when Matt was about ten years old, Mike and Matt were invited to see an Eagles game in Atlanta. They flew with the team on their plane and stayed in the same hotel with them. The players mostly kept to themselves, but a few of them chatted with Matt. He even was allowed to go on the field with them while they practiced. Every so often, someone would toss a football to Matt. At one point a ball came his way that was meant for another player, not Matt, so it was thrown pretty hard. Matt caught it, but it knocked the wind out of him and he went down—seriously. The paramedics came to check him out and give him some oxygen. Matt's favorite player at the time, Randall Cunningham, had thrown the ball. Cunningham felt bad about knocking Matt out, so when the offending ball was presented to Matt, someone asked him whose signature he wanted on it. Without a thought Matt said, "Randall Cunningham." And so Cunningham signed it.

I think that trip was Matt's finest moment. Ever since then, whenever he was playing soccer, football, baseball, or whatever, he seemed to have a habit of taking a hit and dropping to the ground. I think he fantasized about suffering a sports injury and being airlifted to a hospital.

CHAPTER FOURTEEN

In 2003, after a few more alcohol and marijuana incidents, Matt finally started to see a private counselor during his junior year of high school. The school social worker gave us the name of a counselor the school dealt with a lot, someone who seemed to have a good rapport with the students. He was a guy, and Matt saw him weekly. Sometimes Matt failed his drug tests; sometimes he was clean. He always went willingly to see the counselor and said they had good talks and felt he had a connection with him. But the minor arrests for possession of pot kept coming, and so did the drinking incidents.

An intervention was suggested; I'm not sure whether the school social worker suggested it or the counselor did. It wasn't really explained to us what would happen, just that Mike and I would each write letters to Matt and then meet with him, the school counselor, and the private counselor and read our letters to Matt. There was no talk of rehab or increasing the counseling. This was just a session for him to understand how much we loved him and were hurting for him and wanted to help him.

The intervention was set for a Tuesday morning; we would all assemble at Matt's school, and Matt would be called down to the school counselor's office. Matt had seen his private counselor the week before the intervention would take place. When I saw the counselor for a minute in the waiting room, he had seemed a bit fidgety, but I thought maybe he was nervous about not letting on that there would be an intervention. A few days before the intervention, in our local paper, I'd read a short article about someone having been arrested in the area for possession of—and being under the influence of—crack cocaine. Of course you see things like that in the paper, but this person happened to have the same name as Matt's counselor. My husband, Matt, and I all looked at each other and thought, *it couldn't be…*

The day before the intervention, the counselor called me and said he wouldn't be able to attend the intervention. He said I may have already heard or read about the incident and that things aren't always as they seem, but it would all be resolved. When we got to the high school, I told the school counselor about this turn of events, and she made some inquiries in her professional circle. Yes, it was Matt's private counselor who had been arrested. (This was while Matt was in high school, remember. Years later, after Matt was out of college, I needed to call his office to confirm some dates of Matt's counseling, and at that point, apparently, he was still practicing, or practicing again.)

The letter I read to Matt during the intervention went as follows.

November 19, 2003
My dear Matthew,

I've told you so many times before, and I know you are sick of hearing it, but you are the child of my hopes and dreams. I don't mean for you to feel pressure when I say that, but it's true. You're the one who will take me for a drive in your first car, the one

I will watch proudly as you receive your high school diploma, possibly visit colleges with, and lend a hand to as you move into your first apartment. You're the child I will cry for when you and your bride exchange wedding vows, the one who will someday perhaps have a child for me to hold. If these aren't the dreams you want, that's fine. Whatever your dreams are, I will support your choices and do whatever I can to help make those dreams become a reality.

I'm so scared of what might happen to these dreams if you don't get a grip on what you've been doing and work hard to make changes in your behavior. You say that this time you know that you have to stop and that you will stop. I hope that's true, but I think you can understand my hesitation in believing that. I feel so sad that I can't trust you right now, and I hope you can understand that as well. I can't make you fully realize just how much I love you. I care so much about what you do, both good and bad. When you are hurting, I hurt just as much—more maybe, because I can't do anything to stop it. Only you can make it stop. All I can do is continue to love and support you, and I do, with all my heart.

Mimi told me once that when Timmy was born, and it became clear how many problems he had and always would have, the light went out of my eyes. You brought that light back into my eyes, and nothing will take that light away—not the problems you have been having, not bad grades, not the long hair. I'm just so afraid that something will happen to you, and I wouldn't be able to stand that.

Everything I've read tells me that being a parent is a hard job. I knew that, but I thought it meant it was hard deciding what schools to send you to, how to pick a doctor, how to make sure you eat right. No one told me that my child might have a bad group of friends or try drugs, drinking, or whatever. Once a child reaches a certain age, the parents can't make all the choices anymore. It's so hard to stand by and not be able to step in when I know your child is making a bad choice.

Every so often, I tell you "I wish you were four years old again." Maybe I mean that I wish we had the relationship we had when you were four. We had fun together then. You made me laugh so much. I guess I could make you laugh then too. Hearing you laugh with real, uncontrollable laughter just cracked me up.

We talked a lot up until you were in eighth grade, I guess. High school changed you. I know Dad found rolling papers in your pants in December of your freshman year. That started the suspicion, but I don't think I really noticed a change in you until after the fight you had at the end of ninth grade. You were never a fighter or an angry person, but some of the things you said after that fight really scared me. You wanted to hurt that other boy in retaliation and said that your friends would do it if you asked them to. And, as you told us later, that was around the time when you first started smoking pot on a regular basis. I never knew about all the times that summer you were smoking, and I still don't know how often you were drinking then.

September of your freshman year was when I really started to lose trust in you. That was when you arrived at school reeking of pot and then, just two weeks later, ended up in the hospital because you were so drunk. I kept trying to figure out what I did or didn't do. So many times I asked myself whether I should stop working and be home in the afternoons. Realistically I knew it wouldn't matter—I knew you and I wouldn't be sitting at the kitchen table together every afternoon while you did your home-work. But I couldn't help think that it was my fault you were going astray. I still think that. Was it because I was trying to deal with my own emotional issues? Was it because I was doing too much work in the evenings? Did I pay too much attention to Tim and Laura and not enough to you? Did I give you too much freedom? Did I give you too many "things"? Did I spoil you?

I love you and want only the best for you. Of course I am hurt and disappointed to know that you have said you "made a bad choice one time but won't do it again" and then did it again after all, but this is only because I know how much good you are capable of. You are a good person. Everyone who knows you says that, and I agree. You are polite, respectful, caring, and compassionate. I don't want to see you risk your future for the sake of good times. I know this is a really fun time in your life, and you have a lot more opportunities than I did growing up. But you can still do all of these fun things.

I wish I knew what kind of stress you feel—not just now, because I'm sure this is all scary and overwhelming to you, but your day-to-day stress. Is it schoolwork? Household chores? Or is it something more? Do you feel more confident when you drink or smoke? Does that mean you don't feel confident otherwise? Why?

The next several months will be really hard for you. I'm sure it will be tough to resist temptation. I imagine it must be overwhelming for a sixteen-year-old to think that there are some things he cannot do again. I will always be here to help you if you feel you can't get through this alone. You aren't alone. Always remember that. In fact I would be so happy if you would ask for my help. What really hurts is the feeling that you're shutting me out. Never, ever feel that you may have let me down, caused me any pain, or caused conflict in our family. All families have their ups and downs. No matter what you've done or what trouble you may get into, I will always love you, no matter what, and I will always be here for you.

Mike's letter to Matt reads as follows.

November 19, 2003
Dear Matt,

I want to start by saying that I love you. I may not always show it, and you may not always believe it, but I absolutely love you!

The past two years have been difficult and disappointing. Not only have I watched you struggle with the challenges of growing up, but I've also had a tough time trying to figure out what to say, how to act, and what I could do to help you deal with these hurdles.

For the last sixteen years, I've watched you grow. Unlike Tim and Laura, who will never truly grow up, you've grown up fast—too fast! And I haven't been able to keep pace, or maybe it's that I've been too reluctant to give you your space.

Back in 1987 I was scared to death as I waited for your arrival. I prayed you would have opportunities that Tim would never experience. As I reflect it seems you've been going full speed ever since. You went from a cute, full-of-energy, curly-haired toddler who spent hours watching those crazy Teenage Ninja Turtles to a young man with long hair who sometimes drives me crazy. You bolted from the driveway the minute I took the training wheels off your bike, not giving me the pleasure of running alongside as you learned to ride. Now you're dashing out of the house to cruise Monmouth County with your friends. It was a quick jump from Goodnight Moon to The Autobiography of Bob Marley. I worried when you rode your bike to town and played manhunt at the school playground at night. Now you're taking the train to New York and going to concerts in Asbury Park. You went from counting my beers (remember, two was the limit), to my having to pick you up from the emergency room or the police station. It seems like you went from the Point Road classroom to the Freehold courtroom overnight.

As I look back, there were lots of signs that you were spreading your wings. Some were cute; some I missed; while others broke my heart, and I hoped you would learn from them. You wanted to roam around Yankee Stadium like you used to walk around Little Silver. You wanted dreadlocks when parting your hair in the middle used to be cool. Your style went from sweatpants to baggies, from bright-colored muscle shirts to black T-shirts. Your tastes went from candy cigarettes to smoking pot and Parliaments, from drinking Gatorade and sipping a Slurpee to chugging beer and whiskey. Your speed was "fast-forward," while I tried to keep my finger on the "pause" button. Somewhere along the way, you stopped being my tough little guy but never stopped being the son I love.

Now you're my not so little guy, and you're facing not so little challenges. How you deal with these tough times will say a lot about the kind of man you turn out to be. Instead of your going "fast-forward," I think it's time for a slower, more determined, and deliberate pace. It's time to make good decisions.

I'm not sure if you know it, but the whole time you've been sprinting toward adulthood, I've been struggling to keep you in my sights. If you'll take the time to look over your shoulder, you'll see I'm right behind you.

No matter what happens, you'll always be my son. I'll always be your dad. I'll always love you. I'll always be behind you. And if you'll let me, I'd be proud to walk beside you and be your friend.

Matt, I want nothing but the best for you. The world is full of possibilities and pitfalls; realizing its full potential is all about making good choices. The choices you make are up to you, and I know you can do it. I want to help you, if you'll give me the chance.

I love you,
Dad

Matt was pretty angry during the intervention, which he viewed as our ganging up on him. He didn't feel he had any sort of problem—nothing that couldn't be taken care of in weekly counseling sessions. He did take the letters with him as he left the office, which I later found in the trashcan in his room.

We tried.

And we immediately found another counselor.

Matt and I recently talked about this incident. He said he was really hurt and upset at the time; he felt betrayed, maybe, by his counselor's drug use. He felt he really had connected with the counselor, really opened up to him, and talked a lot about his feelings. I wonder if this caused any setbacks. At the time it didn't appear to; he started to see another counselor and seemed to be comfortable with him. But I wondered later if it set the tone for any reservations he might have had with future counselors, and if it was part of the reason he tended to keep everything bottled up inside him.

CHAPTER FIFTEEN

There was so much fighting going on at home, beginning in high school, when Matt started to experiment with pot and alcohol. Mike and Matt seemed to go at it all the time. Maybe they have the same temperament, and that's why they clash so hard. I can't say exactly what the arguments were about—everything and nothing. Drugs and drinking, certainly. Matt ruining his life. His not doing the trivial things we asked of him (cleaning his room, doing small chores). Not studying enough. Not going to sleep early enough. Not showing us enough respect. Matt would listen and promise to change, but eventually he would get to the boiling point and fire back.

I couldn't take it. It actually wasn't because of the drinking or drug use, although obviously I hated that he was using and was terrified that he'd do something irreparable. But I couldn't—and still can't—deal with all the yelling. Timmy and Laura always had been affected by yelling; Laura usually put her hands over her ears and got weepy; Timmy got very excited and sometimes would cry; other times he would wet his pants.

Several times, starting when Matt was in high school, I ended up huddled in a ball in a corner of the kitchen, my arms over my head; I was curled into myself, crying my eyes out and trying to escape it all. All I wanted to do to was disappear, to block out all the noise. I hated what my life—our family's life—had become, and I didn't know how to process all the painful emotions.

All I could do was hope something would help me process everything and bring answers and closure.

CHAPTER SIXTEEN

Matt and Mike occasionally found common ground by attending sporting events together, usually baseball or football games. These events involved other dads and their sons, as well as tailgate parties, especially during football season. There was a lot of beer drinking at tailgate parties, so very early on Matt saw that drinking was a big social thing. Matt also occasionally went to Mike's intramural softball games in town, which was another social outing for Mike. Mike was always in charge of bringing the beer; he said that was because he had the reputation of packing coolers really well. That meant he spent the night before the game buying the beer and preparing the cooler so that the beer was extra cold by game time. Matt saw that this was a big production. And of course, at the games, the beer flowed freely. The team would sit at the field for a couple of hours after the games, drinking, talking, and rehashing the game, while Matt and the other kids ran around playing tag and softball, and going to the local market for gum and candy.

How much of this affected Matt's view of partying and social drinking? Did he learn that in order to have a good time there had to be a lot of beer? That more booze meant more laughs? And did his exposure to all the beer lead to his experimenting with other substances? I hoped that one day we could have this discussion with Matt, to finally unravel the truth about this and so many other things.

What I was concerned about, although I didn't have a name for it at the time, was the "gateway drug" theory, which states that an introduction to drug-using behavior through the use of tobacco, alcohol, or marijuana could possibly be related to subsequent use of other drugs. The theory suggests that an adolescent who uses any one drug is more likely to use another drug. Tobacco and alcohol are considered the first "gateways" for most adolescents; these two, as well as marijuana, are all considered "gateway drugs" and often lead to the use of illicit drugs.

So, yes, Matt fits the gateway theory. Did that make his behavior any better? More excusable? Of course not.

CHAPTER SEVENTEEN

Matt worked hard during his junior and senior years of high school, both in school and at his summer jobs He worked off and on at the office where I worked, worked at a local fish restaurant for a while, and then worked at a natural food store. He continued to see his new counselor regularly until shortly before he left for college. He felt as if he had things under control, and it seemed to us that he did too, although he told me much later that he drank regularly throughout high school. He also told me—again much later—that the night before he left for college was the first time he had used a drug (other than using something called "numb gum," which supposedly gives your mouth the same feeling it gets when using cocaine) in more than a year.

He headed off to the University of New Haven in September 2005. There were no tears on our end when we dropped him off, and certainly none on his end. He already had spoken to both of his roommates by phone and had met and hit it off with one of them over the summer when the new students spent a few days on campus. He was ready to be on his own.

Mike, Tim, Laura, and I headed to Ocean City, New Jersey, for a week, where we stayed in the first-floor apartment at Mike's father's house. During our week in that little apartment, we realized a small one-story house was all we really needed. Furthermore the two-story colonial where we'd lived for fifteen years was no longer safe for Tim and Laura. Tim struggled to get up and down the stairs, and Laura was starting to have drop seizures. Either of them could fall down the steps with no warning. We hoped that after we sold that house we could buy a smaller home in Little Silver and also buy a small home in Ocean City; since I'd spent most of my childhood summers there, it had always been my dream.

We were concerned about what Matt would think, since he had spent all but his first four years in that house. We talked to him about it, and he said was fine with the idea. Most of his friends were away at college, and those who were still around town actually lived closer to the new house. We made it clear that the new house would still be his house, and he'd have his own bedroom; he wouldn't be sleeping on the couch when he came home on vacation from school. So we began preparations for selling the "big house" and looking for a smaller, one-story house.

My mother's health was failing quickly during this time. We had moved her into a nursing home over the previous summer, and her memory was failing quickly. She had been going downhill since my sister passed away four years prior. My mom eventually passed away in early December, and Tim had a flurry of shunt failures (Tim's body had to rely on mechanical tubing to prevent spinal fluid from building up on his brain, and occasionally the shunts got clogged or infected) that landed him in the hospital several times that winter, including the week before and the week after my mother's funeral, as well as the closing week on our new house. Matt did not attend her funeral, again due to his needing to take his final exams in the first semester of freshman year. He never insisted, never voiced that he wanted to be there.

Through all of that rough winter, we managed to get our house sold and purchased a smaller one in the same town. Laura was still having the drop seizures, and we had to take her to the emergency room several times for stitches, but finally our life was starting to be on an even keel.

We painted the new house before we moved in and took our time to get things set up. Matt's room came first; we made sure he knew that was a priority. If nothing else got done, we wanted Matt's room to be ready for him. When he came home for the first time after we moved in, he commented on the fact that his room was all set up for him, and he was very appreciative. He loved the other house, but he also said he liked the location of the new house. So it seemed like we had gotten it right, and Matt seemed to suffer no psychological scars from our picking up and changing homes.

That spring we started to take day trips to Ocean City to look at houses down there. We certainly couldn't buy our dream house on the beach, but we did find a really nice house in a lovely, quiet, family-oriented neighborhood, just a few blocks from where I'd spent most of my childhood and teenage summers. We closed on that house on August 2, 2006. It was already rented through the end of August, and we continued to rent it for the next few summers, but after it was ours, we always spent the week leading up to Labor Day there, as well as most weekends during fall, winter, and spring, fixing it up but also just enjoying the slow pace of Ocean City during the nontourist season. When Matt went back to school in September 2006, we went again to Ocean City for a week, but this time to our own house!

Later that month, Matt called from school, saying he wasn't feeling well; he was suffering from severe diarrhea and vomiting.

My first question was whether he had been using drugs or drinking. He told me honestly that he had done some shots a few nights prior, so the first day of his illness, he thought it was a delayed hangover. But after a few days, it didn't go away, and he was getting weaker and weaker; he said his roommates were worried about him. This was during the very beginning of the E. coli outbreak, which started in Connecticut, where he went to school. So Mike and I told him to think about going to the emergency room at the nearest hospital, Yale-New Haven. A couple of days later, we received a call at about 1:30 a.m. from Matt, telling us his roommates were taking him to the hospital. We were in constant touch with him and his doctors, and I felt really guilty about not being there with him, but he was emphatic about not wanting us to come up, because all he wanted to do was sleep. One of us always stayed with Tim and Laura while they were in the hospital; that was one thing; I thought that an eighteen-year-old adult male probably did not want his mommy sleeping a foot away from him, although he never told me that.. Matt gave his permission for the doctors to tell us anything we wanted to know, and they assured us that this illness had nothing to do with drugs or alcohol.

Matt was in the hospital for five days. He received no diagnosis other than viral gastroenteritis. His back was also quite sore—perhaps from his being in bed so much. Upon discharge, he received a prescription for Oxycontin upon discharge (because of his backache) and was told to eat bland food and to take it easy for a while. After he returned to school, he called me a lot, asking what he could and couldn't eat. He really wanted to eat normal food, and I think he was hoping I'd say, "Oh, go ahead and have pizza." But he pretty much took it easy and finally got back to his normal self.

But for a hospital in a college town to give Oxycontin to a college kid who had a backache? Maybe there was no reason not to, but I wonder whether that fueled his eventual sampling of other drugs. Matt never has given me a straight answer about that. Maybe this question is something that never will be unraveled. Maybe he just couldn't even remember the timing.

CHAPTER EIGHTEEN

Shortly after Matt's fourth birthday, he caught a cold he couldn't shake. He was really dragging, and then he started to complain about aches and pains—at the creases of his knees and elbows and in his armpits. He was so weak and sore that he couldn't climb into his bed or sit on the toilet, and I couldn't lift him onto it because that meant picking him up under his armpits. I had to find a little step-stool he could use to get into bed. The areas that ached were very red, almost like they were sunburned, but sunburned in places that wouldn't even be exposed to the sun. A couple of times, we went to the pediatrician, who had no idea what was going on. She suggested that if it continued, we should take Matt to the ER at CHOP. (Yes, another child was giving us more ties to CHOP.) It did continue; he didn't want to eat or drink, or maybe he was just too weak. He wanted nothing to do with food.

Finally, on a Sunday morning, I told him he could have whatever he wanted for breakfast, even soda or ice cream, but he wouldn't eat anything. That's when I knew he was really sick. The pediatrician made a call to CHOP's ER, telling them to expect Matt, and off we went. At this point, his face and lips were swollen, the redness was everywhere, and areas of his skin were starting to peel. Wearing clothes and shoes hurt him; he wore soft summer pajamas to the hospital.

Matt's illness was a puzzle. Dermatology was there, taking pictures of his various areas of redness. They ran all kinds of tests. They admitted him, and after he'd spent twenty-four hours in a room with three other children, they decided they probably should place him in an isolation room. We saw all kinds of doctors, and passed Tim and Laura's doctors in the halls, who did double takes when they saw us, saying they hadn't received word that Tim or Laura were in the hospital.

Meanwhile Matt was beginning to eat, but it was food he never had wanted before, like hard-boiled eggs. Then he quickly figured out that he could have Popsicles whenever he wanted them. He knew he wasn't supposed to come out of his hospital room, so he'd sit in bed, watching TV, while I went to the little kitchen to get him yet another Popsicle. During one of my trips to the kitchen, I paused at the kitchen door, because I sensed someone was behind me, and I didn't want to knock anyone down. There was Matt, shuffling along, pulling his IV pole with him, patiently waiting for the Popsicle. So he was quickly back to his old self. He was there for five days with what they finally determined was staphylococcal scalded skin syndrome, which is caused by certain strains of staphylococcus bacteria, becoming a skin infection in which the skin becomes damaged and sheds. This is treated with intravenous antibiotics that fight the infection and intravenous fluids to prevent dehydration.

CHAPTER NINETEEN

Matt seemed to be doing very well during his sophomore and junior years at UNH, which was a good thing, especially since Laura had two bouts of aspiration pneumonia and seizures, which put her in the hospital for three weeks each time. Things seemed to be on track with Matt—thank God—because we wouldn't have been able to take care of Laura at CHOP and Tim at home, and handle any problems with Matt all at the same time.

He told me much later that he started using pot pretty much right away in college; he also was drinking and using cocaine like crazy. He already had been introduced to painkillers, first from the broken jaw and teeth when he was almost fifteen, again when he had his wisdom teeth pulled when he was almost eighteen, and finally when he was in the hospital during his freshman year of college.

Matt started working at PNC Bank Arts Center during the summer of his sophomore year, for the catering company that prepared food for the bands that played there. During the summer after his junior year, he secured a position doing an internship (one of two he had to do for his Music Industry major) at MTV in New York City, and he was still able to work some shows for the catering company.

His internship wasn't a paid one, and he took the train to work and ate lunch in the city, so it wasn't a cheap summer for us, but he enjoyed being at MTV. And although he didn't enjoy getting up at 6:00 a.m. to go to work, he did seem to like the feel of taking the train into the city, running around to different locations in the city when he was sent on errands, participating in conference calls with locations in California, making calls to bands, and doing whatever was asked of him.

For his music industry major, he was required to do two, 125-hour internships. MTV didn't work that way. They wanted someone full time or not at all. So Matt had to commit to 350 hours at MTV, and it still counted as just one internship, not two. I suppose it was enough of an honor to be at MTV, and they weren't going to invest any time in training people who wouldn't be there enough to make a difference. That made sense. He called in sick a couple of times and had requested a couple of days off right off the bat, to attend some sort of music festival out of state. Matt finished his required time there, but it was down to the wire.

So he went into his senior year with one internship under his belt, and he could do the other during the school year. Matt had started to see someone in the spring of his junior year, a very nice girl named Daniella. She had graduated at the end of that summer, so she wasn't living at school during his senior year, but still they managed to see quite a bit of each other. He would go to Brooklyn and Long Island to see her, or she would come visit him in Connecticut. In addition to wanting to be with Matt, she had a couple of other friends still there. He didn't find an internship during his first semester of his senior year, but through a friend, he was able to line up an internship in New Haven during his second semester, for a small company that booked entertainment acts for various venues. The owner, Johnny, had some medical issues, including blindness, so he needed a lot of help. At one point, Matt said, Johnny had talked about needing someone to run the business and that maybe Matt and his friend, who gotten him the internship and also had done an internship for Johnny the previous year, might be just the people for the job. As Matt had completed seven semesters of college, while maintaining his 3.0 average the entire time, we were all feeling pretty good.

In October of his senior year, Matt had been involved in a car accident in Ocean City; it was completely not his fault. He and Daniella were OK, but the car was totaled. He was without a car for a couple of months, which cramped his style, I'm sure. The car was originally Mike's, but along the way, once Matt got his license, we turned the car over to Matt and replaced Mike's car. So he was without a car, but unbeknownst to him, we received the check from the insurance company, and Mike's father gave Mike an additional check to use toward a car for Matt. Mike looked around and did his research, and when Daniella drove him home for winter break, there was a very nice used car with a bow on it waiting for him in the drive-way. He was ecstatic. He had his freedom back!

CHAPTER TWENTY

"I have something to tell you."

When a conversation starts like this, there's a pretty good chance it won't be good.

In January 2009, about a week before Matt went back to college for his final semester, he approached us with this sentence. A few things went through my head. Daniella was pregnant. He had failed a class. He had been in another car accident.

Mike and I listened in disbelief as he told us that he had started to gamble—first online and then via a bookie. At first he thought he was OK, but his gambling started to get out of hand and he needed help, because he owed the bookie $1,000. We were shocked and disappointed, but part of me thought, *If that's all it is, that's not so bad.* Matt added that the guy needed the money right away. OK. Not knowing anything about bookies but not wanting to mess with one, Mike went to the bank and was able to get the money together so Matt could be done with this bookie.

Then the stories began to get fuzzy.

It turned out it was really $1,500, so he asked us for $500 more. He didn't want to ask for it all upfront, he said; he was too embarrassed.

Of course, we gave it to him. Off he went, back to school. He needed money here and there all of that last semester—for books and supplies for an art class he was taking, to get his computer fixed, to get his buddy's computer fixed because Matt accidentally stepped on it, to repay a couple of people from whom he had borrowed money. He told us he owed the bookie even more than he told us, so he had borrowed from friends to pay him back, figuring that once he got back to school and his job he could pay them back. But business was slow at the restaurant, and he was laid off. And the bookie actually had him on a three-hundred-dollar-a-week payment plan of sorts. I told Matt I felt like I was supporting a three-hundred-dollar-a-week drug habit. He looked me in the eye and promised that it wasn't drugs; he just had gotten in over his head gambling. He and I spoke about it much later, and he admitted that he had just figured out some easy lies in order to get drug money from us.

I'm not sure at what point he told us that his total debt to the bookie was $30,000; some time after Mike had added up the amount we already had given him, we realized it was already into the tens of thousands. We had a million different thoughts and emotions. Why would a bookie keep taking bets from a college kid who had no job and couldn't pay his debt to begin with? Mike couldn't understand that, but I thought the bookie knew exactly what he was doing. He saw a little college boy who had Mommy and Daddy to get him out of a bind.

And he was right.

I once had a coworker who had a gambling problem, and I knew he had been in a similar situation a while ago. I asked him a lot of questions about gambling, bookies, etc., and the answers he gave me kind of reassured me that the way Matt was telling it really was the way bookies worked. We still do not know if he ever had any contact with a bookie, or just stumbled on a great reason to keep asking us for money. Even so, the lies rolled off Matt's tongue so easily. He always had a ready answer as to where he was, why he had to go somewhere unusual, what he needed money for. And he *always* needed money. He constantly asked for money during his last semester of college and also the entire following summer and fall. A couple of times he actually had me deposit the money into Daniella's bank account, not his, explaining that he owed it to her. We later found out that his account was overdrawn, so any money deposited into his account would be put toward his overdrafts, and he never would actually get the money.

CHAPTER TWENTY-ONE

Matt had wanted to get a credit card for a long time—ever since he started college. He thought it would be a good way for him to establish credit. We always had advised him against getting a credit card until he got a job. During his senior year of college, he told us he had gotten one that had a small line of credit. He also had opened a credit card at a jewelry store to buy Daniella a special necklace, and as it turned out, so he also could buy a few other pieces of jewelry and then sell them at a pawnshop to get more drug money. He had a great time Christmas shopping, buying me a nice candle from a fancy store and getting Mike a leather-bound set of books about cocktail making. Apparently he was also charging gas here and there and stocking up on snacks at the convenience store. Later we found out that he also had opened a couple of other credit cards so he could take cash advances to get even more drug money!

Clever boy.

Matt never gave a thought as to how he would pay off these credit cards. It wasn't real money to him. All he cared about was the cash. I don't think he figured that we would cover his debts, and he didn't figure that collection agencies would come looking for him.

He didn't think beyond the next bet, or whatever was going on with him; just as when he was a kid, his motto was "Act now. Think later."

By the time he admitted his gambling problem in January 2009, he had amassed several thousand dollars in credit card debt, in addition to the money he owed his bookie. Mike and I took control of the credit cards, closing them out and paying them off. This action enabled Matt, yes, but because all of the harassing phone calls that were coming to our home phone rather than Matt's cell phone, it was easier to just be done with it all. We also did it to restore Matt's credit, so that when he got out on his own he wouldn't be denied an apartment, or whatever, because of bad credit.

Then, one day in February 2009, as I was going through the mail, I saw a letter for Matt from an attorney's office in Connecticut. I figured he was starting to get junk mail for his soon-to-be life in the real world. Additionally he already had signed up to get free issues of gambling magazines. Every time one arrived, we'd make calls to get him off their mailing list.

Something made me open this letter. It said that the attorney knew about his arrest in Connecticut in early February for attempting to purchase narcotics. The attorney was offering her services. What? What arrest? I waited for my shaking to subside enough so I could call Matt. I was furious! I was screaming so much he could hardly understand me. As he told me the story, I couldn't really write down the facts because I was still shaking. He said yes, it was true, and he hadn't wanted to tell us about it because he was planning to take care of it on his own. "How?" I asked him. "Borrow more money from someone?" It was a stupid thing, but not a big deal, he said.

He was trying to buy some pot. An acquaintance was taking him to a dealer, and one of Matt's roommates had gone along for the ride. Matt was planning to purchase $50 worth of pot, so when the guy came over to Matt's car, Matt handed over the money and the dealer gave Matt a bag, supposedly with the pot inside it.

As soon as that happened, several policemen surrounded Matt's car, with guns drawn. The police had been watching the dealer and were waiting for the next deal to go down. Off Matt and his friends went to the police station. The dealer was picked up later, just a few blocks away. As the police took the bag of pot, it became evident that the dealer had scammed Matt. He had taken Matt's money and given him a bag of waxed paper with nothing in it—well, not quite nothing. Unfortunately the waxed paper was the dealer's trash and had remnants of heroin on it.

So Mike helped Matt out again and hired a lawyer in Connecticut; one of Matt's professors had referred him to this attorney. All court proceedings concluded around April 2009. Matt was sentenced to having to take a series of eight drug-education classes, which he had to take in Connecticut; paying a fine; and doing sixty-seven hours of community service, which he could do anywhere, as long as they fit the criteria of community service. He had to complete all of this by April 2010. The community service was originally supposed to be just thirty-seven hours (we have no idea how the judge came up with that random number), but the judge was pissed and sort of suspected there was more to the story, so he slapped on an additional thirty hours.

The judge had good instincts.

As the story unraveled much later, I found out from Matt that he was attempting to purchase heroin and did, in fact, make the purchase; he wasn't scammed at all. Somehow, before the police reached Matt's car, he was able to hide the drugs in his sock. And then, while the police were questioning Matt's friend *at the police station,* Matt managed to swallow his purchase—a bag containing a gram of heroin.

The scheduling of the community service and the drug-education classes became difficult, as Matt tried to work out times for both. Mike, Matt, and I all determined that it would be hard for him to do the community service right away, before graduation, since he had to study and needed to complete his second internship. The internship was moving along but slowly, since the man he was working for was ill and had to frequently go to the hospital and therefore sometimes couldn't give Matt the hours he needed.

Meanwhile the drug education classes were set up, but the first class coincided with graduation weekend. So Matt rescheduled and was assigned to the next series of classes, which would take place on Saturdays in August and September. Even with allowing extra time for the traffic, Matt arrived late for each of the first two classes and wasn't allowed to enter the classroom. After missing those two classes, he was told he had to wait for the next series of classes to start at the beginning of October. Well, that was OK.

He walked up to the podium at graduation, although a few days before graduation we found out that he still had a few more hours to complete for his internship. So, on May 23, 2009, he was handed an empty folder, instead of one containing his diploma.

CHAPTER TWENTY-TWO

So what did Matt do all summer? We had a family graduation party for him in Ocean City, so he had graduation money, which he used to pay back money to still more people to whom he was indebted. Our gift to him was a Tag Heuer watch. He worked for the catering company at PNC Bank Arts Center again, but they were cutting back and needed him less and less. He went to a few concerts, went to see Daniella, and went to the beach, all the while keeping his eyes and ears open for jobs.

As we became more and more frustrated with Matt's "I don't care" attitude, he seemed more determined to do whatever he felt, and nothing more. We hardly ever saw him; the hours he kept were the complete opposite of ours. The only way we communicated was by leaving notes. Here's one that Mike wrote out of frustration and left for Matt at the end of June.

June 30, 2009
Matt,

You wrote me a long letter on Father's Day, saying how sorry you were for everything, so now I am writing you a letter to say how disappointed I am in how you have handled yourself in the five-plus weeks since you've been home from school.

Mom and I are both sick to our stomachs, not sleeping well, and can't believe how you're acting—or not acting!

We have asked for the following things for five weeks:

1. *Write thank-you notes to all the people who gave you graduation money—nothing!*
2. *Set up the drug education classes, other than one evaluation—nothing!*
3. *Set up community service—nothing!*
4. *Provide us with copies of bank statements and all credit card statements—mostly nothing!*
5. *Devise a plan to complete your internship—practically nothing!*
6. *Work on your resume—nothing!*

You are showing that you really don't care about our feelings, no matter what you say or write in a letter. We want you to stop going out every night, staying up half the night, and sleeping half the day and get these things completed.

You're an adult now, but you're not showing any signs of being grown up.

You need to show some respect for us and realize you are back in our home and not living at school anymore.

Like I said, our patience is wearing very thin, and we are not going to continue to put up with this.

It's time to get your act together…now.

—Dad

Matt made no comment to either of us about the letter from Mike.

Over the course of the summer, Matt's car window got smashed, right in our driveway apparently. (We weren't at home, and he said he hadn't heard anything.) He had heavy plastic taped over it until it could be fixed, and in those few days, someone stole his watch, which he had left in the car while he was at the beach. (Later he told us that the broken window was the work of a "friend" who was retaliating for something Matt had done to his car.)

All this had been over drugs.

And then our bank accounts started to go haywire. Checks from our account and those of Tim and Laura had been taken and cashed. The person who did this was somehow able to cash them at our local bank, and it set off a chain of bounced checks. Someone at the bank called me about this, as there always had been very little activity on Tim and Laura's accounts—one check each per month, written to us. My first thought was the babysitter, although I'd never had any reason to think she wasn't trustworthy. The woman at the bank was kind enough to fax me copies of the checks. I just couldn't imagine who had managed to get their hands on our checks, and I wasn't prepared for who it was. The person who had forged and cashed these checks was Matt.

He was so clever; all the checks had notes in the memo area saying, "Happy Graduation." I guess no one questioned it, because it was, after all, graduation season, and Matt also had about ten legitimate checks from relatives to cash over the course of early summer.

Once we started looking, we noticed that cash was missing. Mike was the treasurer for his softball team and, as such, had several hundred dollars on hand at any given time, from dues, money to be used as donations, prizes, and the like. Matt used that stash as his own personal bank account as well—but only withdrawing, never depositing.

CHAPTER TWENTY-THREE

In July, for Matt's birthday, we took him to a Yankees game. He originally had plans to go to a different Yankees game with Daniella (for which he had borrowed money from us for the tickets; later he said that Daniella actually had paid for her own ticket), but they'd had a fight, and she was no longer going, so he needed to pay her for the ticket she had bought. Matt was going to take a friend instead to that game but never did. The story came out later that he had conned the money for Daniella out of us; he never really owed her the money because they never had purchased tickets for the game. He also told a good friend of his that he had an extra ticket if the friend wanted to go, so the friend paid Matt for a ticket that never existed. He sat through the game with us, knowing all along that he had conned us and a friend out of several hundred dollars. Just that day, he also had stolen and forged more of our checks.

He also wasn't sleeping well—who could sleep during such a time? He had so much on his mind: his debts, his lack of a job, his lies, the upcoming drug classes, his fights with Daniella, and the internship he needed to complete (he only had a few hours left to finish). So he was up a lot at night, sitting on the porch with the dog, smoking, and falling asleep out there for a few hours. He seemed so depressed-how could he not be? The legal stuff from Connecticut was still hanging over his head. His internships hadn't led to paying jobs. Nothing seemed to be going right for him.

How did we not realize that this could be about something more than gambling? He had told us he had a gambling problem, and we continued to believe him. But why did we continue to keep check-books and cash accessible to him? We vowed to buy a safe but some-how never got around to it. Once we discovered his activities, he promised that it was all out in the open now and that he wouldn't do it again. Eventually he agreed to go to Gambler's Anonymous, but at the time, we were told that it was only a one time big gambling incident, and he did not need help.

Love is truly blind.

Throughout the summer Matt would wake us up during the night, saying that one person or another needed his $300 *right now*. Sometimes it was for a friend from whom he had borrowed, and the friend was going on vacation in the morning and wanted the cash that night. Sometimes it was the bookie who was sending threaten-ing text messages to Matt, saying his boss needed the money and he didn't want to have to do anything to Matt, but he might have to do something to his car. We'd get calls from Matt during our very rare evenings out, saying that someone needed the money immediately. Matt generously would offer to come meet us wherever we were—a party, a dinner, whatever—so that we wouldn't have to leave our enjoyable evening and come home (as if we could continue to enjoy it after getting the call from Matt). While we were in Ocean City for our one-week vacation there a year, Matt drove down there to get money. He'd said he had driven down to visit and then said he needed gas money to get home. More than once we sent him money via Western Union. Why did we do it? Why did we give in and give him the money? Because we wanted to believe it was the bookie who needed the money. Yes, we could have, should have shown some tough love, but we didn't want Matt to get physically hurt.

He ran into one of his cousins at a local shopping center around that same time and asked her if he could borrow some money. She gave him $50 (he wanted $300), then she immediately called us. She knows someone who's a policeman in the narcotics division, and she had been talking to him about Matt. He told her it sounded like Matt was a heroin addict, but I assured her that he was just in deep with a gambling debt.

How stupid do we sound? How naive?

We thought Matt's being a compulsive gambler was bad enough, and every time we gave him money, he reassured us that it had nothing to do with drugs. Talk about blind faith.

His car was finally totaled one night, while he was coming back from meeting a friend to pay him back. He says he ran over a tailpipe or something on a dark road, and it damaged the underside of the car, causing all the fluid to drain out of the car and the engine to seize up, effectively ruining the car. So once again Matt had no car.

CHAPTER TWENTY-FOUR

So many questions. Someday I want all the answers. I think I know a lot of them, but I want to hear them from Matt—for closure, I suppose, and maybe just to know that the lies are all out in the open. He probably doesn't even remember most of the lies, or maybe I mean that he probably doesn't even remember what the truth to all of the stories is.

After he said he had paid off all his debts, Mike and I tried to avoid giving him cash. We still suspected something was going on, so if he said he needed money for gas (to go to Connecticut for the drug education classes), we'd take the car and fill it up. Or if it was time to get the oil changed in his car, we'd take it to be done. But we couldn't always do it ourselves, or even go with him, so sometimes we had to give him the cash and ask him to bring us a receipt. Of course the receipts always got lost. Then we'd discover that he never got the oil changed. Or the money he said he needed to buy new pants for job-hunting somehow got spent—and not on pants.

Yes, we were stupid. A part of us knew there was something other than gambling going on, but a bigger part of us refused to believe Matt could be a drug addict. We never saw any paraphernalia. And when we did see things, we didn't know what they were. For instance one time that summer we found a packet of drugs in the mailbox (he had put them there one Sunday while Daniella was visiting for the weekend because he didn't want her to find them) after coming home from the shore. Matt managed to talk his way out of that by telling us he was holding the drugs as a favor for his bookie, who would knock some money off his debt. Since we still believed he was tied to the bookie, it made sense that he had turned into the bookie's delivery boy. He claimed he didn't know what the packets were—that he was told they were pain pills. I asked why they were in powder form, and he said that sometimes they get crushed to split the batch more and that other substances are added to it to stretch it out.

CHAPTER TWENTY-FIVE

A hurricane was predicted for our area on August 9, 2009. Prediction of a hurricane meant nothing to Matt. There was absolutely no reason to stay indoors. Being the beach bum and bodyboarder that he was, Matt said his plan for the day was to check out the waves at some point, knowing that there would be impressive waves due to the hurricane. He also was going to drive around, looking for help wanted signs. He had a free day so he figured it was a good time to do some job hunting. I called him in the early afternoon, but he didn't pick up. That wasn't unusual, if he was with friends or in the water. (I hoped he wasn't in the water, with the hurricane churning things up and picking up strength.) I had no particular reason to call—maybe just to see if he would be eating dinner with us.

I got home from work shortly after 5:00 p.m. I let the sitter go home and started to think about dinner, when I got a phone call from Daniella on the home phone. She had last talked to Matt around lunchtime but hadn't been able to get in touch with him since then. She said he had an interview at a bakery around 4:00 p.m. that afternoon, and then he was going to drive up to see her—either to her family's home on Long Island or their summer home in Brooklyn.

She was starting to worry, and if *she* was worried, I knew something was up.

I tried getting in touch with Matt's friends, but they all had cell phones, and of course I didn't have those numbers. I called the home numbers I could find, but I only managed to get in touch with one mom, who said her son was at work, and he didn't have a cell phone anyway. Daniella and I kept in touch, but neither of us knew anything.

By now it was 7:00 p.m. or so and very dark; it was raining like crazy, and the winds were picking up. Mike drove down to Monmouth Beach to check out the places where Matt usually bodyboards. We were scared to death, for a few reasons. First, we were afraid he was in the water and had run into trouble. Second, we worried that he was more depressed than we thought, that he might have considered throwing himself into the ocean. And, finally, was the bookie involved somehow?

So, in the middle of a hurricane, Mike drove slowly up and down every street in Monmouth Beach, looking for Matt and/or Matt's car. A policeman eventually pulled Mike over because his actions seemed suspicious. Mike explained that Matt was missing. Ordinarily a missing persons report couldn't be filed until the person had been missing for twenty-four hours. The policeman asked if Mike had any reason to suspect foul play or if anyone might want to harm Matt. Matt had told us that the bookie had left some vaguely threatening messages on his cell phone, so once the policeman heard that, he did file a missing persons report. That meant all of the local precincts would keep an eye out for him. Mike finally drove home to sit and wait with me.

The phone rang around 9:00 p.m., and we were afraid to answer it, not knowing what to expect. It was Matt. He said that his phone had been giving him trouble (which he had been telling me for some time) and that he and one of his old friends from elementary school had decided to go to Point Pleasant to check out the waves there; they had decided to just hang out there for the day. What? He had blown off an interview and his girlfriend to check out the waves? He said he was taking his friend back to his house and then would come home.

He finally came home around 10:00 p.m., sat in the family room with us, and listened as we told him how scared and worried we had been, afraid that the bookie had done something to him or that he did something to himself. He said he was fine and was sorry; he said he should have tried to get in touch with us. But he was OK. It had nothing to do with the bookie, or gambling, or anything bad—just two boys kind of playing hooky from responsibility for the day. I told him that Daniella was very worried, so he called her and spent several hours arguing with her. He had to get up early the next day to drive to Connecticut for one of the drug classes, so I knew he'd be tired. And Mike and I had to drive to Ocean City to check on our house after the storm.

I called Daniella the next day from Ocean City, because Matt wasn't answering his phone. I wanted to make sure he had made it to the class on time. She didn't know any more than I did, either about his day and evening in Point Pleasant or his drive to Connecticut that morning. Matt told me later that they pretty much broke up that weekend because Daniella couldn't deal with his being so irresponsible. But, at the time, we were concerned when he didn't answer the phone, again afraid that he had done something crazy Friday night or Saturday morning—overdosed, committed suicide; who knew what? A good friend of Mike's ended up driving past the house. If Matt's car had been there, we were prepared to tell the friend to break into the house. Not to worry. His car wasn't there; Matt must have been on his way to Connecticut for his class.

More lies unraveled. We later found out that Matt (and his friend) had been arrested that day, for buying and selling heroin. For some reason the police made a deal with them, and Matt was apparently going to lead the police (at a later date, to be set up by the police) to the dealer. We didn't find out about this until several months later. Matt was always the person to get the mail first, so if there was any legal correspondence, we almost never saw it.

CHAPTER TWENTY-SIX

The beach was Matt's favorite childhood playground. Sea Bright, New Jersey, was his venue. He christened the Sea Bright beaches before his first birthday. He took in everything that the beach club had to offer him: the sand, the pool, the ocean, the snack bar. He had been to Ocean City a few times as a toddler, but once we moved back to was Little Silver, he was back in Sea Bright. He on the go all day long, loved every minute of it. And with Tim and Laura in their school programs all day, I could pretty much accommodate Matt—from ten to two thirty at least—until I started working full time. As he got older, he started to push the envelope, asking to walk down the street to 7-Eleven to buy a Slurpee, to walk across the street to the surf shop, and to go to the public beach a couple of blocks away, where he and his friends were allowed to surf or bodyboard.

The beach club was a nice, if pricy, alternative to the public beaches. For the season, we had a "cabana." It was actually a large locker, but it did have a shower in it. Other cabanas, for which there was a long waiting list and an even bigger price tag, offered electricity, sinks, and cabinets. We were fine with what we had; we kept our beach chairs, toys, boogie boards, and towels in there, and didn't have to lug everything back and forth all the time. The membership also gave us access to a guarded beach, adult and kiddy swimming pools, restrooms, a snack bar, and a lobby where we could cool off. A huge raft was anchored just off shore, and that was usually Matt's destination. Maybe he felt like he was on an island? If I were his age, I would have felt that way.

At the time, one of the members was Bruce Springsteen who lived with his family in the area. People mostly left him alone, and really he was just another one of the members. Matt knew who he was and knew that he was "famous" but couldn't put that fact into any real context. An eight-year-old really doesn't listen to that kind of music. So he and Matt occasionally chatted when they were both on the raft at the same time, the rock star asking Matt if he liked surfing better than bodyboarding, etc. One day, Matt, already a social butterfly, told the rock star that we were having a fortieth birthday party for Mike that weekend and asked him if he wanted to come. He said "Sure! Where do you live?" probably thinking or hoping that Matt would name a town some distance away. Instead Matt came right out and gave him our address in Little Silver, which was only four miles from the beach club, and even closer to the star's home. The rock star quickly back-pedaled, saying he forgot he had something else to do that night. It was no big deal to Matt, who for all I knew could have invited everyone at the club to come to the party! Later that day, as we were driving home from the beach, I had the radio tuned to a classic rock station. As one of this Springsteen's songs came on, introduced by the DJ as "the icon of America's Everyman, but one of the greatest rock 'n' rollers of all time," Matt's jaw kind of dropped, and he said, "Wow! He's on the radio?"

On weekends, for several years, the whole family went to the beach club. Tim always liked going, just to hear the happy sounds. Laura enjoyed the going to the pool and taking walks on the beach for a few years, but then became fearful of the water and didn't like the feel of the sand. By then Matt was only using the beach club to take a shower and spent the rest of his time at the public beach, so we reluctantly relinquished our membership.

I hated to give it up. What I really hated to give up was the innocence of our time there. Matt and I would pack a lunch, eat together, get a snack later, and really enjoy the day. He was with his friends for the majority of the day, but he'd check in with me periodically, so it was also just an outing for Mom and Matt.

It was part of our special routine, which he grew up and out of all too quickly.

CHAPTER TWENTY-SEVEN
September 2009

The US Mint started to issue state quarters in 1999. I had a candy dish in my office at work, and whenever I'd get one, I'd throw it into the dish. I got them all the time, so I'd throw several into the dish every week. My little dish filled up quickly, and I moved them to a wooden keepsake box that one of my employees had given me one Christmas. It was a fairly big box that could hold *a lot* of quarters.

I wasn't saving them for any particular reason; I wasn't keeping track of what I had and didn't have, and I wasn't on a mission to collect the entire set. Mike had one of those books, so he was trying to collect one from each state. I wasn't doing that. I didn't care if I had every one, or duplicates. I never really even looked to see what state I was throwing into the box. I just kept throwing them in.

After a few years, too many people at work were starting to borrow a few quarters here and there for the soda machine. They replaced the quarters with dollars or other change, but even though I didn't have any goal in mind for the quarters, my goal was for the box to be full of state quarters—not regular quarters, not any other coins, and not paper money!

So I brought the box home, and Mike eagerly went through all of them, finding a few for his collection. The box was on my bureau and had pictures under the glass top—pictures of me with each of the kids, and one of Mike and me. It was a nice keepsake. After throwing at least a dollar's worth of quarters in the box every week for almost ten years—well, you do the math. There should have been several hundred dollars' worth of quarters in the box. I'd throw the quarters in and hear a nice, satisfying "clink" as the quarters hit the ones already in the box.

Then one day in September 2009, I threw some quarters in, and there was no satisfying clink. The box was empty! Or very nearly so. Of course the first person I confronted was Matt. We'd just had (yet another) heart-to-heart talk, and he said he wasn't going to take anything from us anymore and would stop lying. He said yes, he did take them, but it was a while ago, before he'd made this latest promise. He probably had stolen the quarters a few weeks prior, likely while we were on vacation in Ocean City, just before Labor Day. That would have been the only time when I wasn't throwing quarters in the box every day or so. He insisted then, and still insists, that it was only about $50 worth of quarters. I figure it had to be a lot more than that—at least a day's supply of heroin for Matt. Maybe he took them in several "withdrawals," and maybe it's true that the last time was only $50. That would explain why I was still hearing the clink of coins up until this last time.

That really hurt. I was angry, but I also felt I had been violated. It wasn't the amount of the money; certainly he had taken larger amounts from us. More so than taking checks, though, he had taken something personal of mine. For some reason it hurt more than if he had taken a piece of my jewelry (which, by the way, he never did).

When I confronted him, I told him I had been saving them since they were first introduced in 1999, and he actually looked a bit distraught, like it somehow sunk in through his drug-induced haze that he had taken something important to me. He said he didn't realize that; he thought it was just a place where I kept loose change. I asked if he didn't realize that there was nothing but state quarters in the box and that therefore it might be some sort of collection. He said no; he never had looked. Another lie. There were a few nickels that had gotten mixed in with the quarters (maybe when my coworkers were using my box to make change); Matt had actually left the nickels in the box!

CHAPTER TWENTY-EIGHT

Every day, or more like every night, there was an argument. Matt slept all day and was out or up all night. We'd often get a call from him, asking for gas or food money, or sometimes money to continue paying back the ever-present bookie or others to whom he still owed money. He pretty much checked in with us to let us know where he was and what his plans were, but he spent no time with us.

Our family limped along through August and September arguing and nagging. Always there were requests for money here and there, to repay people who were still coming out of the woodwork, but he finally had started the series of drug education classes, and he'd be finished by the end of November.

Matt finally agreed to see a counselor for his compulsive gambling. I believe his first session was one on one, and after that he went to weekly group sessions. Mike and I were still struggling with it all. The counselor recommended that Matt also attend Gamblers Anonymous meetings, and Mike and I went to GamAnon meetings at the same time. We tried a couple of different meetings but never felt quite comfortable. Everyone else in the group had spouses with a gambling problem. They talked about moving out or kicking the spouse out of the house. We always felt that Matt was our son, our flesh and blood, and we couldn't divorce him or throw him to the curb. But even though we couldn't quite relate to the majority of the group, it did feel good to be able to vent a little and to vent to people who knew the pain and frustration we felt. Matt was comfortable in his group at first, but then he went to one particular meeting that he said became a little confrontational. The argument didn't involve Matt or a gambler and his spouse; I think it was between two longtime members of the GA group. At any rate Matt wasn't sure he wanted to return to that group and said he'd maybe try to find a different meeting. We said we'd go wherever he wanted—not that we would be in the same meeting, but we kind of thought the car rides to and from the meetings were good for a little bit of bonding; they were really the only times we were together. Plus Matt no longer had a car, so it made sense to carpool. I did call a woman from our group—she was younger than us but lived in the same town—and her husband had kind of befriended Matt initially. I wanted to let her know that Matt was upset about something that had transpired at the one particular meeting and asked her whether her husband could talk about it a bit with Matt.

I believe her husband did talk to Matt, and Matt said he would try one more meeting with this group and see how he felt.

Matt, however, never got the chance.

CHAPTER TWENTY-NINE

When I started to put pen to paper in May 2010 to write down all the thoughts and actions of the past several years, I wrote like crazy. I remembered everything so clearly.

I felt I needed to catalog everything up to this point right away, while the events were still fresh in my mind—well, as fresh as they could be. There were still things I was sure I didn't know about, lots of lies to unravel. Matt did say once that I didn't need to hear everything. I guess if I thought back hard enough, I could pinpoint lots of signs that I'd missed. Maybe that part was just too confusing to write about.

I'd already jumped around a lot, so I couldn't start completely in chronological order, but I decided to write it as the thoughts came to me, and make sense of it later.

Stupid statement. There was no sense to this mess.

Yet at this juncture, I was hesitant to actually start writing about the main events. Did I not want to relive those days? They were never far from my thoughts. Maybe I would rather remember the cute moments of that innocent little boy, before things started to go so wrong. Maybe the cute stories would cushion the blow. Or maybe they would make the pain even worse.

I was still resisting, still not ready to write about the sequence of events that started in November 2009. I wanted to write more about the young Matthew, the cute Matthew, the innocent Matthew. I had to keep remembering that person, so I didn't lose sight of who he could be again. He wouldn't become innocent again, of course, but he could be the happy boy who loved life and being a part of it. Sometimes I could no longer remember the cute stories, though I knew there were hundreds. Every day with Matthew during his preteen years was full of cute stories. Now the bad memories were clouding my mind, so I was no longer seeing the cute parts.

CHAPTER THIRTY

I was thinking about the times, or if there even were any times, when I couldn't be there for Matt—the guilty-mother moments. One was Matt's first day of first grade. There was no bus transportation for families who lived less than two miles from the school (which was just about every family), so the children walked or rode their bikes, while the younger ones were driven. Matt and I waited for Tim and Laura's bus to come so we could scoot off to his big day, but their bus was very late that morning. We waited, then waited some more.

Finally we couldn't wait any longer and had to find a ride for him or he'd be late. How would that look on his first day? Matt got a ride with the mother of a friend who lived a couple of doors down from us. I got to school as soon as I could, and I watched him for a while. He seemed very comfortable, but later he said he had wanted me to take him. I don't know how much of that was an act, but I felt terrible about that for a long time. I felt angry too. I knew the driver of Tim's and Laura's bus couldn't help it, but I felt like I was robbed of an important milestone in Matt's life.

CHAPTER THIRTY-ONE

Thursday, November 11, 2009 was one of those really busy days. Mike left early, as usual, to spend the day in his office in North Jersey (a commute of more than an hour each way). I had to do a training session in North Jersey, also about an hour from our house. Laura went to school on the bus as usual. Tim's day program was open but had no transportation due to some holiday. Or maybe just the county had given their drivers the day off. Matt and I worked out the schedule. He would drive me to my office, where I'd get a ride with a coworker to the training session. Then Matt would take Tim to his program at eight thirty, go to community service for four or five hours, and then pick Tim up around two thirty. It was one of those crazy days, but it seemed like everything would fall into place.

And it did, as far as I knew, until about three thirty or four, when I received a call from Tim's day program, saying that Tim was still there but that an aide, who lived near us, would be bringing him home. What about Matt picking Timmy up? Well, the program got a call from the state police, saying that Matt had been "detained," but that he had pleaded with the police to please get a message to the program about Timmy needing a ride home. That's all I knew. I called Mike, who hadn't heard anything. My hands were tied—I had no car—and shaking like crazy. My coworker and I finished up our work, cutting short a late-afternoon meeting and rescheduling the training session. Rather than her driving me home, she dropped me off at a rest area on the turnpike, so she could go straight home; Mike would meet me there and give me a ride the rest of the way home. We still knew nothing by the time we got home and spent an hour or more pacing the floors. Mike called a friend of his who's a policeman to see if he could find out anything. What did "detained" mean? Was he in a car accident? Was he stuck in traffic as a result of an accident unrelated to him? Did my car break down? Did something happen at community service?

We finally got a call from Matt around seven thirty or eight. He was in jail, or maybe still at the police department. I didn't know where he was; I didn't even know what county he was in. He had been arrested for buying and selling drugs. It was mostly heroin, but he had some other drugs in his possession as well. Apparently he would buy the drugs from a dealer for people who were too timid to approach a dealer. Then Matt would raise the price a bit and pocket some extra money—and maybe pocket some drugs for himself as well. Oh, he wanted to tell me one more thing; he had tried heroin a few times.

So began the nightmare of the unraveling of Matt—and of this mess.

We didn't bail him out that night. At that point the bail was set at $50,000, which meant we needed to pay ten percent of that to get him out. Luckily Mike had the name and number of one of the best criminal attorneys in the area and had actually gone on golf trips with him (and others) a couple of times. The attorney agreed to take Matt's case and said to wait and see if he could get the bail reduced.

He also said that if it were his kid, he would have had him stay in jail until his trial.

By morning we learned that instead of the bail being reduced, it was actually raised, I think due to the amount of drugs in Matt's possession and the amount of money in his pocket, which was indicative of trafficking. The bail was now so high that the ten-percent issue no longer held true. Mike and I spent all of Friday starting the paperwork to have a lien put on our house as collateral for getting him out of jail. We also had to figure out where my car was, since it had been impounded when Matt was arrested.

Meanwhile we got a couple of calls from bail bondsmen (whom Matt was allowed to call from jail). The bondsmen would call us while Matt was on another line, and Matt could sort of talk to us through a middle phone. The bail bondsmen kept telling us, and Matt, that all we had to do was give them $10,000 and they'd get Matt out of jail. What they were really doing was putting up the collateral, and $10,000 was their fee. We never would get that money back after the trial. Eventually I figured out how to set up a special prepaid account for calls from inmates at correctional facilities, so Matt could call collect right to my phone. The next time Matt called via the bail bondsman, I was able to tell him to go ahead and call collect on my cell phone. The bail bondsman realized that we had figured things out and immediately disconnected the call, and we never got any more calls from them.

Mike kind of broke down that first full day that Matt was in jail, sobbing and saying he didn't think he could do all of this. He was about to start a new job and had that on his mind, and now this. I told him to get a hold of himself because I couldn't do it alone. So, slowly but surely, we did what we could on Friday, but our hands were tied over the weekend. The one really hard thing for me was calling his internship boss; Matt had said he had just a few hours left and was planning to finish them on Saturday, up in Connecticut, after his drug-education class. So I called Matt's boss to say that something had come up and that Matt couldn't get there that Saturday. He was quiet for a moment and then said, "Matt Laverty? I haven't seen him since February. He showed up a couple of times and never returned. Good kid. Nice, smart kid. He told me about his disabled brother and sister. I was wondering if something had happened to him. I called him a few times, and he didn't return my calls. I thought maybe he had died or something."

Throughout that entire weekend, that was the only time I cried. I completely fell apart. I couldn't stop crying as the reality of it all set in. I could barely compose myself enough to mumble some sort of thank-you to his boss. To hear that the internship was just another elaborate lie that Matt held onto for nine months was more than I could handle. All the Saturdays he had driven to Connecticut for drug-education classes and then his internship—God only knows where he really had gone and what he really had done while he was there. Yes, he did go to the classes, of which he had three left, and which he would now miss because he was in jail.

Matt was able to call periodically over the weekend; he seemed scared to be there, very tearful. He also was going through withdrawal and felt lousy. He said there were five people in his cell and only four mattresses, so he had to sleep on the floor. He said he cried the whole time, huddled in a corner of the cell, scratching into the wall with the top of a pen, "I love my family." He seemed a little panicked that he couldn't get out of jail right away. He couldn't have visitors until he had been there for a week, so we could only talk to him when he was allowed to make calls. Newcomers were on twenty-three-hour lockdown and had just one hour a day to come out of their cells. So we talked to him on Friday and Saturday but heard nothing from him on Sunday. (We later found out that there had been an incident in a different cellblock so the entire facility was on twenty-four-hour lockdown.)

When we weren't arranging everything that had to be done to get him out of jail, I was looking into drug-treatment facilities for him. Finally we realized he had a drug addiction. Our attorney had given us the name of a facility not far from where we lived. I called but couldn't answer many of their questions, as I didn't really know what drugs he had been using, or how much. Up until this point, Mike and I had thought he was just a compulsive gambler who had dabbled with marijuana in high school but had moved past that. So we finally arranged for him to be admitted into Bayview House's Central New Jersey location. Assuming the paperwork would be completed and he would get out of jail on Monday, he had an appointment for that day for the intake evaluation. Matt knew nothing about this, but we weren't going to give him a choice about it; he would go to rehab, or he would stay in jail.

But first we had to do more paperwork regarding our house in order to get him out of jail. First thing Monday morning, Mike and I had to go to Middlesex Court, then to Freehold Court, then back to Middlesex Court. We finally arrived at the correctional facility at 1:28 p.m., gave our name and Matthew's and were directed to the person who needed the bail paperwork. This person kind of took her time, then looked at the clock and said, "It's one thirty—lockdown time. We can't let anyone out during lockdown. Lockdown will be one to two hours." As it was, we were already late for the intake appointment at Bayview House, but they said they'd wait for us. They changed the location, however, and said he would need to go to the North Jersey location, because he was still detoxing and needed to be at the location that had twenty-four-hour medical care.

Matt was finally released around 4:00 p.m. The delay was caused by an incident that kept the facility on lockdown longer than usual.

He gave me a big, hard, hug; cried; and said how sorry he was. I responded with hugs and tears of my own, although the stench from his not showering for five days (by his own choice) nearly knocked me over. Mike hugged him too, but he was really pissed. I offered to drive, thinking that if Matt wasn't cooperative and tried to jump out of the car or something, Mike would be better able to restrain him. But Mike wanted no part of sitting in the backseat with Matt. So I sat in the back with Matt and his body odor. Matt was very busy going through his wallet, hoping that the $600 he had collected when we was arrested was still there. His backpack had been confiscated, along with everything in it, including checks he had stolen from our checking accounts as well as Tim and Laura's. The backpack and its contents were never returned. He also was playing around with his phone—not really checking messages but maybe erasing messages. It didn't matter. I was sure the authorities already had listened to every message and seen every text. I think he was still out of it and just fidgeting with things. His mind wasn't very clear. We told him we were taking him to a place so he could get help. He agreed to that but wanted to go home and take a shower first. We said no. He later told us he really wanted to go use one more time. Did that mean there was a supply of drugs somewhere in the house, or was he going to quickly try to get in touch with a friend who could get him something? That one is still a mystery.

We finally got to North Jersey around 6:00 p.m. I'm so grateful to my good friend, Janet, who went to our house to relieve the babysitter, feed the kids and the dog, give Laura all of her medications (as per my step-by-step phone instructions), get them in bed, and stay at our house until we got home. There were a lot of forms for us to fill out and calls to our insurance carrier to make, and then Matt's intake needed to be completed. I asked if Mike and I could be there for the intake. The nurse looked at Matt who said, "Yes, they need to hear everything." So right away I had them document in Matt's chart that Mike and I were to be told anything and everything throughout his stay and that we were to have full access to everything about him—doctors, nurses, therapists, etc. And so the questions came. "Did you use this drug? This drug? How often? How was it administered? When did you last use? How much?" Matt had trouble following some of the questions or took them too literally and got sidetracked easily. For example, when asked, "Did you ever swallow anything that wasn't meant to be swallowed?" he answered "toothpaste." At times it was almost comical.

Matt asked how long he would have to stay, and I said, "That depends on you and how hard you work." The intake worker said, "No, it really depends on your insurance." Then the person making the insurance arrangements said our insurance wouldn't approve an inpatient stay, because Matt had to have first tried and failed outpatient treatment. We said to do whatever it took, but he wasn't coming home—not that night or anytime soon. So the facility billed the insurance as if he were receiving outpatient counseling for twenty-eight days, and we paid the room and board charges for the twenty-eight nights he was there. That meant that once he actually was an outpatient, most of his outpatient benefits for this admission already would be used up.

Meanwhile Matt was starving. He hadn't eaten much for six days. Mike drove down the street to a mini mart to get him something. Just after Mike left, an outpatient client came in for the Tuesday-night group meeting, bearing three pizzas. I thought Matt was going to faint when the smell hit him. The gentleman generously offered Matt a slice, which Matt initially politely declined but was easily talked into taking. And he still ate the sandwich that Mike brought back for him.

So Matt got checked in. The staff went through everything I'd brought for him; he could bring toothpaste but not mouthwash, an electric razor only, and no T-shirts that had alcohol or drug logos on them. For the twenty-eight days and nights he was there, it was hard for me to concentrate on much besides Matt and his legal and substance-abuse issues, but it was actually a very nice month. We didn't have to worry about where he was, who he was with, what he was doing, or when we'd get a call from him asking for money. We knew he was safe and that we were safe from him. Mike left for a week in Wisconsin to train for his new job.

We talked to Matt weekly and attended the group-counseling sessions. Matt cried a lot his first couple of weeks there and was initially very distraught over what he had done—his breaking the law and also what he had done to us. He admitted to us that he had pawned the watch we had given him for graduation; it hadn't been stolen from his car. While he was there, he learned to share his feelings, made some good friends—both patients and counselors—worked hard, and went to a lot of meetings.

CHAPTER THIRTY-TWO

Matt read the following letter to us one night at the beginning of December 2009, after about a month in rehab, during family group at Bayview House.

> *To my mother and father, who have been nothing but good to me my whole life,*
>
> *The instructions of this assignment say to state the negative attitudes, behaviors, thoughts, and emotions I've displayed to the two of you. I could be wrong, but I know I've displayed plenty of negative attitudes and behaviors. My thoughts and emotions were always positive toward you, though, at least in my head. I have always looked up to the two of you and have envied the things you do and have done. I've learned since I stopped using that I can now show my emotions, but in the past I was holding back. I am an emotional wreck these days, but it feels good. I always felt so bad about hiding so much from you guys; I was just caught up in living the fast life with quick fixes and living in an altered mindset.*

Now that I am thinking 100 percent more clearly, I realize how negative my attitudes and behaviors toward you were. You both tried so hard to get me to change my lifestyle, and even when you weren't always including drugs in the conversation, I knew you were thinking it and knew what your intentions were. If I'd changed any aspect of my lifestyle, it would have changed all aspects of it. I was in complete denial and living a routine of destruction. You would always tell me to go to bed earlier and stop staying up till 5:00 a.m., but I never listened. You would ask me to come home for dinner, but most of the time, I'd be doing something stupid and blow it off. You pushed me to play sports and do things I was into before drugs, not because you wanted me to play, but because you knew I loved these things. You would practically beg me to come visit the family and spend time with you in Ocean City, which I miss more than anything now, and I constantly did what I thought I wanted to do, but it was the complete opposite of what I want. You pushed me through counseling, which I thought I didn't want, and now I wish more than ever that I had followed through with it; it would have saved me many wasted years.

Without your assistance, I wouldn't have applied to all the schools I did, nor would I have loved music like I do now. You allowed me to pursue my true passion and were supportive of it all, but then I started to listen to my stupid alter ego and went down a spiral and path of destruction. I behaved the past few years the way I wanted, destroying and ruining everything good I once had. I thank God you pushed me about that academic scholarship, which at the time I didn't care about, but now I'm so proud that somehow I made it out with about a 3.0 GPA, even though I have to redo the second internship part of the curriculum. Now

I'm trying to look at it in a positive way, though. Maybe I will find something in music that I'm even more passionate about.

With negative always comes positive, and that's how I'm looking at the arrests, as a rebuilding process of our relationships and just about everything else I've screwed up in the past. You are truly amazing parents, and now I'm thinking about you and the family every day, so excited to show you the new me that I'm ecstatic about waking up to every morning. There won't be any more stealing, lies, manipulation, putting you into depression, avoidance, or any of the other negativity I've expressed and displayed.

I'm going to prove to myself and to you that I can do this. I'm going to make you smile like you used to. I'm going to make you proud of me once again. I'm going to love you the way you have loved me throughout my life, because you and I both deserve better. I can't wait to get home and start over with you two, and have the great relationships we once had. Thank you for pushing me to do another thing you know I want—to recover from this terrible situation I put myself in and love my life the way I used to.

Your extremely thankful
and loving son,
Matt

This letter made us feel so hopeful. It sounded like Matt truly realized the error of his ways and was determined not to let it happen again.

CHAPTER THIRTY-THREE

We attended one last group meeting before Matt was discharged. We had a contract to show him and have him sign, outlining what we expected of him once he got home—everything from attending meetings and going to counseling to household chores.

Matt came home on December 16, 2009, happy to be home and ready to stay away from the people, places, and things that had influenced him to make bad decisions. He also would try to attend ninety NA or AA meetings in ninety days. He had made a few friends while in rehab and kept in touch with them for a while. The program's holiday party was just a few nights after he was discharged, and he eagerly met up with his buddies, proud to be clean. Fortunately Mike's new position came with a company car, so Mike's old car was now available for Matt to use.

As it happened, the group of friends met at one location and took just a couple of cars to the party. Matt rode with someone else, who also had just gotten out of rehab, and Matt felt that he wasn't acting "right." He wasn't sure what it was, but he did tell one of the counselors, who told Matt he could tell right away that the guy had relapsed. Shortly after that, the guy came up to Matt and said he was leaving;

could Matt get a ride back to his car with someone else? That wasn't a problem, but Matt had left his jacket in the guy's car, and worse, the journal he had been keeping since he had been admitted to Bayview House. He never got either back. The coat was one thing; it could be replaced, but Matt's journal held a lot of his thoughts and feelings. It would have been a nice thing for Matt to keep so he could read back about those early days and reflect on them. I also would have liked to read it to see what he was thinking in those early days. He went to a lot of meetings, went to outpatient counseling, got together with the friends he'd made in rehab, and started working on his community service requirement again.

My only complaint, through his first couple of months at home after rehab—and I don't know if it was justified—is that all he did was go to meetings—four or more a day sometimes. Some days he would drive to a meeting thirty minutes away, come home, and drive to another meeting that night at the same location. Or he'd drive to a location thirty or more minutes away, only to find there was no meeting. I felt he should be using some of that time to do something more productive, like job-hunting. But I felt guilty even thinking that. I mean, wasn't his recovery the most important thing?

I never questioned whether he actually attended these meetings. I knew he was determined to accomplish the "ninety meetings in ninety days" challenge, which meant one meeting per day. I think he went to more in order to have some meetings "in the bank" as it were. It kept him busy, and maybe that was what he needed to do in order to not think about drugs.

For Christmas—and, I must say, against my instincts—we gave him another watch, similar to the one we had given him for graduation. It was to symbolize a new time in his life, a fresh start, and to show our faith in him.

CHAPTER THIRTY-FOUR

Matt posted the following on his Facebook page about a week after he was discharged from Bayview House in December 2009:

Live Easy, but Think First
By Matt Laverty, on Thursday, December 24, 2009, at 6:02 p.m.

The past few years of my life have been a little crazy to say the least, and the past eight months in particular have been a roller-coaster ride that seemed as if it were on a never-ending down-ward slope. Do I regret it? No, but would I have done some things a little differently? Yes. I've been thinking a lot lately, and actually giving a fuck, unlike the way I used to go about life, not really caring about what would happen. There was one thing I cared for, and it wasn't something that was worth the time I put into it. I let it grab hold of me and squeeze tighter and tighter every day, strangling the little life I had left out of me. I was no longer in control of my life. My destiny maybe, but my everyday life? No. The little energy I had left in me was finally pulled from my body. I was exhausted—physically and mentally exhausted from the torment I inflicted on myself.

In my head I knew there was one of two places I'd be going; it was just a matter of time before I'd reach that point. Well, I made it there finally. As brutal and shocking as it may have been, it was needed, for if not that, the other of the two places would have likely come at some point, and this place you don't come back from (to my knowledge at least). I have to say I'm happy where I was placed, and the unbelievable and exasperating pain I went through is something I will keep in the front of my head for the rest of my life.

This is something I can't and won't forget. I will bring it to the grave with me, and what I thought was a misfortune and bad luck is actually what saved my life. I was sick and tired of being sick and tired, and my much-needed rest was finally in my eyes' view.

Things have changed drastically for me in the past month and a half or so. Some of you may know; some of you may not, but know this—life is an opportunity we only receive once. It is too short to spend like a caged animal, or a prisoner to your own misery. Don't let your life be controlled by someone else, or something else. Learn from your mistakes, and take the signs you are given and act on them. Don't dwell on the negativity that you have caused yourself; look at the bright side of things. I had a hard time doing this for a while, but I can see now—being as I'm still here—that I'm here for a reason. Despite the hardship and struggles ahead of me, all I have is today—more important, now. I've learned that I can't plan too far ahead, because honestly I don't know where I'll be in a month or two. But what I can tell you is that today I will strive to do all I can and work to be the better person I know I can be.

To all those who are supporting me and care about me, thank you. You have no idea how much you're helping me with my struggles and how much easier you make things for me. I'm growing stronger by the day, and it's because I finally see clearly and don't ever want to go back to the way I was living. I hurt everyone who cared about me; I lost almost everything important to me; and I lost myself for a while there. For those of you who know me on a personal level, you know that how I've acted over the past few years isn't the person I really am. Life is simple, and I've noticed that it's only complicated when I make it that way for myself. Its complexity lies unsolved for what comes next for me, but all I can do is what I am doing and plan to continue doing. I've got a new beginning, a new outlook on what's to come, and overall a new life to live. A life that I'm excited to experience in the state I'm in now. A life that I want to grab hold of, not let grab hold of me. Thank you again to everyone who's been helping. And remember, live easy but think first.

This post was very insightful. Again Matt seemed to realize he really had messed up and had learned some hard lessons. He always kept everything inside of him. I was so happy to hear some of his thoughts and feelings and to hear that he did realize how to turn his life around.

CHAPTER THIRTY-FIVE

I hadn't really researched heroin and its side effects and symptoms, because I'd had no idea that Matt was involved with heroin. But I soon would.

This is what I saw happening to Matt, from the time he had told Mike and me about his gambling problem in January 2009 and over the next two years.

Matt changed from being a social person and having several groups of friends, depending on what he wanted to do (skateboarding; bodyboarding; playing baseball, basketball, or football; playing "manhunt" as a preteen; and then, later, playing poker) to being a loner. He has since told me that using heroin isn't a group activity, not part of a social atmosphere, not something to do at a party or as a part of a party. It's just about the addict's feeling of euphoria that he or she gets for a couple of hours and about the thinking and planning regarding how to get the money to buy the next packets of heroin. The addict no longer has any rational thoughts. It's as simple as, *I want/need drugs. I see a checkbook. I will forge a check. I will get drugs,* or *I see cash in a drawer; I will take it, and then I can buy heroin,* or *I need drugs. I don't have money. I'll make up a story to tell my parents or my friends about why I need money right away.*

Matt had no concept regarding how ridiculous his stories sounded. For example he might say, "A friend needs me to pay him back right now, (at midnight), so he can pay his rent," and then he'd come to a party or meet me at a bank—or at McDonald's or anywhere—so he could get the money quickly. Once he even had the nerve to say that if it was inconvenient for me to leave work, I could just give him my bankcard and PIN. (I know I've done a lot of stupid things with regard to Matt, but even I'm not that stupid.) With all of this, Mike and I still stupidly, naively, believed it was a bookie putting pressure on him.

Addicts don't care about work, even though a paycheck would give them money with which to buy drugs. They don't care about their appearance. They will go for days without showering or changing their clothes. They only care about drugs; getting them is their sole purpose.

Later, while Matt was in recovery, I think his brain had been so scrambled, so bruised, that it took a long time for it to start functioning properly again. Would it ever function properly again? I saw that Matt couldn't multitask—couldn't cope with more than one issue, problem, or discussion given to him at the same time. He lost his train of thought and took longer to process a question. Or maybe I was being naive again. Perhaps he was acting this way because he was back to using drugs.

I was thinking that, in a way, drug addicts have to be pretty damn smart—obviously not smart in that they use, but they must have a bit of a chemist's mind, a pharmacist's, a mathematician's, a nurse's. I read about how they cook and mix their drugs; the knowledge they have regarding how to probe around for a vein; which drugs to take to get them up, bring them down, prolong the good feelings, and take the edge off the bad feelings. And they're also cunning. They're wonderful actors and skillful liars. They have the ability to lie and cheat and steal so smoothly that they can pull it off.

Until they can no longer pull it off.

They're smart and stupid at the same time.

CHAPTER THIRTY-SIX

Matt hadn't been to the dentist since 2006. He finally agreed to go after suffering through a couple of toothaches, due to cracked or broken teeth. The initial evaluation showed that he needed one tooth extracted and likely a couple of crowns and root canals, and he had fourteen cavities. I had heard that heroin wreaks havoc on dental health but never understood why. This is the question that led me to do a bit of research about heroin.

I learned that dental issues are especially common in heroin addicts, as they tend to crave sweet foods, which can increase the risk of tooth decay if dental hygiene is neglected, and it usually is neglected, since addicts typically don't care about their appearance.

Addicts gradually spend more and more time and energy obtaining and using the drug(s). Because heroin abusers don't know the actual strength of the drug or its true contents, they're always at risk of overdose or death. Heroin use via intravenous injection takes effect in seven to eight seconds; intramuscular injection takes five to eight minutes; and snorting, sniffing or smoking takes about ten to fifteen minutes.

Potential signs of a heroin addiction include confusion and lethargy, poor performance at work (if one is able to continue working at all), mood swings, unexplained absences, and possibly criminal behavior.

Long-term effects of the drug include collapsed veins, infections of the heart lining and valves, abscesses, cellulitis, liver disease, pulmonary compromise due to the overall poor health of the addict, and heroin's side effects of depressed respiration. Their overall health is poor, as they don't care about eating or taking care of themselves. Poor hygiene is common.

Higher and higher doses quickly bring physical dependence and more intense withdrawal. Withdrawal symptoms peak between forty-eight and seventy-two hours after last use and usually subside after about a week. Symptoms include bone pain, vomiting, constipation and/or diarrhea, insomnia, intense restlessness, and of course cravings for the drug. Some individuals may show persistent withdrawal symptoms for months. Matt later told me that this was, in fact, how he felt; in particular he had leg spasms that persisted for a long time.

Interestingly, for an addict who wants immediate inpatient help to get through withdrawal, I have found that an emergency room doesn't seem to be the way to go. On more than one occasion, Matt had agreed to go into inpatient treatment, but the facility couldn't take him until the next day. Where would he go that night? We didn't want him staying in our home, and he was already starting to feel the effects of withdrawal. I called several emergency rooms, looking for one that had a detox unit. Several told me there were no beds available. Frustrated and near panic, I asked what an addict was supposed to do; Matt was ready to seek help and was about to go through withdrawal. I was told that heroin withdrawal isn't usually life threatening and that he could wait. (If he went to the emergency room, he would get worked up and treated as if he had a viral syndrome.)

Heroin cravings can persist for years after drug cessation, particularly upon exposure to triggers such as stress, or people, places, and things associated with the addict's drug use.

The following is the most depressing picture I have read of an addict.

> *To be a confirmed drug addict is to be one of the walking dead.... The teeth have rotted out, the appetite is lost, and the stomach and intestines don't function properly. The gallbladder becomes inflamed; eyes and skin turn a bilious yellow; in some cases membranes of the nose turn a flaming red; the partition separating the nostrils is eaten away—breathing is difficult. Oxygen in the blood decreases; bronchitis and tuberculosis develop. Good traits of character disappear and bad ones emerge. Sex organs become affected. Veins collapse and livid purplish scars remain. Boils and abscesses plague the skin; gnawing pain racks the body. Nerves snap; vicious twitching develops. Imaginary and fantastic fears blight the mind, and sometimes complete insanity results. Oftentimes, too, death comes—much too early in life.... Such is the torment of being a drug addict; such is the plague of being one of the walking dead. (Deadly Shortcuts, 1962)*

This description depressed and worried me more than ever.

CHAPTER THIRTY-SEVEN

February 2010

Matt and Daniella saw each other a few times in that first month after he was out of rehab. They exchanged gifts at Christmastime, and for a while, it looked like they were going to give their relationship another try. Eventually, though, they went their separate ways, remaining friends but nothing else. I contacted Daniella recently (to ask for permission to mention her in the book) and actually had to go through Matt, who went through one of her friends, via Facebook, to get in touch with her. I wasn't surprised that she was hesitant to respond. Finally she responded to Matt—with just a quick answer to my question—and then she did respond to me. Again, she gave just a quick answer at first and said that she hoped things were much better for everyone. After that we did have a few back-and-forth exchanges, just about information I needed for this book. She said she didn't know much about what happened and what Matt went through; she said they had broken up shortly after she had found out that he was using heroin.

She also said she really didn't know anything about his drug use during most of the relationship; she thought he just liked to smoke pot. Certain things he did or said didn't add up for her, but he always had an excuse, and every time she questioned anything, it would lead to a fight. She couldn't remember exactly the way everything happened, but around the time of his first arrest, in August 2009, she got fed up and contacted one of his roommates (there were four). She said it was a struggle, but she finally got a little bit out of him, probably not the full story, but enough. When she went to Matt about it, he said that this roommate was using also. Matt was able to convince her that he had stopped and that it never had been that bad to begin with. She said that she did start searching his bags but never found anything. One time, while they were at her family's vacation home on Long Island, she heard him in the bathroom, apparently cutting up drugs in lines—or whatever gets done—and sniffing, which led to a huge fight. He completely denied everything.

By the second time he got arrested, in November 2009, she'd had enough. She never learned how bad it was until after he got out of rehab the first time. I suppose he came clean with her then, told her everything in an attempt to make a fresh start. As I said, they saw each other briefly then but broke up for good, and she moved to New England for her own fresh start. I told her she was the only good thing about Matt's life during that otherwise horrible period. I said I was so sorry that drugs took control of his life and that he couldn't be the boyfriend she deserved. I told her to be happy.

Daniella and I were in touch again a few months later, again about this book and for her approval about what I'd written about her. I think she had a lot that she'd kept inside her and wanted to "talk" (via e-mail). This is what she told me.

> You wrote about how you didn't know if he ever lied to me. Well, he lied to me every day. I gave him roughly $1,000 that summer: gas money (that was a big one), money to pay someone

back—I'm sure there were more times; I just can't remember. The more involved he got into drugs, the more irritable he got, which of course let to fights, mostly about nothing in particular. I can't remember fighting before the drugs. He'd come over and pass out. Always tired. All we did that summer was sit around. I was almost a year out of college and had nothing to show for it. And my parents didn't make it easy on me! Always getting on my case about a job! That last summer he never left his phone on with me around.

It's hard to remember now, but there is no doubt in my mind that whatever lies and stories he told you and Mike, he told me. Maybe modified or entirely different, but there was always something. I knew he was in trouble with money, I offered countless times to help him figure it out, and his response was always the same—"It's complicated." He blew me off more and more, or he'd show up late (hours), always with an excuse. Job interviews, community service, filling in for the sitter, something. And maybe sometimes it was true. Knowing what I know now, I can't imagine it was often.

One night after he blew me off and ignored my calls for hours, I actually drove down to your house, with absolutely no idea what I was going to do or say, of course. When I saw Matt and Mike talking in the living room, I figured he was safe, not out with another girl or friends or something crazy, I ended up sitting in my car for a while down the street and drove home. After a while he stopped making sense. He was always at community service, but every time I asked how many hours he had left, the number would go down by an hour or two. I couldn't question him; he had a comeback for everything, and it always seemed to make sense at the time. It wasn't until later, after he'd left & I was alone that I thought about it and nothing added up.

Maybe I just couldn't handle the fighting so I chose to believe him just to make it stop. Looking back, I feel like an idiot for not realizing it was drugs. All the signs were there; it was so obvious but I never put it together. Maybe I always knew in the back of my head but couldn't bring myself t believe it, to say it out loud.

I'm still in [New England]. I hate to say it, but yes, the decision to move here was to get away from him. I knew if I didn't get away I would continue to be caught up in his web of lies. I wouldn't get myself a job, and I'd keep throwing money at him, yet not trusting him almost at all.

I wonder about Matt sometimes, whether he's sober or not, what he's doing, stuff like that. I just don't think I could bring myself to talk to him again. Unfortunately I don't know if I'd be able to trust him again.

I felt so terrible for all of the pain that Matt has caused her. I told her not to feel like an idiot, that we didn't see it either, or maybe we just didn't want to believe it. I told her I wished she and I could have talked more, during the relationship and after. Maybe we could have given each other some amount of comfort.

CHAPTER THIRTY-EIGHT

Matt finally started looking for work and found a job as a waiter at a fondue restaurant. Matt told me about interview process, and all of the applicants were asked, "What is the hardest thing you have ever done?" There were a few answers like "I went bungee jumping," "I ran a half marathon," or "I had a job digging ditches." When it came time for Matt to answer, he said, "I got arrested, realized I needed help, and went to rehab." He was hired on the spot.

He also did assorted community service work during this time and finally completed the required sixty-seven hours in March at Lifestyles for the Disabled on Staten Island. The drug-education classes were finally rescheduled, for the third time, and he was attending them on Saturdays, the last one being on May 1, 2010.

Matt met a girl in March, at an NA meeting, and they started spending time together. She was several years younger than him, just out of high school, I think, and was attending culinary school some place locally. He saw her quite a bit, but I think he had a hard time adjusting to someone local who was always around. He seemed to do better with long-distance relationships. Or maybe she just wasn't Daniella.

Work was going just OK for him. They only needed him a couple of nights a week, and he said they were still only giving him small tables, since he was the newest employee, so the tips weren't great. Finally, one morning in April, he told us he had been fired the night before. The supervisors told him that he wasn't encouraging customers to order side dishes, desserts, etc., to drive up the cost of their meal, which would bring in extra revenue for the restaurant. In short his sales were down.

During February and March of 2010, Matt started to rebel. He avoided taking home drug tests when we requested him to, got more lax about going to meetings, and was cranky. The post rehab honeymoon period had worn off. I talked to his counselor. I was afraid that he had relapsed; actually I was convinced he had. She tested him when he went to counseling, and the test came back clean. Matt said he was just tired of taking drug tests and going to meetings and counseling sessions. He just wanted his life back. He stopped seeing the new girl in his life, saying he needed a break and not so much togetherness. It was around this time that he had gotten fired from the waiter job as well.

He kept looking for other work, was starting to make calls and send out letters about his internship, and had a few court dates for the New Jersey issues. These were finally all settled in April 2010, and he received a sentence of two years' probation, with regular check-ins with a probation officer. Matt stood in front of two judges and told them he had made some poor choices in the past, and he realized how lucky he was, how many opportunities were ahead of him, and how he was in the process of turning his life around—working, attending meetings, attending counseling, and doing community service at Lifestyles for the Disabled, and that he was enjoying that so much that he planned to continue to volunteer there even after he had completed the required time.

Based on information I gathered later, he was high at the time.

My father-in-law was very ill at this time and ultimately passed away just after Easter. It was a tough time for the entire family, but we all pulled together and spent a few nice days together. Matt attended the funeral, drove to the cemetery, and then headed back to Little Silver.

He was high then too, although I didn't know that until much later.

I rode out to the cemetery with him, and my sister-in-law, in the car behind us, was very worried about us because of his erratic driving. I thought he was just tired (which is what he told me). After the burial he drove home, but not before driving to Elizabeth, New Jersey, so he could buy more heroin.

CHAPTER THIRTY-NINE

Still we stuck it out, and it seemed as though we would get through it. Matt babysat for us one night in April so Mike and I could go out for a quick dinner to celebrate our anniversary. We talked about how crazy the past six months had been for our family but that things finally seemed to be on the right track, and we were beginning to see the light at the end of the tunnel.

The next afternoon I told Matt that I needed to run to the bank, to get the money he would need to get to Connecticut the next day. He told me no; he still had some money from his last paycheck, and I didn't need to bother. Immediately I saw that as a huge red flag; Matt would never turn down money. It turned out that he didn't want me to see the recent activity on any of the checking accounts, but of course I checked. I noticed some checks missing from Tim and Laura's accounts. When confronted, he admitted he had taken the checks, and he had relapsed a week or two earlier. He said that he only wrote the checks for amounts of money that he knew were in the checking accounts. (He checked the ledgers; wasn't that considerate of him?) He also cashed a check or two from our checking account. He didn't check that ledger, but fortunately nothing bounced.

How could he do that? I was more astonished than angry; I was still in a cloud, thinking that the heroin use, his subsequent arrest, and rehab would be a one-time thing; I thought he would be "cured" after that. I just couldn't understand how he kept doing these things.

That same night, on his own, without Mike asking, Matt admitted taking cash that Mike had tucked away for his upcoming annual golf weekend in Florida. Mike was crazed; he grabbed Matt, threw him down on the bed, and pinned him down by the shoulders; he screamed and yelled at him, and shook him. I was crying and yelling for Mike to get off him. That was another moment when I wanted to curl into a ball and hide in a corner.

Instead I immediately called his counselor. I told her Matt had relapsed, to which she replied, "There's a surprise," so she obviously had seen it coming, starting as early as when he had gotten out of rehab, when he was determined to go to a couple of concerts (but they had NA meetings between sets, he had told everyone, as if that justified his going) and pretty much easing back into his old social lifestyle. Just that day his counselor had discharged him from the outpatient program because he had stopped attending his sessions for the last month. Since Matt was over eighteen, the program wasn't required to tell us if he missed a counseling session, so we didn't know he had stopped attending. Once I learned about that, again I was astonished but still not angry. Somehow I still had blind faith in Matt and what he told me.

The plan was for him to go back to outpatient treatment, five days a week, as per both Matt and his counselor. But would the plan work? He was still working at this time, so there were days he wouldn't go to outpatient treatment because of work. Additionally he was still completing the few remaining drug-education classes he had left.

CHAPTER FORTY

Mike scraped some more spending money together and went on his golf trip the first weekend in May. Matt had his last drug-education class that Saturday, so he would be in Connecticut for a good part of his day, and I had arranged for a babysitter to stay with Tim and Laura so I could spend the afternoon with a college friend, having lunch and shopping. It was a really nice day. We talked a lot. My friend has two sons about the same age as Matt and has had some rocky times with them, so it was a nice break to talk to someone who really understood. Although Mike and I had just been sucker-punched yet again over the past week, Matt was out of the house and occupied for the day with the drug class, and I felt that I didn't need to worry about his activities that day.

After my friend and I went our separate ways, I met up with Matt at the local produce store to do some shopping there and then at the grocery store. It was a nice couple of hours with Matt on neutral ground, with no fighting, as well as a really relaxing day for me in general—a break from all of the mess we'd been dealing with.

Then I reconciled my grocery purchases in the checkbook and realized that more checks were missing.

Matt of course admitted to taking the checks. I yelled and cried, and as I was figuring out the money, he said, "I want to go back to inpatient rehab."

He was so close; he had finished his community service as well as his drug-education classes (although he apparently had attended both while under the influence of heroin). He had an upcoming court appearance the following Tuesday, and then all of the legal mess would be done with. He already had received probation and fines from his New Jersey arrest, and this court appearance was just a formality for Connecticut.

And so Matt only had to deal with me and my wrath, such that it was. It was more tears than wrath—a lot of words about wondering how and why he kept doing this. Of course I called Mike. As it happened, Matt's attorney was also on this golf trip, so he was kept informed. The attorney said that whatever negative effects there might be, it would certainly look good to show that he voluntarily had checked himself back into rehab.

I have to say thank you once again to my good friend Janet, who canceled her Saturday-night plans in order to drive up to North Jersey with Matt and me, as well as Tim and Laura, to get him checked in to begin round two.

Matt got settled in, only to be taken out again three days later for his court appearance. I called Bayview House a lot, trying to make sure everything was arranged for him to leave to go to court. No one was calling me back, so I just kept calling. Someone finally said that I had to stop calling, and when Mike picked Matt up, someone told him I was out of control. I guess I was. Being in control over whatever I could be was the only way I could cope. Anyway, leaving the rehab facility to go to court wasn't allowed, so basically Matt had to sign out AMA (against medical advice) and then be readmitted. At this point Matt didn't think he needed to go back; he said he only had needed to go there to be detoxed. Mike convinced him to stay for a few more days so his attorney could figure things out.

By the end of the weekend, Matt's counselor said that Matt was very emotional but knew he needed to be there for the long haul, which meant a sixty-to-ninety-day stay. He had some things he needed to work through, she said. "The lies," I replied. She agreed; he needed to work out how to stop lying. The truth might hurt us a lot, but it would be better to know the truth than just know in our gut that he was lying. He felt closest to me, he told the counselor. We had talks. Or we used to. He told me things he was excited about—concerts, music. But the things he worried about, the scary thoughts, he didn't share. Maybe he shared them in group counseling, during one-on-one counseling sessions, or maybe at AA or NA meetings, but they were locked away from us.

Knowing he was safe again gave us great peace of mind and a nice respite. The household was a lot more peaceful. A part of me felt we should take advantage of this time and do something fun with the family, knowing that Matt was well taken care of and would be safe, much like we did when Laura was a toddler and in feeding and behavior-modification rehab. But we didn't. We just used the time to regroup and collect ourselves, trying to relax after the crazy last few months.

CHAPTER FORTY-ONE

When Matt was six, we took our first trip to Disney World, which was wonderful. Laura was at Seashore House at that time, and part of the protocol for the feeding rehab and behavior-modification program was for her to see her family only once a week. So after clearing it with the feeding team, we booked a four-day trip to Disney World—just Mom, Dad, Tim, and Matt.

It was February of first grade for Matt. He was just learning to read and sound out words, so when we were ready to tell him, we showed him the airline ticket and had him sound out the destination that was on the ticket (Orlando). It took him a minute or two, but he finally got the word. Then we asked him if he knew what was in Orlando. Of course he knew. It was spring vacation time, and there were all kinds of commercials on TV for Disney vacations. He was ecstatic. He loved his first plane ride and was thrilled with his first stay in a hotel. The amenities were endless: the game room, the kid-friendly restaurants, the pool. One thing he really thought was cool was that he could sit (or lie) in bed and watch TV! I think this spoiled him for all future hotel stays.

Matt didn't have any idea what to expect from Disney World itself. By that time he had been to small local theme parks, but they were his only point of reference. When he saw the castle from a distance for the first time, he was speechless. No, not quite speechless—he kept saying, "Oh, my. Oh, my." The way his eyes lit up with the joy of childhood innocence is something I'll never forget. He kept hugging us, saying how much he loved us. It was a great trip. There was no need to say no to anything. We were in the Magic Kingdom to go on rides, so why would we say no? We were on vacation, so why would we tell him he had to go to bed early? We went into the trip knowing we'd be eating on the run, so if he had a preference for pizza versus hamburgers, it didn't matter. And Tim was with us, using a wheelchair when needed, so there was no reason to cut back on anything because of his immobility. I felt bad that Laura wasn't with us, but I don't think we would have been able to handle her getting through an airport, let alone a place like Disney World. She was where she needed to be, getting excellent care and therapy. I didn't have to worry about getting a babysitter, and we had a stress-free vacation.

I was delighted that we were able to make a dream come true for Matt.

CHAPTER FORTY-TWO

Mike and I met with Matt and his primary counselor in May 2010, after Matt had been in round two of rehab for just a couple of weeks. We talked about general feelings, but his counselor wanted to include Tim and Laura in the discussion, so since they hadn't come with us, she added two chairs into the little circle. We discussed Matt's feelings of creating extra burdens when we already had so much to deal with regarding Tim and Laura, and he confirmed that he was keeping everything inside rather than burden us further. His counselor asked about Tim and Laura's abilities and disabilities, and what their understanding might be of the situation with Matt. We felt that they did not comprehend anything, except that the yelling and fighting when he was at home upset them. She also asked what their life expectancies were, to which we replied that they had normal life expectances... She brought up the point that we really had three children with disabilities, not two, because Matt's addiction was certainly a disability. She hypothesized that we could actually lose one of these disabled children—Matt—if the addiction couldn't be brought under control. Obviously only Matt could do that, but Mike and I needed to think of it in those terms. We needed to understand that he, too, needed special considerations because of his disability.

Matt shared his thoughts that he tends to do better with deadlines when he's on his own and no one is banging on his door and telling him to get up and get going. We knew we needed to stop enabling him, even if we were doing it with the best of intentions. We all agreed that Matt needed to be out on his own. So the plan was for him to finish his inpatient treatment and then live in the facility's step-down house, for as long as it took, until he was ready to be on his own and had secured a job and an apartment.

It was a pretty powerful meeting. I said that I loved him and never would give up on him; I'd do whatever I could to help him. I said that Matt's disability was killing us, but his stealing from us was also ruining us. And we couldn't trust him. So we needed to step back, stop enabling him, and stop putting the pressure on him, whether it was to find a job, get an internship, cut the grass, or whatever.

I admitted that the contract we had written and had Matt sign upon his discharge from his first round of rehab was a farce. Obviously the things like "Go to counseling" and "Go to meetings" were important goals—things we expected Matt to do to stay strong and clean—but things like "Keep your room neat" and "Help around the house" were items I would put on a chore chart when he was seven years old. You know, if he got ten gold stars for the week, he could pick out a piece of candy from the drugstore. The best one on the contract—"Come up with a plan to start repaying us"—was the biggest joke of all.

Matt said he wanted to be able to talk to us when he was feeling vulnerable, scared, and itchy, and we needed to listen. And we could offer comments and suggestions if he wanted them, but we couldn't lecture or judge him. I thought I could do this, but I didn't know if Mike could. For as long as I could remember, most of their conversations had turned into a lecture, with some kind of moral coming out of it. I've always mostly felt sadness through this struggle; Mike has mostly felt anger.

We knew Matt was very closed off and didn't express his feelings much. Maybe he was trying not to burden us further, but he didn't want to talk to a counselor and didn't want to take antidepressants. I worried about the relationship between Mike and Matt, but I couldn't do anything about it. That was about them; I could only work on *my* relationship with Matt. I told him he could always talk to either or both of us, but he couldn't play one of us against the other, which he had done many times. Countless times he had called me, asking for "gas money" and wanting to stop by my office to get it, even though Matt and Mike were both at home, and it would have been more convenient for Matt to ask Mike.

I also told him we wanted him to be independent and have fun, but he had to temper his expectations. He would come to me, bursting with excitement because his favorite band was playing in Baltimore or New York City, and he really wanted to go. And it would mean so much to him and make him so happy, and there were NA meetings there between sets, and it would be really good for him to be there because it would keep him being noticed by the music community. So was that supposed to make it OK and keep me from worrying? And was that supposed to justify my giving him $100 or $200 so he could attend? It's always hard to say no to your child when he's excited about something—always, from the time he's three years old and wants a balloon at a carnival. But where do you draw the line? In return for the money, he wanted for the concert, or to go out to dinner with some buddies, he'd say he'd cut the grass for us or clean the house. Of course he never did it. And still I gave in. Mike would give in too; he would just give Matt a twenty-minute lecture first.

During that same meeting, Matt's counselor helped us unravel a few more lies. After Matt left the room, she told us he apparently had relapsed at the beginning of March, just a couple of days after he had met the new girl in his life, but we didn't find out until April. Ironically the new girl had no part in the relapse; he had done it by himself. And the counselor confirmed that he had pawned the watch we had given him for Christmas. So that's how he had funded his habit for a while—that and his tips, until he got fired. I guess that's when he started to steal from us again, and from Tim and Laura.

So maybe now I was angry enough, fed up enough, to really say no and mean it. It finally slammed into me that the drug abuse and rehab weren't a one-time thing—and that the stealing and lying were an ongoing pattern for Matt. How could he do this to our lives? To us, his parents? To himself? I was still sad and frustrated, more than angry. Matt was my son. Moms are supposed to be able to fix everything. Why wasn't he listening to my advice?

Having him out of the house for the next couple of months would help a lot. We needed space from him. We needed to make some changes in the house so he couldn't access our financial information, and we needed to plan to put the Little Silver house on the market, in preparation for our move to Ocean City.

I had to remember to keep thinking of Matt as our third disabled child, and his lifespan could be much shorter than Tim and Laura's. It was all up to Matt. And all Mike and I could do to lengthen his lifespan was to find him rehabs, support him in his recovery, and love him. I told him that when we decided to have children I knew there was enough room in my heart for as many children as God saw fit to bless us with. And it's true. There wasn't a finite amount of space in my heart that would get divided into smaller pieces as the children came along. The space would expand and multiply, depending on the number of children we had and depending who needed the extra strength at any given time. I'd told him that during our meeting with the counselor. I was sure I had said, in moments of frustration, "I can't take any more!" But of course I could. I would. There was always room for both the good stuff and the bad stuff. And we could do this. The person who had the greatest challenges ahead was Matt.

CHAPTER FORTY-THREE

During the times when Matt was at Bayview House (for round one and round two), Mike and I attended group meetings there for addicts and their loved ones. The first meeting we attended while he was in for round two was the first time I had seen him since he had gone in for this round. He still looked pale and thin and had dark circles under his eyes. He told us he knew he had to be there for the long haul and asked whether our insurance would cover a long-term treatment. Then he thanked us for coming.

Two addicts who were finished with the inpatient part of their treatment read letters of apology to their families that night. One man, married, was being discharged right after the meeting. I could see in his face and by the way he looked in his wife's eyes the entire time, hardly glancing down at his letter, how badly he wanted this. He wanted to make it work. He said he had gone to Bayview House for his wife, but after a few days there, he realized he wanted to do it for himself. The other addict who read his apology was a twenty-year-old boy (one of Matt's friends), who read a letter to his parents. He showed no emotion, and the parents could have been us. The story was the same; the parents even said the same things we've said—"The words don't mean anything. We've heard them before." The only difference in their story is that apparently the boy had lost a brother to drugs—an overdose, maybe; it wasn't clear. The boy referenced his own four weeks in the hospital (also due to an overdose?) with his parents not knowing whether he would live or die. He mentioned that he had been arrested a couple of times and that his parents had bailed him out.

We heard no apology from Matt that night. Maybe he wasn't ready. Maybe it wasn't the way it was done. Maybe the apology letter was read closer to discharge. His counselor said he was still very emotional and had to work through some things.

These were the best groups I've ever attended. They were comprised of addicts and their loved ones, all together in a room, maybe forty or fifty people. It was helpful for us to hear other addicts' points of view—not just Matt's—and the addicts were very blunt. There was no mincing words or watching language for the benefit of the parents. And it was great for us to see how other parents interacted with their addict children. (Maybe we learned something, maybe not.) But it was the best place for us to feel like we weren't alone. Bayview was the only rehab that offered this type of session, and they offered them weekly, whether the addict was an inpatient or in phase one or phase two.

At the end of May, Matt received a notice in the mail stating that he needed to appear in court on June 25, 2010, for failing a drug test and missing several probation check-ins. It looked like he had been skipping probation check-ins as early as the beginning of March. So I guess he started using again around mid March. We weren't missing money until a month later, so he had gotten money from somewhere—or someone—else. I'm guessing he made better tips at the restaurant than he let on. After that, I guess he sold the watch. And after that, he started to steal from us again. This cycle was never-ending, and neither were the revelations. This was what our life had become, and I think I was starting to become desensitized to it.

So Matt had to appear in court, but he was still in rehab. His attorney said the best thing going for him was that he voluntarily had put himself back into rehab and was still there. We got word at this time that our insurance wouldn't pay for any more inpatient treatment; twenty-eight days per admission was it. It had nothing to do with how much help the person needed. It was all very cut and dried to the insurance carriers—at least our carrier. This meant that even though we had planned for two more months of inpatient treatment, our insurance would pay for those two months only as outpatient, while we would pay for room and board in their halfway house (phase two); so by the time Matt would actually be ready for outpatient sessions, that benefit probably would be all used up.

CHAPTER FORTY-FOUR

At the beginning of June 2010, while Matt was still in round two, we attended another group-counseling session. The topic was "enabling." We had listened through these sessions before, but this time we were in the middle of the circle, along with Matt. We listened as Matt told us how we had enabled him—for example by Mike paying his legal bills, court costs, and fines—and said he wanted to pay us back somehow, someday. He said he knew he could always come to me for something if Mike said no, and he said he would stop putting me in that position.

Mike said he certainly was guilty of enabling him, by paying the bills, etc. He said we would always support him in his recovery, but that if there were any new legal issues, Matt would be on his own with a public defender and would have to spend time in jail, if it came to that. I said I knew I had enabled him by trying to micromanage his schedule, reminding him to make calls, run errands, or get to an appointment or meeting on time. I vowed to pull back and not do it anymore, but I also added that if he was going to just lie around and do nothing, he wouldn't do it in our house. I thought if I said I would stop enabling him enough times eventually I really would stop.

At the end of the week, Matt would be moving to Bayview House's halfway house program (phase two), where he would stay for a couple of months. This meant that once he got acclimated he would be required to go out during daytime hours and look for a job or an internship. He had to be back at the house at 5:45 p.m. and would be randomly tested for drugs. He'd be allowed to go to the library to use a computer to look for jobs and send resumes and e-mails regarding employment or internships. I wondered how or if they monitored Internet use and cell phone use.

Matt's new counselor in phase two thought he was doing really well. He said Matt often talked to a lot of other inpatients, convincing them to stick with the program when they felt like giving up.

At these group meetings, we went around the room, using one or two words only to describe how we felt. I said I felt comfortable and safe, because Matt was there but also because he seemed comfortable there. He seemed very at ease, in no rush to get out. I prayed to God that it would work this time. Even so, I knew the odds were against him.

As Matt worked on his recovery, Mike and I spent a lot of time pondering the next steps for him. He wanted to be independent, to live on his own. We wanted that for him as well, and the truth was that we didn't want him living in our house, wherever that house may be. We didn't want to live in fear that he would steal from us again. We didn't want him to have access to our wallets or banking information. Yes, an easy fix would be to get a safe, and we kept saying we were going to do that. But an addict will find a way to get what he wants. Of course I wanted Matt fairly nearby, close enough to come and visit us, but would I always be watching him? Would I always be afraid to walk out of a room when he was in our home, fearing he would pocket something he could pawn?

Sadly the answer to all of these questions was "yes."

Mike and I went around and around. I wanted to get the [second, smaller Little Silver house on the market and sold. Mike said he couldn't just sell the house out from under Matt because Matt would have no place to go. At one point, before drugs had taken over Matt's life and ours, Mike had contemplated buying a condo in Little Silver after selling the house, so he would have a place to stay when he was in the area on business, and Matt would have a place to live. I thought we should find an apartment for Matt—obviously not until he knew where he would be working or interning—and pay his rent until he was on his feet. Call that enabling, but enabling him by paying a modest monthly rent on an apartment would be cheaper than enabling him by keeping a house with a large mortgage just so that he would have a place to live.

Matt had said he was more efficient and responsible when he was on his own. Really? Then what were we waiting for? I knew Mike wanted to make some repairs and improvements on the house prior to selling, so was he really just dragging his feet about starting the projects? He knew the financial situation better than I did. I was (and still am) constantly worrying about not being able to pay the bills—more so now, with Matt's legal bills, credit card bills, college loans, and out-of-pocket rehab expenses. Mike expressed his worries all the time as well. But then he'd bring up the idea of buying a condo in Little Silver as an investment property. It was no wonder I'd wake up at 4:00 a.m. and not fall back asleep. No wonder I always had a stomachache. No wonder I kept four different to-do lists going at all times. No wonder I sometimes felt like I was losing my mind.

CHAPTER FORTY-FIVE

June was a busy month for Matt. As I mentioned, once he was in phase two and living at the step-down facility, he was expected to be out during the day, making productive use of his time by looking for jobs and/or an internship. He wasn't allowed access to his car or phone until he had secured a job or internship, so he had to make use of public transportation and his feet. His counselor, Terry, confirmed that it was appropriate for us to give Matt some money every few weeks, as he would need it for bus or train tickets, as well as lunch when he was out, but he added that he and the other counselors do not recommend giving addicts more than $60. Mike gave him $50.

Right off the bat, Matt was starting to get a taste of freedom again. He was playing by the rules and was only talking about work and internship; he wasn't talking about going to concerts yet. He called me one day from a pay phone while he was job-hunting in Red Bank to see if we could have lunch together. Another day he hoped he and I could go shopping for clothes that would be more appropriate for job-hunting. I wasn't sure what that was about, since Mike had dropped off nice shirts, pants, and shoes for him, but maybe

Matt hadn't received them yet. Or was Matt playing us—trying to get around the rules again?

Would I always be suspicious? I wondered whether he just wanted to get more money out of me. Maybe it wasn't really about shoes or clothes. What if he really wanted to get more drugs that day? Just one more time?

One day I had to take him to his doctor because of a sinus infection. It was a bonding day for the two of us. We did a lot of talking, which I really missed once he had started using drugs. He talked about what he was looking for in an internship, updated me on where he was with that process, and sort of showed me around town on the way to his appointment. We discussed future living arrangements. He said that he would love to have an apartment and that it would be cheaper if he had a roommate or two. He mentioned that a couple of friends from rehab also would be ready to leave phase two soon. I wondered whether it would be a good idea for him to live with other addicts. Matt said it could be good or bad. They could support one another or tempt one another. There would always be risks. He told me about a girl in rehab whom he had mentioned a couple of times. I expressed concern about his getting involved with an addict, because as he told me once, "Two sickies don't make a wellie." He assured me that he was only saying she was really nice and a good person. He said they were just friends but that he couldn't say that he would never get involved with an addict.

He also asked me what my reaction would be if he came home with a tattoo someday. I just shrugged. He said, "That's it? No reaction?" I asked whether he was still thinking of a shamrock, and he said no, maybe a saying on his chest, like the serenity prayer or something along those lines. I said I had no problem with his getting a tattoo. But after he had helped himself to so much of our money, the fact that he would think to spend his first "extra" money on a tattoo was disheartening. He just nodded. I tried not to always bring up the money, because I couldn't see, at that stage, how he could possibly be able to pay any of it back. But it hurt to think that he was already thinking about how to his spend spare money and seemingly not giving any thought to paying some of the money back to us.

Terry had mentioned to me early in June that Matt had finally had some sort of breakthrough, and he was very pleased that Matt was able to talk about it. It seemed that Matt had been upset about his grandfather's recent death and how he had handled the day. He had told Terry how much it had moved him to see Mike and his brothers openly crying at the funeral service and then at the cemetery. Since Matt was high during the entire day, he was just numb and didn't feel sadness or emotion. Apparently he had a lot of guilt pent up inside him and was finally able to let it go this week, crying and talking about it for quite a while.

I guess he was finally starting to see what his actions had done to others.

That week, at our meeting with Matt and Terry, right off the bat Matt said he had something to tell us. He said had some wrappers (remnants from heroin) and also some Suboxone pills hidden in his room. He told us exactly where they were hidden (very well hidden, I might add) and asked us to get rid of them. *Another good sign*, I thought. He knew the wrappings would have enough residue on them for a small high, so he had hung onto them. And he knew that if he used again, he would need help stopping, so he hung on to the Suboxone to help him through the withdrawal. It appeared that he wanted to come clean and also get the temptation out of his reach.

At that point I wondered whether I should tear his room apart, looking for more drugs or drug paraphernalia. Was I supposed to open every book to see whether more wrappers were hidden between the pages? Or should I look at the positive in this—that he was coming clean?

That night at family group, Matt shared that he felt good but was in no hurry to leave. He said he was grateful for the time he and I had spent together the day I had taken him to the doctor and also was grateful that Mike and I hadn't given up on him and his recovery. He knew we wouldn't support him through this financially or legally, once we were finished with the current legal matters. He was still covered under Mike's insurance plan, so of course we would give him that kind of support. He knew he wouldn't be living with us and was looking forward to getting a place of his own.

Matt added that he was grateful that we had never given up on him and said he was sorry. Words were just words, though, and we had heard those words too many times over the last six or more years. It was time to see him put those words into action.

We had a two-hour onsite visit with him at the end of that week. The counselors said we could take him out, but not back to our house. So we picked up subs at a place nearby and ate lunch at a picnic table near the marina. Tim, Laura, and Molly (our dog) came too. I think he was happiest to see Molly! Matt showed us the halfway house where he was currently living and saw a sign for a one-bedroom apartment for rent near it. We had talked about his hopefully getting an internship in Freehold, and I suggested that he might look for an apartment closer to Freehold. He said he kind of wanted to stay around the area of rehab and that it was only a fifteen-minute drive to Freehold. So maybe that would work out. He was scheduled to go on a job search again the following week.

Matt told us that a friend of his from high school—and fellow addict—had been admitted to Bayview House earlier in the month and had been asked to leave the previous night. Matt said the only reason he knew of for someone being asked to leave immediately was if a client gave a dirty urine test and wouldn't own up to it. This client had a job and therefore a phone and transportation, and had been out all day. After I thought about that for a while, I became concerned about the amount of freedom that Matt was allowed at that point. I felt he should be kept on a short leash. I was relieved that he was getting drug tested daily, and I also was relieved that he was sleeping at the halfway house and not our home. I felt Matt should let Terry know how loose his internship schedule could be and that there would be days when he'd be able to go bodyboarding at the beach or stop at my office so I could put gas in his car.

After we dropped Matt off at Bayview House at the end of our day together, Mike said he was sad that Matt was living there and sad about what he done to himself and to us that had gotten him there. I said he should be glad that Matt wasn't at home because Matt's time in rehab was giving us a much-needed reprieve from him and the tension. I told him to think about how he got upset and tense even when Matt wasn't around, when Mike just did something as small as opening up Matt's car and seeing the mess. Mike had no reply, but maybe what I'd said would make him think about it some.

And, I told him, we mostly should have been glad that Matt was in rehab, getting the help he needed.

CHAPTER FORTY-SIX

In the middle of round two, in June, 2010, Mike attended one of the group sessions alone; I wasn't able to be there. Matt and Mike sat in the middle of the circle, while Matt read his letter of apology to Mike.

Dad,

I'm writing this letter to you, not as an apology but as what I see that I've done wrong and how I would like our relationship to change. Obviously, I am sorry, but saying that to you in this circle, which we've sat in before, does not seem very genuine. The word "sorry," coming from my mouth, has no weight behind it; it is simply a word I've used time and time again with nothing actually changing after my saying it.

This time around, I want everything to be on the table. I am sick of lying and having to lie to cover it up. When everything is in the open, and I am not trying to hide anything, I feel there is far less walking on eggshells. With that being said, I'm going to tell you something I'm sure you know, but I need to get it off my chest, to let you know, and because it's something that eats me up inside. The watch you and mom got me for Christmas—I sold it. I'm sure that doesn't come as a surprise to you, but I know that by giving me that watch, you were really hoping for a change. I actually remember that the card you gave me with it said something along the lines of "It's time to change and start over." I regret being so ungrateful, and this is a prime example of the lows drugs take me to. Also, you already know about the money you had saved up for your golf and the checks I took from you, Mom, Timmy, and Laura. I owe them an apology as well. In the right frame of mind, without drugs driving me to maintain a high all day long, those checks and money would've never been touched. Using for the month or month and a half that I did was more painful than the last time I went into treatment. Even though I was doing a lot less, the guilt and shame I felt was worse than ever. You and Mom have your hands so full as it is, and you don't deserve to have me putting you through hell, making you physically and mentally sick with my behaviors and actions. You deserve a son who is willing and wanting to help out as much as possible, a son with integrity who expects nothing in return. After all if it weren't for you, I would be sitting in a jail cell right now, not sitting in a treatment center trying to get better. I'm grateful I made it back when I did. I saw my life beginning to spiral out of control; the unmanageability was becoming overwhelming, and I know if I kept at it I would have ended up catching more charges, landing me in state prison, or worse, in a box in the ground. And I know both of those things would be a great hurt to you.

I have to tell you, Dad, Pop-Pop's funeral was a real eye-opener for me. When we were at the burial, and I looked over at you and Uncle Dan crying, a million thoughts went through my head. I can't imagine what it would be like to lose you, and I can't imagine what it's like for you to lose your father. But this made me think and reflect a lot. My addiction has put so much separation and distance between us. What was once an amazing relationship when I was much younger has turned into me isolating, avoiding what you think are your lectures (although they really aren't lectures; you're just trying to help) and flipping out at you for anything and everything. I don't like the person I become when I'm on drugs, and I know our relationship gets worse and worse when I use.

I'm really excited about my recovery and moving along in my life this time, taking the steps I need to take to get my life on track. I thank you so much for being by my side every step of the way, even if at times I seemed ungrateful. You are an amazing person for sticking with me through all of this, and I'm going to show you the same respect you've shown me. I'm excited to start over, and I don't just mean with what I do when I get out of here, but what we do also. I want to rebuild our relationship. I want to do more things like take fishing trips, catching bluefish every cast. Like going to football games and getting the wind knocked out of me during pregame warm-ups because I wasn't paying attention during passing drills. Like taking Molly for walks and setting up Christmas decorations. I still remember the day you taught me how to ride the wave rather than take the wave straight in. I remember having catches with you in the front yard every possible chance I got. I remember when you helped me build the magic light for that science project and when you helped me make the Oscar Mayer Weinermobile, for which I won first place for the funniest car in the [Cub Scouts] Pinewood Derby. I remember catching a doormat fluke and almost winning the pool on that fishing boat with you.

What I'm getting at is that I miss all the good memories with you. The past few years have been so hectic, due to my using, and all I want is to create new memories, good memories like all the ones I just listed. I envy how hardworking you are, how you put our family ahead of everything no matter what, how you always try to talk to me when I'm upset or frustrated. I truly look up to you and respect you for all you've done in your life and all you've helped me to do. I just want you to know that this time I'm going to work my ass off at staying clean and at rebuilding our relationship. I love you, Dad, and I hope this didn't come off as me just trying to say sorry. I just want you to have the hope that I can stay clean and that we can rebuild the father-son relationship we once had.

Love,
Matt

Our initial, private, reaction was that we had heard this before. However, I would stay positive so that Matt would stay positive. And I prayed that this would be a new start.

Mike had cause to give this letter back to Matt a few months later, after some infraction by Matt, with a sticky note attached to it that read, "Matt: Take this letter and read it again. Then figure out how to tell me the truth for once. Love, Dad."

CHAPTER FORTY-SEVEN

One day, toward the end of June, Matt had a 3:00 p.m. appointment in Freehold with a friend of someone Mike knew who had a recording studio. This meeting hopefully would lead to an internship. I had thought maybe Matt would call me when he had a minute and access to a phone. He didn't call, but that was OK. I got home from work shortly after five, as usual. I was going out to dinner with a friend, leaving Mike with kid duty. I asked if he had heard from Matt. He said no and expressed that he was starting to get concerned. Matt had taken his car, which Bayview House had said wasn't allowed, but we had acquiesced, in order for him to make it back to the halfway house by his curfew. He also had about $100 in cash, which he would have needed in order to take trains to Freehold. Of course all sorts to thoughts started going through my head. I figured, though, that if he went back to Bayview House and failed a drug test, so be it. If he got arrested somewhere trying to buy drugs, so be that as well. We wouldn't be able to help him out of it anymore.

My friend arrived around 6:00 p.m., and I figured I'd go out to dinner anyway. I could do nothing regarding Matt, and being out with a friend might help the time pass more quickly. Besides, we'd heard one thing over and over—that we can't let the addict rule our life or our actions. So my friend and I pulled away from the house, got a couple of houses away, and saw Matt's car coming toward us. What relief I felt! I asked my friend to stop and flag him down so I could speak to him for a minute.

He was beaming as he told me he had gotten the internship; he would start the next day. He asked whether Mike and I would be able to get his car up to Bayview House by then (cars are allowed once the residents have jobs or internships). He wasn't sure how he was going to get back to Bayview House by his curfew that night. But he was happy, he was smiling, and he was encouraged.

So was I. I prayed this would work out for him. He would do the internship for about a month, and these people might be able to give him job leads after the internship was over.

A new start for Matt? Please, God.

CHAPTER FORTY-EIGHT

I've always said I knew Matt had a good heart from an early age. There were so many ways I could tell.

I could tell by the way he treated our pets. No matter his mood, the dogs were always his best friends and constant companions, even when he was in some phase of his drug use (although we didn't know it at the time). He was the same with infants and toddlers. Even if he didn't know the children, he was always friendly and gentle. Gentle? I think that's a good word to describe his relationship with both animals and children. They always came up to him, ready and willing to go into his arms or snuggle up with him. So I've always known he's a good person, even when he was doing bad things.

Watching movies with him when he was young was another sure way to gauge his true character. The *Home Alone* movies brought out pure laughter in him, which brought out pure laughter in us. Conversely *The Lion King* moved him to tears and me as well, with both of us sobbing at the end because, as he said, "The dad died."

Another sign of Matt's character was that he never ratted out his friends. Whether it was the earlier days, when they were trying to sneak booze into our basement, or later on, when the arrests for drug possession started, he never would tell us who he had been with, or where he had gotten it, or who had bought it. He'd just say, "You don't know the kid." I wondered why he wouldn't tell us. Was he simply protecting his friend? Was it fear of retaliation? Or was it that Matt was always the instigator? There were many incidents we still hadn't unraveled, although after his arrest, subsequent days in jail, and round one of rehab, he had said, "No more lies." I suppose that meant that if we were to ask him about something he would tell us the truth; I didn't think he necessarily would volunteer anything. Most likely he didn't remember a lot of what had happened. I had to remind myself that his brain was still pretty scrambled from all the drug use and would take a while to heal—if it ever did heal totally. I thought that, little by little, things would come back to him every so often.

Even as a young child, Matt was sensitive to the feelings of others. When we moved to Little Silver for the second time, he was almost five years old. We rented a furnished house in Allenhurst while our home was being built; our own furniture was piled in the dining room of the rental, and Matt had a great time in that house pretending it was his fort. First when we were in Allenhurst, and then in Little Silver, my mom (Mimi) would come up to visit fairly often. By that point she wasn't driving long distances. My sister would drive her up, or Mike or I would drive down to get her, or my sister and I would meet halfway. My kids were pretty close to my mother. After all we had lived in West Chester for three years, only a fifteen-minute drive from my mom's house, just before our move to Little Silver for the second time, and we saw her almost daily.

Tim and Matt shared a bedroom in West Chester and then for a few years in Little Silver, which left us with an extra bedroom to use as a guestroom. Eventually, when Matt was six or seven, we started talking about letting him have his own room. We thought he would really like it and talked with him about decorating it in a motif of the New York Yankees, his favorite baseball team. While we were planning and window-shopping, the boys were still sharing a room. Then Matt started to come into our room during the night, saying he was having "scary thoughts" and couldn't sleep. He said they were mostly thoughts about Mimi—thoughts about Mimi trying to hurt him. I was devastated! Mimi? Mimi who adored my kids and was around them a lot, being nothing but cuddly and loving? I got the school counselor involved, who talked to Matt once or twice. It came out that he thought that by having his own bedroom, he would be taking away a place for Mimi to stay. I talked about it with him and explained that Mimi could still stay with us and that he and Tim would have a sleepover and share a room when Mimi visited. I also told him it was no big deal and that he and Timmy could share a room until he was ready to move into his own room.

And, after a few months, he was.

Even during his drug use, he still showed caring and compassion. One night, after a particularly loud and ugly argument between Mike and Matt, with me trying to intercede, Matt stormed off on his bicycle. I wasn't siding with one over the other, but Mike was livid and had every right to be. It was about the usual. Matt had taken money that Mike had hidden. I kept telling Mike to calm down; I thought he would have a stroke. As Matt stormed out, Mike said something like, "Don't come home until you can be a good son." So I was really worried about Matt—where he was; what he might do; what might happen to him while he rode around at midnight on a bike, in the dark, probably dressed in black. I texted him a few times, and he replied. Still I slept (or didn't sleep) on the couch in the family room, waiting until he came home.

When he walked in the front door, the first thing he said to me when he saw me on the couch was, "Did he [Mike] hurt you?" While riding around, angry, cold, tired, and whatever else he was feeling, his first thought was that I was on the couch because Mike had taken his anger out on me (which, of course, he never did). That was a comfort to me.

I can't say I felt completely safe around Matt when he was on drugs (of course, for a long time, I never knew he was on drugs; once I knew, I always had my guard up), and he could be an ugly drunk. He's stronger than I am, and I have no idea how drugs could make him think or act. So would I trust my life to Matt on drugs? No. Would I trust my life to a clean and sober Matt? Absolutely.

CHAPTER FORTY-NINE

Laura had a doctor's appointment at the beginning of June, while Matt was still in phase two. She had been under the weather for five or six days, and she also had been agitated and barely sleeping for several weeks.

I briefly filled the doctor in on Matt's status, and then we discussed Laura. I told him that her neurologist was working her up to figure it out. The doctor asked about any potential abuse, from anyone she could have been around when Mike and I weren't at home—babysitters or their friends, or any of Matt's friends.

It was sickening that I even had to think along those lines, but years ago there was a psychiatrist at Tim and Laura's school who was arrested for molesting a student. This occurred while Laura was going through feeding rehabilitation and behavior modification, so we were at Seashore House, seeing psychiatrists frequently. I had asked one of the psychologists there how we would even know if Tim or Laura had been molested, since they couldn't (and still cannot) verbalize something like that. The psychiatrist said we would know; there would be a marked change in their behavior, such as a new fear of men or women, or a habit of grabbing their genitals.

While Laura's behavior had changed, she didn't seem to be afraid of men or anyone in particular; she wasn't afraid of snuggling, or snuggling in a new and unusual way. She was just agitated to the point of not sleeping at all during the night. The neurologist had us try several different medications (Ambien, Xanax, etc.) before finally deciding on large doses of Benadryl in order to get her to sleep. He was concerned that she might go into a state of permanent psychosis if she was sleep deprived.

Laura and Tim's school and day programs were so careful about whom they hired, and their policy was to never to leave a client alone with just one person. Everyone was so afraid of lawsuits. The babysitter was very conscientious and somewhat timid around Tim and Laura, as if she was afraid she'd accidentally do something to hurt them. I had no concerns about their being alone with the sitter. Occasionally she'd had a friend, her husband, or her own child there, but Laura was fine with all of them; no one acted as if they were trying to hide anything, and Laura never acted differently around them. That left Matt and his friends. He had babysat only a couple of times between rehabs one and two. I asked Matt point blank if any of his friends ever would have had a way to be alone with her. He was appalled at the thought and emphatic with his reply of "no."

I had no reason to suspect anyone. There was no one day when I could say something must have happened. And I couldn't even *think* about the possibility that something happened. Who? When? How? And how would we fix it?

I couldn't believe that Matt, even on drugs would have done anything to Laura, or have let his friends have the opportunity. I don't think he would have been able to live with himself, and we would have seen a change in *him*.

It was just one more thing to worry about. I prayed we would get answers and that it would be a simple explanation. Maybe Matt's comings and goings had confused her. Maybe she had gotten used to seeing him at home after he had gotten out of college, and then he suddenly went away, came home, and went away again. She didn't act either overly excited or upset to see him.

A few months later, we consulted with a psychiatrist at CHOP who does a lot of his work in conjunction with Laura's neurologist. He asked a few questions, looked over her records, and said, "She's bipolar. It's actually not uncommon for patients between the ages of eighteen and twenty-one with diagnoses of static encephalopathy and cerebral palsy to have an onset of bipolar disorder." Another puzzle unraveled. After many visits to CHOP, blood tests, and conferences with her neurologist and psychiatrist, it seemed they finally had gotten the balance of medication just right. Laura had good days, bad days, and OK days. But at least we know what it was and what it was not.

CHAPTER FIFTY

Ever since Matt was a child, he had many different things he wanted to be when he grew up, but I don't know that he was ever really *driven* to do anything. Some people just know, from a young age, that they want to be a doctor, or an architect, or a plumber. I think Matt always just lived for the moment, but I hoped he was starting to think ahead to the future.

When he was six or seven, he wanted to be a policeman. For his eighth-grade graduation gift, he wanted a drum set and to take drum lessons. He did take lessons for several years, so I guess he knew at that stage that he wanted to do something with music. Then he took a break from that and wanted to own a skateboard shop. Actually, he wanted to be a professional skateboarder and get sponsored by several skateboard companies, travel the world skating and promoting products, and gathering free products and clothing along the way.

What else did he want to do? He wanted to be a baseball player for a while, and he briefly talked about going to a college that offered a culinary curriculum.

But the music industry stuck in his mind; he kept going back to it, and that's what he finally focused on in college. For a few summers, he worked at PNC Bank Arts Center, although for the caterers that supplied food for the bands, and not with the actual bands. The catering company had a very strict policy about its employees not approaching the bands.

A few of the musicians did actually talk to him; James Taylor invited him to sit on stage while he did his sound check. (Matt said he remembered going to one of his concerts as a five-year-old and falling asleep!) He told us one night after work that there was a really good guitar player playing that night. It was Eric Clapton. And a band with a really good drummer was there another night. It was The Police! He definitely was exposed to music that he previously didn't appreciate.

One of the things rehab was supposed to be teaching him was to think on his own—to think ahead, to look at all possibilities and consequences, and to figure out the best solution. This meant that, for his job search while he was in rehab, he had to plan out his route on foot, by bus, and by train. He had to get to appointments, make efficient use of his time while at the library, and use his money wisely when making phone calls or buying lunch. He was learning the life skills that he should have learned years ago. For years I tried to get him to make his bed by giving him an allowance, gold stars, and small toys. I used all kinds of bribery. Now this was just one of the rules while he in was rehab. He *had* to do it. The same with his laundry. He was doing his own laundry while in rehab. He actually started doing it once he left for college, and he'd do his own laundry when he came home on weekends. He started to let it pile up once he got out of college and was living at home again—and using drugs. Rehab wasn't boot camp, but he had to learn to play by the rules, and it sounded like he didn't get away with much there.

He was there until the end of July 2010. He said that living on his own would be better for him; he did better with time management and deadlines when it was all on him, with no one to wake him up or give him reminders.

I hoped he still had his mind set on his goals—the goals of maintaining sobriety and getting a job. He had mentioned something about taking classes in New York City for DJ and recording. I just wanted him to complete the second internship. Anything in the music industry would do. I didn't care if it was in a recording studio, or at a venue, or as a roadie, or as a booking agent. It was now a full year after his supposed graduation. I just wanted him to get it done.

CHAPTER FIFTY-ONE

One night during Matt's junior or senior year of high school (he must not have had his driver's license yet, or he would have driven himself to work), Mike wasn't at home. I was awakened by a phone call about 11:30 p.m., saying that Matt was at the police station. He was in a car that had been pulled over for having a broken taillight, and the police had found pot in the car. Thinking this was another infraction on Matt's part, I asked if he could stay there until morning, but they said that because he was a minor, I had to come get him. I figured I could quickly drive up to the Little Silver police station (which was less than a mile away) and leave Tim and Laura asleep at home for those few minutes. I arrived at the police station, only to be told that Matt wasn't there and hadn't been there at all that night. Perplexed, frustrated, and angry, I had to drive back home to look at the caller ID on the phone in order to figure out which police station had called. It turned out that it was the Sea Bright Police Department, which about five miles away, which made sense, since Matt worked at a restaurant in Sea Bright.

The police report had been filled out incorrectly, initially identifying Matt as the driver, even though it also listed his location in the car as being in the backseat on the passenger's side. Matt's friend (the driver) and another passenger had given Matt a ride home from work, but otherwise Matt and the other passenger had nothing to do with the pot in the car. The driver told the police that it was his and no one else's, but still Matt and the other passenger were taken to the police station and given a court date.

Because Matt had to appear in Sea Bright court, we hired an attorney. Matt, of course, was totally in the clear. The driver, who had no attorney to represent him (his parents were smart enough even that early to make him handle his mistakes on his own) was sentenced to a $100 fine and community service time. We put out much more money than that for Matt's legal fees. (As an aside, Matt has gotten into trouble with the law several times since then; this time, at least, he was blameless.)

CHAPTER FIFTY-TWO

Once Matt moved into phase two of Bayview House and into a new phase of his recovery, I started to think about his situation—our situation—with clearer eyes and a clearer mind.

I wondered what I would like to have said to Matt but hadn't, maybe because I didn't want to start an argument, or cause a relapse (I know, I know, we don't cause it), or be the cause of hurt feelings.

I would tell him I felt violated when he went through our things and stole from us. And because of that, I was afraid to have him in our house. He knew ways to find money that we didn't even know about, so we couldn't leave him alone in our house. He said he never had taken any of my jewelry to sell. Frankly I couldn't imagine why not. Why did he think forging checks was acceptable, but he wouldn't stoop to stealing and selling my jewelry?

He was my son, and I would do anything I could to help him in his recovery. But I was uncomfortable around him. I didn't want to delve into sensitive topics with him, but I didn't feel I should have to walk on eggshells around him either. So what if he was an addict? That was no reason for us to have to put up with crankiness, swearing, and other abuse. If anything I felt he should be more open about it and apologetic for his mood and behavior. In addition to working toward recovery, he should have been working on regaining our trust and patching up our relationships. Working on recovery wasn't an excuse to slack off on everything else, like pulling his weight around the house. Working on recovery wasn't a free pass to do nothing else. He should have been bending over backward in an effort to make amends to us.

The unraveling of Matt, and of any addict, goes hand in hand with the unraveling of a family. Parents are bound to be united by the desire to get help for their child, but ways of dealing with it are different for everyone. Ways of reacting are different. Ways of hearing and interpreting the lies of the addict are different as well. And even though the parents are in it together, and united in their ultimate goal, it's possible to be on different pages at the same time.

Here's how a typical morning started while Matt was still in phase two.

Mike drove back to Little Silver from Ocean City early in the morning. He called me when he got there to tell me about the mail. A bill from Matt's attorney had come—no surprise. A notice from probation also had arrived, saying that Matt hadn't paid his fine for three months, since May 3. No surprise there either; I reminded Mike that the lawyer had told us to put that on hold for a while, since Matt was currently in rehab, but that he should call the lawyer and double-check that we were proceeding appropriately.

I asked Mike he thought Matt would pay it in the first place. He certainly wasn't working while in rehab. He'd been in rehab since the beginning of May, which was when he had stopped paying his fines. Then Mike started in about how Matt never paid for any of the fines before he had relapsed. He said that Matt had paid for his fine one month and had used the rest of his money for drugs. I told him that was in the past—let's be positive and move forward. Then he said he wondered whether Matt ever contacted the probation department after he had gotten out of rehab and moved into phase two. And he wondered why Matt tended to answer or return my calls but not his.

We should both have been on the same page with this, yet we weren't. I think in some ways Matt knew I could be a pushover, but I looked at it as my dealing with the situation more logically and rationally. It may not have been the healthiest way, because it meant I kept a lot of things bottled up inside. It also meant I tended to be the peacemaker and the middleman, so when something negative happened to—or because of Matt—I reacted from hearing it initially, and then again, when I heard Mike's reaction to it, so it was like a double whammy of negative emotions. I always had believed in the "pick your battles" philosophy, and the stress I felt often was made worse because of Mike's reactions, or potential reactions, rather than from whatever it was Matt was or wasn't doing. It was no wonder that their relationship wasn't great. I wondered whether it would ever be good again.

I wouldn't say this had caused our marriage to unravel, but it certainly hadn't made it stronger. Tim and Laura's numerous medical issues may have been what had kept it together initially. But because Mike and I approached Matt's issues differently, we processed and dealt with them differently. Clearly they hadn't served to unite us. But they should have.

CHAPTER FIFTY-THREE

In June, on Matt's first day of his internship, he finished up early and came to the house to say hello before heading back to Bayview House. He got here just a few minutes before Mike, and I arrived right after that. He sounded excited about the internship.

Mike checked the cash in the house, and thankfully all was accounted for. Matt left to go back to Bayview House, and Mike left for a softball game. At about 7:00 p.m., I got a phone call from Bayview House, asking for Matt. I said, "He's not living here. He's living at Bayview House." The woman said he hadn't shown up for group counseling. I said I didn't understand and told her he lived at phase two of Bayview House. I asked her to please make some calls and have someone call me back.

Oh, the thoughts that raced though my head! And the knot that took up residence in my stomach! I was immediately anxious and upset, so I called them back. Apparently the woman who called was reading from the list of people attending an outpatient group, which wasn't the group Matt attended. Matt was fine, was where he was supposed to be, and wasn't MIA. I called back again about an hour later, just to confirm.

That initial call sure gave me a couple of hours of panic. How could he blow this chance so quickly? Then again I wasn't really shocked by the possibility, just very disappointed. I didn't even let myself think what this could have meant legally for Matt. All I could think about was that if he really did take off, he must have been strategizing for quite a while. And, again, that he was a great actor.

But my faith in him was restored.

The woman who called, on the other hand, needed to have been reprimanded. That wasn't the kind of phone call to be made in error.

At the end of June, Matt went to New York City to talk to one of our friends who had been instrumental in getting him his first internship with MTV. Mostly he gave Matt some advice during this visit, but he also said he would get in touch with some other departments who may have openings for Matt.

Matt called from the train, on his way home. He sounded good, excited. Did he feel like he was finally on the right track? Or did he just feel good to be out and about, feeling somewhat like he was living his old life of taking the train and subway and walking around the city? He was back in the area by midafternoon, spent some time looking on the Internet at our house while the sitter was there, and met me for a slice of pizza as an early dinner. He would go to his internship the following day for just a couple of hours, as he had a doctor's appointment.

I hoped he understood that now that he was allowed to use his car and cell phone, he couldn't just wander around all day. The rules of Bayview House said that if he wasn't interning, he needed to be job-hunting or doing something else that was productive. We didn't want him coming back to our house just to hang out and definitely didn't want him moving back in.

We didn't give him the run of the house. We still couldn't trust him, even though he had obtained an internship. It was a start, but it would take a lot more than three days of an internship for us to think our son had been reformed. He and I had a nice conversation at a local pizzeria, and that always made me suspicious. Was he being overly cordial in order to distract me from something? Would it always be that way? I thought I was well within reason to be cautious. I just didn't want him to have access to our possessions, which meant I didn't want him in the house unless Mike or I were also there. As soon as I got home, I checked online to make sure our banks accounts were all OK.

I didn't know whether he would ever talk to us about his cravings, urges, or fears, so I wasn't expecting that he would tell us when he felt like he wanted to use. Of course we didn't want him to ever use again, but the reality was that he might, and we had to protect our family against that possibility. So Mike and I were always on our guard. Always.

And that's a terrible way to have to go through life with one of your children.

CHAPTER FIFTY-FOUR

One of my nieces, Lily, found a lot of pictures at my mom's old house, which was a renovated barn on my brother's property. She had divided them all up by families and gave us each a box full of pictures of our families. They were mostly of our kids.

I spent an evening sifting through them, and I pulled out all the pictures of Matt. Some had dates stamped on the back; for others I had to guess what year they had been taken and how old he was. They were pictures of the innocent Matt, before his shift to the darker side, when there were no secrets to unravel.

I saw lots of pictures of a one-year-old Matt, spending time in my sister's pool. As the day wore on, I watched as the photos progressed into a more and more tired-out Matt. There were lots of outdoor pictures, with his chubby belly hanging over his shorts. There's a picture of him at a Halloween party with his play group, dressed as a devil (did I know something, even at that young age?). There are pictures of a two-year-old Matt, looking so somber and serious at times, on the day that he went to the hospital to see his newborn baby sister. Then there was three-year-old Matt, always inquisitive, a little mischievous, and then four-year-old Matt, when he began to form his style. Certain haircuts were important. He had certain clothes he wore *all the time*—a red bathing suit, Ninja Turtle T-shirts, army fatigues. I saw adorable Matt, watching fireworks on the fourth of July, a baseball hat on backward, his eyes wide and shining with awe, his cheeks red from a day in the sun.

There weren't so many pictures of Matt from eight to ten years old. He was still a cutie but ready to hang with his buddies by then. There were photos taken at birthday parties at sporting events, his Little League baseball and football games. I saw Halloween costumes of his choosing: a vampire, a pirate, a punk—any reason he could carry a "weapon." There were pictures of Matt and Mike playing football in the front yard, Matt at the zoo, Matt on the amusement rides in Ocean City.

I knew I had a million pictures, but this batch of my mom's seemed to stop right around when he was ten years old. Was he just not around as much? Or did we stop taking pictures in the late '90s? There must be more, another box I already had been given.

I was looking at an open, fun, loving, carefree, innocent Matt up until around age ten. It saddened me to see how he had changed just a few years later. It would be interesting to find pictures of the ten-to-fourteen-year-old Matt and see how that transformation played out—unraveled, as it were. To me his formal, posed, college graduation (or not graduation) picture showed it all—scraggly hair and beard, beady eyes, a poster child for drug addiction. Thinking back, knowing all I know now, I'm sure he was on drugs when his graduation pictures were taken. Every time I saw those pictures on the mantle, I wanted to lay them facedown, or replace them with pictures of a five-year-old Matt, watching fireworks.

Ann Taylor Laverty

CHAPTER FIFTY-FIVE

Laura had an MRI scheduled for mid-July, as we were still seeking clues as to the reason for her agitation. It reminded me that Matt had had a couple of MRIs and CT scans also. I think he was about four years old the first time he had one, maybe five. He had been standing in the kitchen talking to me, and he sort of slumped against the refrigerator, his gaze locked to the right. It lasted maybe thirty seconds. Was it vertigo? A stroke? He said he saw monsters trying to come in through the window. He had a couple more of those "dizzy spells," as he called them, over the next several months, so we finally had him checked out by Laura's neurologist, who ordered the scan. He said everything looked fine, and the events were likely just benign positional vertigo.

Every so often he had another episode, but without visions of monsters or anything else. When he was in his early teens, we took him to a local neurologist who ordered a repeat test. This doctor felt he was likely having small seizures, but for someone having them that infrequently and that mild, he said he would take the person *off* medicine, not put him on any.

So nothing was ever done. Once in a while, I'd ask Matt whether he still had any of these spells, and he'd say he occasionally did. Seizures don't usually occur during heroin withdrawal, so we really didn't have to worry about his heroin withdrawals triggering them. He had physicals while in rehab, and in college, while he was in the hospital, and I was sure he hadn't mentioned these episodes then. But could they have done just enough disruption to cause any damage? I knew they couldn't cause drug addiction, but could they have changed Matt's brainwave pattern, just enough to alter his cravings, willpower, rational thoughts? This was something else I needed to unravel.

CHAPTER FIFTY-SIX

Mike gave Matt a watch that had been his father's. It wasn't valuable, just sentimental, especially because Matt really had a hard time dealing with the fact that he was high during his grandfather's funeral. He had been wearing the watch since Mike gave it to him. One day in midsummer, I noticed that he wasn't wearing it; he said it was in his backpack, which was in his car. Did he take it off because he was skateboarding while he was in Philadelphia with me earlier in the month? Or did he sell it for a few dollars?

I found out that summer, between tips and a lump-sum paycheck from the restaurant, at one point Matt had $700 or $800 in his wallet. This was before he had started using again. Why, then, was he always telling me that his tips sucked and that they only gave him small tables? Was he already setting the scene for when he started using again, saving the money but not telling us about it, so we wouldn't question what he was spending his tip money on? He was so secretive about the money he really had. And finally that story has unraveled.

Could I ever trust Matt again? I already was thinking ahead to where he should go if he relapsed again. Maybe Bayview House wasn't the best place for him. But how would I find "the best"? I even searched the Internet for drug rehab facilities by ratings. There were a million to choose from. Who assigned the ratings anyway? What were they based on? I could narrow the facilities down by state, but that shouldn't factor into it at all, except that maybe the farther away Matt was from the bad people, places, and things, the better. Or should I talk to our insurance carrier and just follow the list they gave us? Somehow I didn't think they would tell us which place was "the best." They would only tell us what they would pay for.

I was so worried what Matt would do once he started to collect a paycheck again. Would the temptation be too great? When he was discharged before and had found a job, I told him I thought Mike or I should control or manage his checks. He disagreed with that idea, and we never saw one. There were always the stories that he started in the middle of a pay cycle so he wouldn't get paid until next time, or that all of his taxes and uniform cost were taken out of the check so there was no check. He started lying about it before he started using drugs again. So would it always be in the back of his mind? Did he have a plan in case he wanted to use again?

I would have felt a lot better when or if I saw the watch on his wrist again, but I didn't want to start an argument. That was my way—always trying to keep peace. And that was another thing I didn't understand. I would think he'd be bending over backward to rebuild our trust in him, whether it meant getting his watch out of his backpack, or keeping his bedroom door open when he was just sitting in there watching TV. I never suggested that he do those things; maybe I should have, but maybe I wanted him to do it in his own to show us he was trying. I finally asked him about the watch, and he told me the band had broken.

I was looking forward to family group that week, as we had kind of touched on these subjects the previous week, and I wanted to continue the thread. Plus at this point I was thinking that it may be our last family group, since Matt would be discharged from phase two soon. We could still go as long as Matt was still going to outpatient treatment. But once Tim and Laura got placed in a day program in Cape May County, they and I would head to Ocean City permanently, to live full time in the house we had purchased in 2006. Our lives, at least, would not be in limbo quite so much.

CHAPTER FIFTY-SEVEN

The kids and I relocated to Ocean City at the beginning of July 2010, living in an apartment at Mike's father's house, so the kids could get situated in their new adult day program.   We still had summer tenants in our Ocean City home, and as soon as summer was over, renovations would start on the house. My employers were so generous, restructuring my job description so I could work from home and therefore work my hours around things that need to be done regarding Tim and Laura. So it was just Mike at home in Little Silver now, commuting back and forth on weekends.

Matt's ninety days of inpatient rehab and living at the halfway house would be finished on August third, and then he would be released. He could go to an Oxford House, sort of a three-quarter-way house, where newly clean addicts lived together. There would still be curfews, rules, chores, and drug tests, if someone in the house suspected that someone was using, the residents in the house would vote to have the test done. Rent is low at Oxford Houses—about $125 per week.

Matt, though, wanted to get an apartment with a couple of other guys. I had told him that, without his having a job and therefore no guaranteed income, he couldn't expect us to put out a few thousand dollars upfront for security deposit and first and last months' rents, plus his already established bills (fines and cell phone). I told him we would paid his fines and phone bill as long as he was in rehab, and of course the fees for room and board while he was in phase two, but when he got out, he would be on his own. We didn't want him living at home, nor did he want to live there.

I was getting anxious about his possibly relapsing, because I knew the odds were against him. I knew, from all of the addicts' discussions in the multifamily groups, that they all had hiding places for their stash, in case they really felt the need to use again. They had ways to get around a urine test. And they had ways to get to their family's money. I also knew they weren't sharing the specifics of these secrets in group. There were some secrets that didn't get told, no matter how much "sharing" went on in these sessions.

In mid-July, as Matt's time in round two of rehab was winding down, we attended an interesting family group meeting, in which each family did a "finish the sentence" exercise. We had to complete phrases about the other members in the family. Matt completed phrases about Mike and about me, and we each completed sentences about Matt. The lesson was also about listening, and each person had to repeat what the others had said about him or her. It was also about body language while speaking to the other person and about the other person really listening well enough to repeat the answers back to the group.

The first phrase was "I love…"—not "I love you" but something we loved about the other person. I said that I loved Matt's inherent caring and told the story about my knowing what his true self is because of the way he is with his pets. Everyone in the group really liked that. Mike said he loved Matt's "potential." Matt said he loved his dad's work ethic, but he struggled to find the right words to say about me. He said either "genuineness" or "gentleness." I asked what he meant, and he said that when he's with me it's like being with one of his friends.

The second phrase was "I miss…" Mike said he missed the lost time—time when Matt had been absorbed in a world of drugs. I said I missed the trust. Matt said he missed the openness he and I had shared. He also said missed the fun things he and his dad used to do together, such as fishing or going to ball games.

The third phrase was "I am thankful for…" Matt said he was thankful for our continued support. I said I was thankful that Matt is still alive to get another chance. Mike also said he was thankful that Matt is alive.

I knew I needed to be a better listener. So many times when Matt was talking to me or telling me something, I'd only half listen while doing other things. And then I'd sort of wake up and focus more on what he was saying. I thought Matt had become a better listener. At least the clean Matt had. I think he had his eyes opened some when he went with me to take Laura to get her MRI. She wasn't really bad, but watching her get sedated, trying to keep her still, and seeing me go through the waiting period—well, maybe he got to see a little bit more of how tough things are for us sometimes.

CHAPTER FIFTY-EIGHT

As I mentioned, Matt would finish the inpatient part of his rehab on August 3. I'd hoped he would go to an Oxford House and stay there for a few months until he found a job. But he and two friends at the halfway house had found an apartment and really wanted to put a deposit on it. The staff at Bayview House spent a lot of time talking about Matt and his two friends during their regular meetings. They talked about the fact that they were all working or interning and how they had taken the initiative to find a place to live. The staff there thought they had a good chance of making it work. Matt had his one bump in the road; I prayed that he could stay on an even keel from this point forward. Mike and I talked about it a lot and ultimately decided we would pay for some form of rent until he found a job. He planned to finish the internship the next month, and he'd already sent out a lot of résumés and inquiries, so hopefully he would have a job lined up for when he had finished the internship.

Maybe we were enabling him. Clearly we were taking a big risk, but we decided that we would help him out until January 1, 2011; ideally he would collect a paycheck long before that. He knew he would have to drop out of the apartment at that time if he hadn't found a job. He seemed very motivated, though. He had to complete the application, which could have been a problem if the landlord had done a credit check. Matt could say he wasn't working because he was currently doing a nonpaying internship. The boys had been to the apartment a few times and had talked to the landlord. If Matt was turned down, so be it. It wouldn't be because we had said no. But if he did get turned down, he'd have to wait and go to an Oxford House until he found a paying job. Maybe that would motivate him even more.

Right before the kids and I headed to Ocean City for good, we had our dog, Molly, put to sleep. She was only about 9 years old, but the vet had discovered a mass on her adrenal gland, and she deteriorated quickly. Matt had said many times that Molly was his best friend. Truly, during his drug days, when he would spend his nights lying on the front porch, Molly was right by his side. I cried a lot, and Matt did too. I think it was cleansing for Matt, and it was a justified reason for him to cry without looking silly. Afterward he said he was going to go right to a group-counseling meeting, so he would stay busy that night. And looking ahead to getting the apartment would help him think positively.

I prayed this all would work out for him. When talked about his goals, I could tell that he saw how close he was to being on his own, and he really wanted that. He seemed so happy when he talked about it.

I'd been to enough meetings to realize this would be a struggle for him for the rest of his life. I couldn't begin to imagine how overwhelming that must be. As he faced so many other challenges, it must have seemed impossible to him at times. But if he could just stay positive for a while longer, I had to believe it would get easier for him once things were looking up for him.

As his parents, we would be in recovery for the rest of our lives as well—always on guard, always double-checking the money, always questioning and never quite believing the stories. Would I ever be able to trust Matt again? He was my son, and I loved him, and I would do anything to take away his hurt and do whatever I could to give him a chance, but I was learning to say no and not give him everything he wanted (concert tickets, new sneakers, etc.). And I wouldn't let my guard down. It was way too soon for that.

CHAPTER FIFTY-NINE

At the end of July, Matt reached his ninety-day anniversary of being clean. He wanted to go to an NA meeting to "celebrate" but needed to go to the multifamily group meeting first. Then he would be discharged. He and his friends would sleep on the floor of their apartment that night and move their furniture in the next day. Matt was running around all day and saying good-bye to a high school friend who was moving to Oregon. His apartment and his social life were his priorities for a few days. He said he would bang out the internship within a couple of weeks, because he would be able to stay later into the evenings without having to worry about curfew.

He already was thinking about having more responsibility and being more organized. He said if he was no longer living at the halfway house, he would have no curfew and could attend later meetings.

So he was on his way. I listened to him with tears in my eyes. I wanted this so much for him. I prayed that he was finally free from his demons, and that he and his roommates would keep one another on the right track.

He had a court date the following week, and who knew what would happen? Matt wasn't concerned; he was only focused on his social life and the apartment. Mike was worried, upset, and a little pissed, so of course I was too. I could certainly understand how excited Matt was. This first apartment wasn't the same as his first dorm room in college. He was on his own at this point, for better or worse. I prayed with all my heart that it would be for better.

Matt seemed really happy to be in his apartment and getting it fixed up. He seemed to be thinking ahead, mentally planning his week by telling me he had to get groceries and get to IOP, his internship, and then a meeting. And he had to get nice pants for court on Friday. The only problem was that he still didn't have any money coming in and wouldn't until he got this internship out of the way. There was always a reason why he only put in a few hours a day. He said his bosses were just leaving for lunch and told him not to come in one day. I hoped this wasn't a red flag. His boss, who knew Matt's background, e-mailed Mike in the beginning and said that Matt was in a safe place there, so I had to believe that if Matt was slacking off, he would contact Mike again.

Matt was in court a couple of days after he had moved into the apartment, because he had violated his probation in March, when he had relapsed). He received no additional fines, no lengthened probation, and no jail time—just a harsh lecture from the judge to let Matt know there were no more chances. "The next time you're going to jail," the judge said. There was another guy in court that day with issues similar to Matt's. He was sentenced to 364 days in jail.

So was this the end of this story? Probably not—just the end of a chapter. After all we'd thought it was over back in March, when the judge had sentenced him to fines and probation. And yet he'd started to use again less than two months later.

He had thirty hours of his internship left, he told us. He had an interview of sorts set up via one of our friends. I hoped his remaining internship time was legitimate. I kept thinking back to the internship he'd said he had in Connecticut and how devastated I was to learn that he never went. Still I felt his current boss would have let Mike know if Matt hadn't been going.   But I had been so naïve over the years. How could I not have questioned his pattern of needing $300 every few days during his last semester of college? I even joked at one point that it seemed like I was funding a $300-a-day drug habit. Why didn't lightning strike me or something? How could I not have seen any of the signs? Why was I so willing to believe that the erratic moods, sleep patterns, eating habits, and work schedules were just his crazy lifestyle and not signs of his growing addiction? I guess a parent always wants to believe the best about their children. Love really is blind. I hoped I was wiser at this point. With him not living at home, though, I wouldn't see these signs readily, unless he started stealing from us again or got arrested. I prayed that neither would happen. This was his chance for a fresh start. He'd had a couple of chances. Not everyone gets more than one chance. I hoped he would use the resources available to him if he started to feel tempted or encountered triggers. I hoped his roommates were true friends and would support him and steer him toward doing the right thing, and I hoped he would do the same for them. He had an internship, a car, a place of his own, and, hopefully soon, a job. Seemingly he was in good shape. I hoped he would keep going to counseling and meetings and that he talk a lot about his feelings and any insecurity he may have felt. I hoped he would use the counseling and meetings for what they were meant and would use them for as long as it took—forever, if that's what it took.

CHAPTER SIXTY

After Matt had come home from rehab the first time, he told me later, he started using again around the end of February, a little more than two months after he had been discharged. We never saw any clues. He said he thought about it a lot and often had urges before he actually relapsed. This is pretty common among addicts, according to Matt. The day he actually relapsed, he had gone to Staten Island to talk to someone at Lifestyles for the Disabled about his community service, and he knew he would be driving home past his usual meeting place with the dealer. He had money from his job at the restaurant, so he contacted his dealer and told him he'd been away and was currently clean but was looking for some drugs. So Matt bought them and pretty much used right away. He had no last-minute thoughts about whether he should stay clean a little while longer, no thoughts about taking one day at a time, no thoughts about going to a meeting or calling his sponsor. He thought he could do it just that one time but quickly realized he'd get right back into it and it would happen all over again.

So, for as long as he was working and making tips, he was able to get his supply. We saw some crankiness, but he'd say he was tired from a long day at work, or that tips were bad, so he was in a bad mood. But the more he used, the less he cared about work and trying to increase his sales. So he was let go. That's the only reason he gave us. Once he was no longer getting a paycheck and tips, he started to steal from us again. He was proud of the fact that he had come to me and requested to go back to inpatient rehab for round two. But the day he asked me was the day I'd found out that he was forging checks again—for the second time in two weeks. Would he have asked for inpatient help if I hadn't caught him? I don't think so. I think he would have kept on at the pace he was going until he got caught, because that's what happens. He was so slick for a long time. Once he stumbled onto the gambling lie, it bought him a lot of time (and a lot of heroin!) until the police caught him. I was hoping Mike and I were now smart enough not to believe any story he came up with. When something seemed off, we realized he was probably up to something—something bad.

I wondered whether Matt really was working the twelve steps. I didn't really understand them. When we went to GamAnon meetings, the members there were working on the steps, but we started to attend those meetings when they were getting toward the end of the steps, so I never really understood them. And maybe I never understood them for another reason. Perhaps, on some internal level, I knew gambling wasn't the real problem, so how could we say we were powerless over the gambler and his addiction when he wasn't a gambling addict? And until we could put a name to Matt's addiction, how could we start to work the steps? How could he? He went to GA meetings and saw a counselor whose specialty was gambling addiction. Matt must have been a really skillful liar to go to those sessions and have everyone convinced. I guess it was easy—he could truthfully say he hadn't gambled in a while and didn't have any urge to do so; he could say he hadn't gambled in thirty, sixty, or ninety days, because he hadn't. That much was true.

Shortly after Matt moved into his apartment, he told us he had completed his internship and received a grade of 4.0 for it. He said there was no reason he wouldn't receive his diploma—even if it was more than a year after we'd expected it. About a week later, he sent me a text with a picture of his diploma. It was official! And he also had a couple of job interviews lined up. *Please*, I thought. *Let this be the start of only good things for Matt.*

Matt's social life kicked into high gear as soon as he got out of phase two and moved into the apartment. During his first weekend, he went to a music festival. He tried so hard to get us to be happy that he was going; he'd finished his internship hours and turned in all of the paperwork to his college advisor, and he told us this festival would be a great opportunity for him to do some networking. Plus he would get in for free because he was working at the "Sober Table," and the festival organizers had mentioned even putting him to work, for which he would actually make some money.

These were all valid points. He was concerned, though, about whether or not he had enough money for the weekend. He would need money for gas, food, ice for his cooler, and cigarettes. I guessed he was hoping I'd say, "Well, I have some money tucked away for an occasion just like this!" But I didn't have it. And if I did have it, he probably already would have found it by that point. I knew he wouldn't starve; I didn't want him to run out of gas, but if he ran out of cigarettes, I wouldn't feel badly for him. If he ran out of food, it would be due to poor planning or shopping on his part.

I wasn't concerned about the festival being a trigger or a temptation. Matt would use again if and when he wanted to. I could only pray that, first and foremost, he remembered that he had no more chances. If he used, he'd be found out, and he'd go to jail. I hoped he had matured and wised up this time around and would be able to resist any temptations that might cross his path.

I wish I knew what Mike and I could have or should have done differently to instill in Matt the work ethic that he so obviously doesn't have. He went to the concert and made a good choice by not continuing on to the next concert in Buffalo. As it was he barely had enough money to eat and drive. Upon his return he went to our house and said he didn't have enough gas to get back to his apartment. He also said there was no food at his apartment, and he had no money to buy any. He said there was no food at our house either. Of course there was no food at our house. He had cleaned us out the previous weekend. He finally said there was one egg and a little piece of bread. I was sure there was also soup and other canned goods. What he meant was that there was nothing he felt like eating. The way I saw it, beggars can't be choosers.

I guessed he wouldn't let himself think things through enough to realize that he would have had money for food and gas if he hadn't spent it on a concert and all the preparations that went with that. He wanted it all—the necessities and the luxuries. But he'd been through some rough times lately; I couldn't understand why he hadn't learned that he needed to change his lifestyle.

What could I tell other parents to do differently? What did Mike and I do wrong when Matt was younger? I tried the allowance thing, where he had to do chores in order to get his allowance. Somehow he always managed to get the allowance first and said he would do the chores later, which usually never happened. The answer, I guess, would be to stick to your guns. And we didn't. We also should have found a way to get him to save his money, somehow get it through his head that he had to save his money until he had enough to buy whatever special thing was in his mind at that moment: a movie, pizza at the mall, whatever. But he spent every penny he got as soon as he got it. If his grandmother gave him $2 for a Slurpee, he'd buy the Slurpee and buy as much penny candy as he could get with the change. We gave him money too readily. Why? Because we couldn't do so many things with him (because of Tim and Laura and our not always being able to find a sitter, especially at the last minute). If a friend of Matt's was going to a movie and had invited him to go, we'd cough up the money so he could go, since he had no allowance saved. I never wanted our friends to take pity on us or Matt, or treat him like a charity case. We could pay our way, or his way. The opportunity for him was there at that moment. We didn't have the willpower to say, "Sorry, you can go to a movie when you have the money." We couldn't go back. But it wasn't too late to do something about going forward. The question was, "Would we?"

Once Matt had gone to round one of rehab, I should have read more about drug addiction and what to expect before, during, and after rehab. I had thought those initial twenty-eight days would be a one-time thing and then he'd be "cured."

Since that music festival, Matt had received more calls to run a booth for the Digital Buddhas, a group that supports sober concert-goers. In exchange for manning the booth, he'd receive two free tickets to the concert. I suggested that he start asking for expense money for gas and food, because it ended up costing *us* $100 or more each time he did this. He agreed that he needed to start doing that. When Mike heard about it, he just went off. He said, "I don't mean to rain on your parade," but that's exactly what he did. Mike was right, but it hurt me so much to see Matt's exuberance get deflated in the blink of an eye. I kept thinking he needed some positive reinforcement.

Maybe Mike actually had a better sixth sense than I did. Maybe I was just a sucker and a pushover, and maybe Mike had a feeling that Matt was using—or getting ready to use—again.

A friend of mine was having trouble with her son; he had been abusing painkillers for a while. When Matt went into rehab the second time, my friend's son decided to seek help to get clean. When I spoke with my friend and compared notes, it brought back memories of all the lies. Her son had told so many of the same lies that Matt had told us—about why he had no money and why he didn't get paid—when all along they both had money, at least until they used it to buy drugs.

When would all the lies be behind us? There were so many that I was still trying to unravel. But even with all this pain, if Matt's experience had served to help one person get help, or helped one family know they weren't the only ones going through this horror, then it had done something good.

CHAPTER SIXTY-ONE

It was interesting to see how drugs could affect a relationship. Matt started seeing Daniella in March of his junior year of college (and her senior year), before his *big* drug involvement. He was with her for about a year and a half. The heroin use started about eight months after he started seeing her. She had nothing to do with it. I don't think she had any idea of the extent of his use. She only knew he smoked pot.

Daniella told me they were very happy the first months they were together; she had good memories of their early times. I knew they had some pretty intense fights later, which I attributed to her temperament and his frustration. He told us from the start that she was an Italian from Brooklyn and didn't take any crap from anyone! And Matt's temper could be worse than I had seen in him before—probably fueled by drugs. There were incidents, I later learned, that had occurred during the course of their arguments. He had broken his hand, at work he said, but later I learned he had punched a treadmill in anger during one of their fights. Then there was the armoire door that had shattered when he said he accidentally had shut it too hard; he actually had hit it in anger. The cracked bedroom door he said he had shut too hard? He had kicked it in because Daniella had locked it during an argument.

As Matt's behavior became more and more erratic due to his increasingly heavy drug use, they fought more and more. That day in August when Matt had gone missing for most of the day and evening was pretty much the last straw for her. Over the next few days, they talked and fought; she said she couldn't deal with him any longer and that he should give her a call when he got his shit together.

Matt did call her when he got his shit together, but it took several months for that to happen. First he had to get arrested, go to jail, and then go to rehab. He eventually told her everything when he was discharged from rehab in December 2009, and they saw each other several times over the next couple of weeks. Initially Daniella was very supportive of his going to meetings rather than going out to a party. But the interesting thing is that when they broke up for good, it was because she said she couldn't deal with it anymore, that everything in his life revolved around recovery. His friends were recovering addicts; his days and nights were planned around meetings and counseling; and even though he wasn't currently using, their life together was still revolving around drugs.

I think they kept in touch for a while, but their relationship was over. Not that she was a big partier, but I'm sure it must've been quite an adjustment for a twenty-four-year old to change her habits merely because her boyfriend changed his. I texted her while Matt was still in his second round of rehab. I told her I was sorry he didn't treat her the way she should've been treated. She said she just hoped he was OK. She was sorry to hear that he was back in rehab but glad that he was getting help.

Would it have lasted? Who's to say? Two strong personalities were colliding. I think Daniella was more of an on-the-go person, whereas Matt sometimes just wanted to "chill." Again that may have been due to the drugs. As of right now, though, he says she won't accept his request to be his friend on Facebook.

It's recommended that an addict not get romantically involved with anyone during his or her first year clean, but hormones don't work that way. Anyone can say they don't want to get involved with someone for one reason or another (it's long distance; it's someone you work with; you just got out of rehab), but I suppose desire is stronger than logic. Every so often Matt would say he needed a good woman to keep him in line. Matt seemed more grounded when he was involved with someone; not running around as much. Maybe it wasn't such a bad idea.

CHAPTER SIXTY-TWO

By the end of August 2010, after just a month of freedom in the apartment, Matt was starting to worry me. I spoke with his counselor, and she was worried as well. He started to attend IOP only sporadically; it seemed he wasn't working his program too seriously. She called him and got no answer, as did I. Finally he picked up. Maybe he was asleep; maybe he was in the shower; or maybe he was screening his calls. He said he was at his apartment. I told him people were worried about him, and it seemed he wasn't too dedicated to his recovery these days.

I told him that if he relapsed but went back into rehab before he actually failed a drug test, maybe he could avoid jail, but if he got arrested, no one could help him. He said he knew that. I didn't want to come across sounding as if I didn't have confidence in him. But I didn't. Something just didn't seem right to me. Maybe it was a mother's intuition. I knew he would be in recovery forever, and I supposed I would be as well. It was far too early to let my guard down and have faith in his strength. The counselors had said mood swings were part of the process, though, so hopefully he was OK. He said he would be going to IOP the next day; he would get drug tested then. If he didn't show up, we'd know we had a problem. If he gave a dirty sample, we'd know there was a problem. If it was clean, then all would be good for the moment.

This was all so difficult. Matt knew we were concerned, yet he didn't do or say anything to reassure us. The counselor mentioned that depression and lethargy aren't uncommon during the early stages of recovery and sometimes last up to a year. I understood that completely, but why would Matt not reach out for help? He had said he didn't want to take antidepressants. He knew he should seek out his sponsor or go to meetings or IOP—anything to help him work through these feelings. Maybe these feelings weren't cravings or urges to use. Maybe they were depression. I wanted him to tell us. How could Mike and I help if Matt didn't tell us? Going back to rehab would be a hell of a lot better than what would happen if he skipped probation—or worse, gave a dirty urine test to the probation officer.

I had a bad feeling about all this. I'd been in Ocean City for several months, away from our house in order to get Tim and Laura settled in their programs. I was working and doing all the normal day-to-day things; I wasn't on vacation. But with Mike down here on weekends, leaving our house in Little Silver vacant, I felt like something bad would happen. I actually was *waiting* for something to happen. I could watch the bank accounts online, and I did so constantly. It wasn't just what Matt could do—and had done—to us. I just didn't want him to end up in jail, or worse, overdosing. He was like a ticking time bomb or someone playing Russian roulette. Every time he used could be the time that he used a bad batch or used too much.

Yes, Matt could be in jail, and he should have been in jail long ago. He did, after all, have a history of getting caught in midtransaction. But he also could be dead. I didn't know how I could go on with my life if that happened.

CHAPTER SIXTY-THREE

August turned into September, and Matt still hadn't shown up for IOP. His counselor called and talked to him. She told me he sounded like he was asleep; he said he had been up all night but that he would be at IOP that night. She said if he didn't show up, he would have to be discharged or moved up to more intense treatment. I said to send him back to North Jersey for inpatient treatment. To me it seemed he was obviously avoiding IOP because there was something he didn't want them to know, and to me that meant he needed to go back to inpatient treatment.

Wasn't it terrible that I doubted my son? Wasn't it terrible that his need for drugs overpowered everything else? It overpowered his love for his family, his health, and his freedom. September 1 should have been his four-month clean mark. Who knew if he would be?

He did pass a drug test. He did go to IOP. The counselor called to tell me about the clean urine test. She said she knew there had been a lot of drama in the apartment that had nothing to do with Matt. (One of the roommates was letting a girl stay there, and she had been using.) Maybe it was stressing Matt out, and he was trying to avoid it. He hadn't told us about this problem; he didn't talk things out with us anymore. I supposed it seemed easier for him to keep retreating into his shell.

Matt and his other roommate wanted to get rid of the third roommate. The three of them were supposed to sit down and talk about it. Matt's counselor called Matt an avoider; he avoided uncomfortable situations. That summed it up pretty well. I guess he got that from me.

One day, at the end of the summer, Matt had said he might drive down to Ocean City for a quick visit. By that time I had learned not to count on him or even ask him to come for a visit anymore. But his wanting to come visit us brought to mind a winter weekend around Christmastime of his senior year in 2008. We were in Ocean City for the weekend, and the Laverty holiday dinner was at Pop-Pop's house. Matt was coming down for dinner. He and Daniella had spent the morning making chocolate-covered pretzels, but she had to leave by noon, and then Matt would be down.

Dinner was set for 3:00 p.m., which was perfect timing; Matt would leave right around when Daniella left. However, apparently Daniella couldn't find her car keys, and her mother had to drive down from Brooklyn with a spare set of keys. Lo and behold, they eventually found the keys under the kitchen table. Matt didn't show up until very late—around 6:00 p.m. or later.

Later Matt told me he actually had been delayed because he and Daniella were fighting and that he had started using heroin about a month before this.

That day, Mike and I were quite embarrassed. All of our other relatives were there, and he could barely get himself down there to see his cousins and to show his grandfather the car he had helped Matt purchase. He did show Pop-Pop the car. It was about the first thing he did when he arrived. At least he had the grace to do that. But he only stayed for about an hour.

Since the age of thirteen or fourteen Matt seemed to distance himself from the family, both my side and Mike's. Why? Was he embarrassed? Afraid someone would be able to see through him? See through his lies? See that he was using drugs and stealing our money? When he was little, he always came along with us. Tim and Matt are the oldest of the cousins on Mike's side, and after Matt, a lot of girl cousins were born. From the time he was a young teen, he always seemed to come up with reasons not to participate and stayed away whenever possible. Did he already see then that he would have golden opportunities to be free to do whatever he wanted while we were away for the day? Were we wrong not to insist that he come? Getting together on holidays is what families do. Was he afraid someone would see something that we didn't?

One day we were at my mom's house, maybe for her birthday; Matt was probably in his early teens. My brother Steve and his family were also there, down from Rochester, New York, for a long weekend. They have a son who's six months older than Matt. When they were younger, they played together and enjoyed each other's company at family gatherings, but at this one, Matt kept to himself; the two boys barely spoke to each other. My brother pulled me aside later and asked me if Matt was all right. He wondered whether Matt had been smoking pot or something. As I look back, I realize he probably was.

So maybe that was why Matt found reasons to stay away from family events. Did he know he wouldn't be able to fool everyone? But why stay away at a point when he was supposedly clean? Was it because of all the drinking that would go on there? If so, he should have told us that. If that were true, it would be a legitimate excuse for someone still struggling to stay clean. Maybe there was no clear answer, and if there was, would we ever know what it was?

CHAPTER SIXTY-FOUR

More erratic behavior occurred one night in mid-September 2010. Mike told me that he had encountered Matt in our kitchen at 4:30 a.m. on a Friday, making himself something to eat, seemingly unsteady on his feet and slurring his words. (Matt knew the code to our garage door opener; we never had changed it.) Mike asked him whether he had been drinking, and he said no, but some of his friends had been; he said they had all been in Red Bank, presumably at a bar. Why was he even at our house? He had an apartment now. Mike and Matt exchanged words. Matt went outside, made a phone call, and proceeded to walk down the street. Mike called him; he said he was walking into Red Bank which was a couple of milesfrom the house... Mike got in his car and went looking for him and/or his car but found neither. Mike kept calling Matt's cell, and finally Matt answered. He said he was heading into his apartment in Keyport. Had he called for a taxi? Did someone give him a ride back to Keyport? Where was his car? Did he walk to wherever his car was and drive himself home, when he was intoxicated? Mike didn't hear from him on Friday or Saturday, until Matt finally returned a text and said he was OK and was getting ready to go bodyboarding.

Was this a relapse? Matt probably would have said no, because he didn't have a drinking problem, and he didn't lapse back into the drug world. I calculated that he lasted four and a half months being clean and sober. That's about how long he lasted after his first trip to rehab. It seemed like a pattern. When he stopped answering calls and texts, something usually was wrong.

So what next? Would he tell his counselor? Would he say something at a meeting? The last time he relapsed, he just stopped going to IOP and meetings. But that was heroin; was this just an isolated evening of drinking? What were the rules here? Substance abuse is substance abuse, and it didn't matter what the substance was, as far as I was concerned. I would say that Matt had a problem with alcohol as well as drugs. He had a problem with saying no. Would he even choose to tell me about it? Would he and Mike talk about it?

Most important, would he do it again?

CHAPTER SIXTY-FIVE

Wednesday, September 22, 2010 was a special day for my family. A celebration was being held in honor of the one-hundred-year anniversary of Taylor Hospital, which my grandparents founded in 1910 in Ridley Park, Pennsylvania. There would be a picnic, memorabilia on display, a garden dedication, and lots of pictures taken with my relatives, Dr. and Mrs. Taylor's descendents. More important to me, several relatives would be there. My brother John and his family—and by brother Steve and his family—hadn't seen Matt in more than ten years, before my sister Beth died, I'm sure. And it would be the first time in a long time that all five of us—Mike, me, and the kids—had gone some place together.

Matt was going to come down to Ocean City on Tuesday night so we could all drive together, but he ended up having a job interview in Long Branch early Wednesday morning, which was a little disappointing. I had looked forward to having him here for a while; maybe we could walk up to the boardwalk together, or I'd watch him bodyboard; maybe we'd get a doughnut and coffee together, but a job interview was more important.

This day meant a lot to me. So Matt texted me at 9:30 a.m. and said he was just getting ready to leave. He should arrive at the hospital around eleven thirty, but even if he was a bit late, it wouldn't be a problem. He stopped answering his phone, however, and never showed up. Mike and I tried not to worry, but by 2:00 p.m. we were frantic. We were sick to our stomachs and of course couldn't enjoy what should have been a wonderful day for my family. I called his counselor, who hadn't heard from him (but didn't expect to, as Matt was only attending counseling once a week at that point). All sorts of images and scenarios went through my head. Matt was in jail or dead. Maybe the roommate with whom they were having trouble had gone postal. I was actually hoping for a minor car accident. I just kept praying, *Please let him not be in jail. Please let it not be drugs.* Mike was thinking and praying the same things, but interspersed with, *I'm done with this crap. I'm not paying any more money for a lawyer. I'm not bailing him out.* Our heads were spinning, and a million different thoughts whirled around in my head. *I'll have to set up the collect-phone call thing. Which phone number should I use? Who'll be able to watch Tim and Laura if we have to go to the correctional facility, police station, or wherever he is?*

Finally, around 4:00 p.m., he called. One immediate good sign was that he had called from his own phone (if he were under arrest, they wouldn't let him use his phone). The story went like this. Right after he had texted us in the morning, a buddy from rehab had called him, crying and very upset. He had taken a lot of pills and was going to take more to end it all. His wife was leaving and taking their child with her. Matt told him to come meet him at our house, and they immediately got in his buddy's car (Matt drove), but Matt didn't even have a minute to grab his phone from his own car. Apparently they drove around all day, looking for a rehab that would take his friend immediately, not just for rehab but because he had a lot of drugs in his system and was threatening suicide. Matt finally got him to a place that could take him right away. He waited with him through the admission process, and then drove his car back to where his wife was. He explained to her what was going on, and the wife drove Matt back to Little Silver, where Matt's car (and phone!) was.

Did Matt do the right thing? If the story was true, yes. His buddy was in trouble and needed help. We just found it hard to believe that in the seven hours that he was unreachable; he couldn't find a way to call us. His friend must have had a phone; he had called Matt, after all. Did I believe him? I thought the story was way too complex to be made up. We told him to get in touch with his counselor because we had called her, and she was concerned. He would be attending group that night and would take a drug test. He didn't touch our bank accounts, so if he was using drugs, I didn't know where he got the money, and if he was using, he would use again and be found out.

He talked about the events of the day a lot, and with a great deal of specifics. He was very upset about it; he was so wrapped up with it all that he didn't even grasp that we were worried and upset and that he had missed the event at the hospital. There was no groveling or apologies, because he felt he'd had no choice. This was something he just had to do.

I hoped Matt would talk it out at group, in meetings, or with his counselor, because if it was all true, it must have been a very emotional experience for him to go through, knowing that preventing his friend from "offing himself," as Matt put it, had all been on him.

When I spoke to his counselor a few days later, the story seemed to add up. Matt's buddy did have an upsetting incident that had caused a relapse, and he had returned to rehab. Matt never strayed from his story or indicated that it was a lie. Why, then, did these things always happen when he was supposed to be at family events?

And would I ever completely believe this story?

CHAPTER SIXTY-SIX

My niece Liz knew a woman who was a medium. She couldn't see the future and didn't read tarot cards or palms; she was just someone who attracted spirits from the afterlife, people who had passed to the other side. I believe in this and had been interested in hearing what my relatives would "say" to me. I felt even stronger about this since my mother and sister had passed. I prayed to God, and prayed to my loved ones who had passed, but I wondered what they would say to me. I wanted to hear from my mom and my sister; I wanted to hear anything that might give me comfort.

So at the end of September 2010, I met with the medium. The conversation was very disjointed, as that was the way she was receiving messages from the other side. I remember bits and pieces of it, but not everything. She told me to take the fee she would usually charge and find myself a counselor, because she was receiving a message that this was what I needed to do. She said she saw that I was pulling a figurative wagon with two people in it and that it was draining me. She said that one was a boy and later said that it was my son and that he was working really hard to overcome his issues, and he didn't realize how much it was taking out of me. The other person in the wagon was smaller and slower—a female, she thought. She said there was a male peer (Mike?) who was sort of in the picture but also off to the side (perhaps because he was still spending the weekdays in Little Silver?).

She also saw that I needed to be by myself for a while—maybe for a weekend, but more time away would be better—to let my tears fall and to let go a little. She said she saw that my mom and dad were both deceased and that they were united now in their support of me—Dad with strength and Mom with compassion. She said she didn't know whether they had been divorced or separated, but they hadn't been physically together for quite a while (my father passed away forty-five years before my mom, so that was true), but that they were now together and were joined in their care and concern for me and everything I was dealing with. She said my mom always had to give my dad a little push on his arm to get him to speak up and "do something about it," and that he was stepping forward now to help me be strong. She felt he had indigestion while he was alive and asked whether he'd had an ulcer or indigestion or something like that (he did have an ulcer). She added that his death had been respiratory related (he ultimately died from pneumonia). She kept grabbing at her throat as if she had to belch, because that was how my dad always felt. She said my mom didn't want to talk about how she had died. (She had Alzheimer's and died at age ninety-two. I suspect she felt it was an undignified way to go.)

The medium also saw a little boy who had passed, maybe a six-year-old boy, named Tim or Tom, and he was scampering around my feet, just wanting to be around me. (I had a brother named Timmy who died before I was born. He was six years old.) When I told her that, she was quiet for a moment then gasped and said, "Oh, I see a greenish car. It was an accident, wasn't it?" (Yes, it was. He had been fooling around with our parents' car and had gotten out; the brake released and crushed him between the car and a stone wall.) What she saw was right on the nose. It's interesting that Timmy wanted to comfort me, since I never knew him. She talked about my sister and said she was there and is always with me. She knew that Beth had died suddenly and that she had suffered before she died. She grabbed her head and said she got the sense that Beth had had a violent head-ache but added that something had occurred with Beth's breathing as well. (A tumor had wrapped itself around my sister's heart, squeezing it until it stopped, and then she had fallen backwards and hit her head hard against the stove.)

The medium then put herself into a trance, where two spirits talked through her. They were solemn older people, and they talked about Matt. They talked about the same thing—that I had done all I could—and said something about Matt not having much time left. The medium said I sighed a lot because my burden was so great. She said my mom didn't necessarily want me to go to parties or have a few drinks but just wanted me to relax and smile and laugh and do something to enjoy my life.

I had the names of some counselors and vowed to call one that day. The medium first thought I should talk to someone in the clergy but then said no; I should just see a medical professional, a down-to-earth woman in her fifties. I felt I should listen to her. She was right on the money with pretty much everything else she had said. It would be interesting to see what my new counselor would be like.

CHAPTER SIXTY-SEVEN

At the end of September, I drove to Little Silver for a doctor's appointment and stopped at the house to meet Matt and go to lunch. His clothes were all over his room. Excuse me—I mean the room that used to be his before we all agreed that his living at home wasn't a good idea. I asked if he had moved back in. He said no, that he had brought his laundry over to do at our house. I told him one of the reasons he was living in an apartment instead of our house was because of the stress it caused. I told him to put all of his clothes in garbage bags and put them in his car. I told him to stop eating his dad's food and to stop having friends over for feasts. Of course I had to be the one to say all this because when Mike talked to him (and to me), it sounded like a lecture, and Matt just tuned out. We'd see if my talk did any good; I knew it wasn't likely.

I also left a message with Matt's counselor, asking him to call me. I wanted to hear what Matt had told him about the apartment situation. I also wanted to know how the counselor thought Matt was doing in general and what, if anything, Matt had told him about the previous week when he didn't come to the family event. I wanted to know what he thought about the night when Matt had gotten drunk.

I wanted to know all of the things he had opened up about to counselors and fellow addicts but not to me.

At the same time, though, I knew I had to step back and let it go, but if all this was affecting us financially, I thought I had a right to know what was going on. Matt needed to know how much all this was affecting me physically and emotionally. I did tell him that I knew he was working hard on his recovery, but I also reinforced the idea that he had to multitask; he had to do more than just work on recovery. He had to get his stuff out of our house and get a job. He had answered an ad from an agency that would train him to be a bartender, and then, once he passed the test, they would place him in a bartending position. It definitely wasn't the ideal job for him, but if I expressed any opinion, he'd fire back at me that we wanted him to get a job, and he was doing something about it. Still I expressed my view that it couldn't hurt to keep looking elsewhere.

I often wondered whether anything I said sank in.

I was working on letting go—one day at a time. Today Matt was clean. I couldn't control or cure his addiction, and I certainly didn't cause it. If he chose to use, so be it. I couldn't live my life waiting for a relapse. I tried to think positive thoughts, for me and for him, that he would be strong enough to resist his urges.

He had picked up a few hours of work for a caterer, a job he had found on Craigslist. I was eager for him to start working more hours; maybe he could start bartending as well. The busier he was, the less time he would have to think about drugs. If he was doing a good job and earning money, I thought he'd feel better about himself. Just having a job would boost his ego.

I expected he would stay clean and was holding that thought, one day at a time. I asked him how long he had been clean. Was it six months now? He said, "Something like that," but he didn't know how many days it had been since he had gotten drunk a few weeks ago. This should have been a red flag. Most addicts know to the day how long they've been clean, even if they haven't used in ten years.

I asked Matt if he had to start over with the counting because of the drinking incident, which he didn't call a relapse. He said, "Yeah." A couple of days after the night he had gotten drunk, he had said it wasn't technically a relapse because drugs were his demon, and he hadn't used drugs. So was it a relapse or not? Did he think so at that point? Maybe he talked to his counselor about it; I didn't know. But I considered it a relapse, and when I asked his counselor, he did as well.

CHAPTER SIXTY-EIGHT

Matt wasn't feeling well; he had another sinus infection. He always had been prone to them, but I assumed that his shoving heroin up his nose for the past couple of years had made them worse. He mentioned what the doctor had said before—that he may have to go to an ENT and possibly need surgery to scrape his sinuses. He had heard it was painful and would require him to take painkillers, and he didn't want to do that.

What was the point of his telling me that? To let me know why he wasn't going to the doctor in the first place? To let me know that he still wasn't interested in taking drugs, even if a doctor had prescribed them? I didn't care whether or not he had surgery, or even if he went to the doctor or not. No, that's not true; I'd always been a proponent of his having regular medical and dental checkups.

Matt always had been one to cry wolf. Maybe he had a low tolerance for discomfort. All through grade school, he'd say he was too sick to go to school, but miraculously he'd feel better by about two o'clock, so he could go outside and "get some fresh air," or even earlier, say lunchtime, because a Slurpee probably would make him feel better.

What I didn't like was when he missed work. He had called in sick numerous times for the various jobs he had held. One time he said he went to work for the caterer and that they had sent him home because he was blowing his nose so much. I just wanted him to work so he'd stay busy. His having a steady schedule would be good for him and me. The only problem with that was that it also meant he'd receive a paycheck, and I worried what he'd do with the money when he got it. When he worked I knew where he was and what he was doing. I was trying not to obsess over him, his actions, and his whereabouts all the time, and I thought I was getting better at it.

Matt hadn't yet passed his test to get his bartender's license. A teacher had been testing his ability to make various drinks, but there was always one drink he'd slightly mess up. He said he could keep taking the test until he passed. It shouldn't have been a problem for him to pass it, as he had taken a bartending course in college and had some sort of certificate for it. I knew bartending wasn't the ideal job for Matt, but since we had paid for this course, we wanted him to have something to show for it. In addition to that, he needed a job.

CHAPTER SIXTY-NINE

In mid-October 2010, Matt betrayed us once again. I learned he had taken $240 from Tim's account over the past six days. I prayed it wasn't for drugs, but what else could it be? I read one of his e-mails (yes, I looked) from someone who said he had waited too long for the money Matt owed him for pills. Pills? I didn't think Matt had used pills in a long, long time. So was he selling them? Was the person who sent him the message a dealer? Was it a friend he had borrowed money from? And how recently or long ago had this happened? Did this have anything to do with Matt's having missed my family's hospital event last month or his missing work last weekend? Or his continuing to fail his bartending test?

Did he come down to Ocean City and go through my things? Or were these checks that he had taken last May or last year? I would have known if he had been here, wouldn't I? Besides, how would he know that I wouldn't be here? The only time I wouldn't be here is if I had gone to Little Silver, but he didn't have a key to our apartment in Ocean City anyway. It had to be checks he had taken a while ago, and it appeared there were still a few more missing. (He did tell me later that he had found them in a box in our closet in Little

Silver—old checks, or temporary checks we weren't currently using, checks so old that we didn't even know they were there.

Was he actively using drugs again? As far as I knew, Matt had only been to probation one time, last week, and wasn't due to go back until November. Was that what he was counting on? Was he timing his probation meeting so he could use but still produce a clean urine test? Was this why he hadn't gone to counseling? Did he think he might as well live it up until he got sent to jail?

I prayed that he just had to pay someone back. But he should have known that although we might not catch him using drugs, we would catch him if he forged checks. If he really did need the money to pay someone back, why wouldn't he just come to us, ask for the money, and tell us what it was for? I couldn't believe he would steal money just to go to a concert or something—unless he was on drugs when he had done it.

What an emotional twenty-four hours. It took quite a while that night for me to get in touch with Matt and actually talk about it with him.

He was alive; he wasn't in jail; and he wasn't using drugs, as far as we knew. He just had gone into his shell. Once we had started to leave messages the previous night for him to come home or call us, he figured that we knew about the checks. So he avoided us all day because he didn't want to have the scene we ended up having. This was the same reason he hadn't come to us to tell us he owed someone money from a couple of years ago. He didn't want that scene, so he thought it would be easier to forge checks. His logic was very warped. He had some form of brain damage, I guessed, from his drug use.

I told him he needed to go to counseling more than once a week, because he was lying constantly and had no respect for the rest of the family. He may not have been using drugs, but some of his old behaviors were still there—and lying was at the top of that list.

I was so grateful he was alive and free—free from drugs, for now, and free from imprisonment. But he had a long way to go to repair the damage he had done to himself and our family.

I vowed I would check into switching the bank accounts, which would involve changing the kids' Social Security direct deposit, and therefore dig up the papers that showed that Mike and I were their legal guardians. It would be a pain, yes, but it was a small price to pay for feeling secure once again. (When was the last time I had felt secure?) I needed do the same with our savings account and have the direct deposit changed on my paychecks. He had not accessed that account, but it was better to be safe than sorry.

I was drained. I prayed all morning. I prayed every morning during my walk. I was able to work, but I felt drained. After that I basically walked around in circles the rest of the afternoon and evening, unable to concentrate, but once again, I thanked God for watching over Matt. The choices he had made over the past week weren't good ones, but he wasn't using; he didn't get in trouble with anyone but us; and he wasn't dead or in jail. For those things I was so grateful.

And of course, as I found out later, he had used the money for drugs.

Through all of this, friends and family told us we should have turned him in for forgery and let him go to jail, but I couldn't do that to my son. I didn't want to be the one who turned him in, who ultimately made that decision, although I thought I would've been OK if the authorities had caught up with him.

Mike and I went around and around. I wanted Matt to get help, and so did Mike, but Mike also said he wouldn't pay for any more legal fees. If Matt hadn't missed a probation meeting and hadn't failed any drug tests, would he be able to check himself back into rehab and tell probation that he wanted to do so because he wasn't doing so well and was feeling the urge to use? Matt ended up being honest with probation and hoped his honesty would work in his favor and that he wouldn't get sent to jail.

We had done nothing but try to save Matt from himself for the past nine or ten years, most aggressively over the past year, since he was arrested and put in jail for several days. How could he do this? How could he not fight these urges, or at least ask for help, when he knew what the consequences were?

I was angry. I was pissed. I felt hurt, insulted, and violated. He had stolen money from us again, and he couldn't even blame his actions on drugs. He was still saying he had owed someone money and hadn't wanted to go through the lectures with us. So he had forged checks from Tim's bank account. He could steal, cheat, lie, and use drugs, but he wasn't man enough to listen to his parents tell him that what he had done was wrong. *For God's sake*, I thought, *grow up, Matt!* If he wanted to be a man, in charge of his own life and his own destiny, he had to learn to take the bad with the good.

At one point he even said to Mike, "I don't know why I do these things." He needed help, but we didn't even know what kind of help. He probably didn't know either, but again he was so closed down and kept everything bottled up. He certainly needed to talk to someone about his lying and stealing. And the forgery! Forgery is a major offense; I couldn't believe the bank hadn't caught on.

Maybe he also still needed to talk to someone about the drugs and alcohol. I had no idea whether he had used anything since the night he had come home drunk the previous month. The thing with drugs, though, is that if he took them again, just once, he wouldn't be able to stop, and he would get caught. I didn't think, however, that he could touch our money anymore.

Obviously I was wrong.

If he chose to use again, he would borrow money from his buddies again? Anyone who would lend him money was a fool. Or maybe he would start stealing—but from whom?

I couldn't do any more for him. He had to save himself. Either that or he would ruin himself.

CHAPTER SEVENTY

From the time Matt was about nine months old, until he was around four years old, we had to tie all our kitchen chairs to each other and to the table. He was always so inquisitive, several steps ahead of where he should have been. His motto, before he was old enough to know about mottos, was "Act first; think about it later." He wanted to use the chairs to climb onto the counters and explore the cupboards. I probably kept lollipops there; maybe he wanted to stick his finger in the sugar bowl. Maybe he just did it do get my attention. My goodness, he did get my attention; he had my attention. He was in a preschool/day care before he was even two years old, so he could be with peers. But he and I also spent a lot of time together, running errands, just the two of us, while Tim and Laura were in their school programs.

He was always pushing the boundaries, even before he could walk.

CHAPTER SEVENTY-ONE

I'd been thinking about what the medium had said when she was in the trance and two spirits had talked through her. It seemed to me that they were older American Indians, the elders, the wise people. They had said something to the effect of my having done all I could and that Matt didn't have much time left and that I couldn't do any more.

So what did that mean? Would he fail a drug test and go to jail? Would he attempt to forge another check and get caught? How would I get through my days if my son were in jail?

Even worse, what did it mean that Matt didn't have much time left? Was he going to die? If so, how? From an overdose? Would a dealer or someone to whom he owed money kill him? How would I survive if that happened? A large part of me would die if something like that happened to him.

Coincidentally, or not, the medium called me a few weeks later, saying I had popped into her head. I asked her what the wise people had said, and she said she didn't ever remember what she said when in a trance, but that the spirits never would say anything that was truly negative; she said it didn't mean anything horrible would happen to Matt. I did remember that the first person who spoke finished talking then said he or she would let another person talk—someone who could say things more gently.

CHAPTER SEVENTY-TWO

My mom told me once that when my son Timmy was born, and it was immediately clear that he would have major health problems, she saw that the light had gone out of my eyes. I wondered what she would say now, because there certainly was no light in my eyes currently. I thought they looked flat, expressionless. No, that wasn't true. They had expression; they were full of pain. Yet I knew they could get worse, and would, if something bad happened to Matt. I prayed for something good to happen to him; that would put some light back into my eyes.

The end of October 2010 brought a turbulent weekend, and we were very frustrated by Matt's lack of communication.... As always we went into panic mode when he didn't respond to our calls or text messages.

Matt finally went to talk to Mike, and it was pretty emotional. Mike was inconsolable afterward, as was I. Matt said he was sick and tired of counseling and sick and tired of our always asking if he'd gone here or done that. The more we asked him to call, reply, or answer us, the more he shut down. I could understand that. But for as long as he was accepting our financial help to pay for his rent, groceries, and phone bills, he owed us the courtesy of responding. He didn't have to tell us his every move, but he owed it to us to be courteous and reply to our calls or texts. All he had to say was that he was OK but a little busy and that he would get back to us later. Instead he completely pulled away, leaving us to wonder whether he was all right.

After hearing all of this, I thought about the day of our family event at the hospital in September and wondered whether he really had been with a friend in distress, or whether he had just blown off the celebration because he didn't want to be forced to do something.

The tears were cleansing for all of us, I think. They certainly were for me. Matt shed quite a few himself. I hoped he realized how much we feared for him, his health, his safely, and his life. I hoped he knew that everything we did was driven by our love for him.

But Matt wanted the best of all worlds. He wanted his freedom and independence, by living on his own, but he also wanted to come and go in and out of our home as he pleased, eating, cooking, showering, and doing laundry. He wanted to come to us for money for food, gas, rent, and bills, but he also wanted us to back off. When would he grow up? He said he was sick of going to aftercare (one day a week of counseling); he said he had heard the same topics and lectures many times. He said he got more out of AA and NA meetings. We asked that he go to a "final discharge" session, to wrap it all up, as a courtesy to his counselor. Mike wanted to have a session with Matt and the counselor, with me there as well, if possible. I thought it was what we all needed. But would Matt be willing to participate?

CHAPTER SEVENTY-THREE

As October 2010 ended, I was still grasping at straws, wanting to hear anything that would give me a reason to hope. A radio show I listened to had a psychic on the air one day a week. On a whim I called the station and asked what one had to do to speak to the psychic. I guess I called at the right time, because they took my phone number and arranged for me to be the person the psychic spoke to that day. The psychic said that Matt wasn't completely on the right path and that he would still stumble, but that I must give him unconditional love and not beat him down. He said he didn't want to air our dirty laundry on the radio but that I knew exactly what he was talking about, and said ultimately Matt would be OK. He asked about the numbers fifty-seven and seventy-five and the dates May 7 and July 5 and whether they meant anything to me. (They didn't at the time, but I later found a journal entry regarding something that had happened regarding Matt on May 7.) The psychic also said that someone who had passed, someone with "Mar" in his or her name, was coming through (my mother and Beth were both named Mary—my sister's given name was Mary Elizabeth) and was sending her love and an apology. He said Matt would be OK, and I would see lots of pennies around, which would be her way of saying hello.

So Matt would stumble, according to the psychic. I hoped that meant he'd get drunk again or get caught in another lie. But please, no jail. Why was I so concerned about jail? Maybe it would teach him something, but I was afraid he would learn more tricks of the trade in prison and come out hardened rather than reformed. And the mother in me didn't want to see my little boy exposed to all that ugliness.

At the beginning of November, I had an epiphany and decided I wasn't going to worry about what may or may not happen to Matt. He was in God's hands. I prayed that God would guide him toward good choices and away from temptation. I wouldn't let his choices affect my happiness. I kept telling myself this over and over, and I hoped I'd start to believe it.

I talked this out with my therapist (the one I started seeing shortly after the medium told me I should), and she said I had a right not to like Matt very much sometimes. I always would love him and always would worry about and feel protective of him because he was my son, but I didn't have to always like him. And I could be pissed off at him. So I was pissed off at him—pissed that he had disrupted, invaded, and violated our lives. Invaded our lives. How dare he steal from us? How dare he forge checks from us?

How dare he not show us the respect we deserved? He was walking in and out of our house at all hours of the day and night, helping himself to food and cooking it, sometimes cleaning up afterward and sometimes not. He wanted to live on his own. He had wanted his own apartment for a few years, and now he had it. Yes, there were a few strings attached because we were paying for it. The deal was that he had four months to find a job. How hard had he been looking? Not at all. What had he done? He had gone out to dinner at an

Italian restaurant/pizza place and put in an application while he was there. He did a little catering under the table and was supposed to fill out an application for more permanent work. He hadn't done that. He had spent entire days skateboarding. He had found ways to get to concerts without having to drive there himself or pay for his ticket. He would work overtime if necessary to accomplish that. He would happily drive his friends back and forth to their houses and help blow leaves or paint their houses to help their parents, but he couldn't lend a hand to help with anything at our house.

There didn't seem to be an ounce of gratitude in him—gratitude for a roof over his head; for a college education; for the money we put out monthly for rent, bills, car insurance, gas, and food. If he got paid any amount of money for working a little on the side, he'd blow it on food or cigarettes, instead of offering to give his dad even $50 toward one of his bills. He made no effort to even see us, just to say hi. I couldn't remember when I saw him last. Sometime in October, I think. We'd had lunch, and of course he needed a little money.

He wasn't around when I was home the previous week. He knew what day I was planning to come up to Little Silver that week. He'd said he would call me but didn't. Screw it. I didn't need to have lunch with him. He would only sit through lunch because he wanted money. I decided I wouldn't knock myself out to see Matt. He wasn't knocking himself out to see me; he just wanted to see my wallet.

I had thought we had a close relationship; I'd thought Matt felt comfortable talking to me, as he would with a friend. It had taken me years to realize I was wrong.

CHAPTER SEVENTY-FOUR

Matt's behavior started to get erratic again at the beginning of November 2010. He missed a scheduled doctor's appointment, and we didn't know why. He'd slept through the appointment set up for the previous Friday and didn't go to a walk-in clinic all weekend, even though he said he felt really lousy. Was he going through withdrawal? Did that explain why he wasn't job-hunting? He also seemed to have gone back into his shell, not answering texts, calls, or e-mails.

Then, out of the blue, he called one afternoon just to say hello. Was that to throw us off? If he were smarter, he would make calls like that every few days. I e-mailed him and said if he was using, he'd better check himself into Bayview House in Central New Jersey so he could get clean before his next probation appointment. I wondered whether he would think about it or if he even read my e-mail.

It's unbelievable how drugs can take over an addict's mind—so much so that the person doesn't even care whether he or she might go to jail. I supposed addicts are willing to risk anything, just for one more fix.

And if Matt wasn't using drugs, why was he so damn lazy? If he was scared of being in the real world and having to support himself, scared that he wouldn't be able to make it, why wouldn't he just come out and admit that?

No wonder I couldn't go to sleep—or if I did fall asleep couldn't stay asleep. I had constant headaches and frequent stomachaches and felt like crying all the time. And I couldn't concentrate on anything.

The days moved along with no word from Matt. Mike had decided that if he showed up at the house he would have to take a drug test before he could come in or get food or money. If he refused, Mike vowed to tell him he wasn't welcome at the house. He planned to give Matt his cell phone bill and tell him he wasn't paying for it any longer, since he wasn't using it to communicate with us.

I was heartsick. I couldn't believe we had lost our son to drugs. What powerful things drugs are. He didn't have enough willpower to try to fight them. I was thinking he had given in. All logic went out the window when drugs were involved. If he went to jail, I wanted it to be for violating probation and not because he had gotten caught making a drug deal, or robbing a store to get drug money, or forging a check. I felt like his life was over, and I didn't even have any facts.

Except for the silence.

Eventually he called and said he was fine; he was just tired of us texting, calling, and e-mailing him with messages assuming the worst. I was glad he called but didn't feel any better, because it wasn't a rational conversation. I told him I was worried how he'd be able to support himself once we stopped paying his bills.

CHAPTER SEVENTY-FIVE

On November 9, 2010, I realized it had been one year since Mike and I had received the news that Matt had been arrested and was in jail. It had been a year of real nightmares, although everything really had started about ten months before that, in January 2009, when he had come to us and said he had a gambling problem. And then he'd had two stints in rehab. I guess about six or seven years before that was when he started smoking pot and drinking. I had aged twenty years in that eight-year period. It—and he—had worn me down.

In mid-November 2010, Matt went MIA again after he'd been living in the apartment for three and a half months. One of his roommates called me on a Sunday night, saying Matt hadn't slept there in several nights. It also came out that Matt was supposed to give his roommates money toward that month's electric bill, cable bill, and cable deposit but hadn't. Mike had given him the cash for these things, but apparently the cash never made it back to the roommates.

Mike was able to get in touch with Matt that Sunday night, after his roommate had told us he was worried. It seemed he had driven down to Hilton Head with a high school friend to visit another high school friend. My guess was that the money that was supposed to go toward the apartment bills had funded his impromptu road trip. Mike frankly didn't see how he could have held on to the money for that long. One of the roommates thought Matt had been drinking from time to time but not necessarily doing drugs. I prayed Mike would remain calm when and if Matt surfaced.

As Matt readied himself for the return trip, of course, he needed us to wire him enough money to get home. But he did say that when he got back, he wanted to talk to a counselor or psychiatrist. I started to do some research, but first I needed to talk to Matt and see how much or how little he was willing to commit to. We only talked about it a little, but he shed lots of tears. He said he was compulsive and had trouble following through with things. He thought maybe he was depressed but wasn't sure he wanted to take medication. I was planning to talk to a psychologist who's a friend of someone at work and see what he thought the first steps should be. Counseling first, then psychiatry, if it looked like medication was indicated? And would Matt go back to Bayview House or start fresh with a new counselor, one unrelated to Bayview House?

Matt told me much later that he had in fact been using prior to this little road trip, and he had left so he could detox on his own, away from temptation. But it didn't work; on the drive back, he went straight to Elizabeth to meet his dealer and buy more heroin. He also started to use needles around this time.

November ended with Matt leaving us disappointed—again. Happy Thanksgiving. Once again should we have believed him or not? Thanksgiving dinner would take place in Ocean City with all of the Lavertys. Matt called early in the afternoon to say his car wouldn't start but said a buddy was going to give him a jump, and he was just waiting for his call. I called him at 3:00 p.m. and 4:00 p.m. but received no answer. I texted him and asked whether this was another disappearing act, or whether he was just avoiding his family. At 5:00 p.m. I received a text from him that said he had fallen asleep and never heard his phone ring, so the friend who was going to jump the car for him never did, figuring Matt no longer needed his help. I told him not to come unless he was staying overnight. I didn't expect to see him. And I didn't.

How many times could he break my heart over a two-year period? Really it had been six years, but over the past two years, he had done some things that had devastated me. So many times he'd said he would be somewhere at a certain time and then would show up embarrassingly late, if at all. I prayed he would go to see a counselor, so he could talk all of this out. But I doubted it would happen.

CHAPTER SEVENTY-SIX

As November ended on a bad note, December started on an equally bad one. Matt was supposed to start a new job with a pyramid type company, where he would start out as a part timer, selling fragrances and then eventually have salesmen working under him... Apparently he didn't go either the first or second day (there was no sign that he had used an E-ZPass, and his car was at his apartment). He later told us he called on Monday to say he was running late, and they told him to start with the next group the following Monday. He had stopped at our house that day because he owed $50 to one of his roommates and would need money to get lunch once he went to work. He already had received the rent check from us. Why hadn't he told us then that he owed his roommate money? After he got the money, he had to go back to his apartment; hence the reason for his being late for work. Or did he really want the money for drugs?

Mike went to Matt's apartment that afternoon. The house was dark, and Matt's car was there. Matt said he was out skateboarding. Mike said that since he wasn't working that week he would be able to keep his appointment with his new counselor (he hadn't been yet). If he started work the following Monday, though, how would he keep his probation appointment? Did he use drugs but time it so they'd be out of his system before his probation meeting? Why couldn't we believe him? Why couldn't we think positively about his actions? Why didn't he try harder to reassure us?

I prayed and prayed that he finally would get it right and get through this. I knew my prayers would be answered—just maybe not in the way I wanted them answered or in the time frame I wanted them. Maybe jail really was the only way he would learn. Certainly it was better than the alternative—death. All his counselors had told us to sit back and let it happen; they said we should have kicked him out and cut him off long ago. But I couldn't. I couldn't live with myself, knowing that my son was living on the streets, because if he was living on the streets, he surely would end up in jail.

Even if he wasn't using drugs at that time, he was a compulsive liar, a chronic relapser, and a manipulator. Had the drugs done this to him? Had they caused him to have no conscience and no feelings? I hoped some of his brain cells would grow back; otherwise, what a horrible way to go through life—for him and for those who love him.

In mid-December he missed his probation meeting; apparently he called to say he was running late for the meeting but also running late for a job interview. The probation officer left a message with Mike, at home, and also left a message on Matt's cell phone. Would the officer finally draw the line and tell Matt it was time to face the consequences? Matt was able to meet with the probation officer the following day, and everything was fine except the PO wanted to see him again in two weeks, then again in January. Good. I wished he had to go every week, since he wasn't going to aftercare or IOP, and I didn't think he was going to NA or AA meetings either. He hadn't yet met with a private counselor, as he said he would.

As it happened, he thought the job for which he was supposed to start training was too much work for too little money. What did he want? What made him think he deserved special treatment? I guess he wanted someone who would let him listen to demo tapes all day and pay him large sums of money. He had two weeks left in his apartment (because we'd stop paying his rent after December), and he had no plans beyond that. He hadn't told his roommates that he would be moving out. Did he know something we didn't? Did he know he was bound for jail and therefore wouldn't need either a job or an apartment? Or was he gambling with the possibility that we'd still pay his bills? He had a great argument for the phone bill. He said that if he didn't have a phone, we wouldn't be able to reach him, and neither would potential employers or probation. He was right.

Would he find some place cheaper to live? Who would pay the security deposit and the first month's rent? Drugs certainly had taken a toll on his brain, because he wasn't thinking clearly—if at all. Of course I never had these conversations with Matt, as once again I didn't want to start an argument. I kept all these thoughts inside. I'd had these talks with Matt before, and his response always had been that I was stressing him out.

Mike had a mini breakdown about what had become of Matt (or what Matt had become) but felt better after he talked to Matt. Mike had reached out to three different groups of friends with whom he was involved, asking anyone and everyone to keep their ears open for job opportunities. A couple of people got back to him with some music-related opportunities, as well as a job that could offer honest hard work at a building-supply company. Anything would be good. A job would be good for Matt's morale and also would take some weight off our shoulders. Keeping busy was what he needed to do. I was so glad that Mike had reached out to his friends. I had gotten jobs for Matt at my office during a few summers or Christmas breaks and had long ago become embarrassed by his work ethic, or lack thereof, and especially his behavior of late, and I wouldn't put my employers in the awkward position of hiring him out of loyalty to me.

One of Mike's contacts came through, and Matt was scheduled to start work at the building-supply company as a driver's helper. The manager of this location used to live in our neighborhood, so Matt knew him from social events (block parties, holiday parties, etc.) and would feel comfortable working for him. I knew he wasn't excited about the job itself. He probably thought it would be too much physical labor for him; I guess he didn't want to get his hands dirty. I was sure Matt wasn't in very good shape, although he had gone to the gym some while he was in rehab. Still this would be work. He had another possible moneymaking opportunity as well; a local person was willing to pay Matt $15 an hour for his assistance in helping her clean out her attic and garage. He also had two contacts in music-related fields to call. Maybe they would lead to more networking than actual jobs, but it was worth a try. I thought maybe he was timid about making the calls. I was sure he would have preferred to have these people go through Mike and just tell Mike to have him show up at a certain place and time. I wondered whether that was it—insecurity. Or it was maybe embarrassment; perhaps he wondered how much these people may have known about his past.

CHAPTER SEVENTY-SEVEN

I was making Christmas cookies in Ocean City shortly before Christmas and had sent half of them home with Mike to give to Matt. I remembered the few Christmas seasons when he really had looked forward to the cookie-making process. There were certain cookies he wanted me to make, and he wanted to help make them as well. For some reason he always wanted us to sip sparkling grape juice while we baked. Maybe he had seen that in a commercial once.

As I made the cookies this day, I wondered whether Matt would even be with us over the holidays. Mike and I had ordered some things he needed, and he knew we had ordered them—shoes, a backpack, and a sweater—and we told him they were his Christmas gifts. I supposed we'd get stocking stuffers for him—some candy and some gift cards for groceries, I guess. Some things would never change. I remembered the Tag Heuer watch we'd given him the previous Christmas, which he later pawned. That Christmas he had only been home from rehab for a week. He had gone to church with Mike and seemed very appreciative of being alive and clean and having a second chance. He had said he had "found God" while in rehab. How quickly things changed. I hoped he felt grateful for another chance once again this Christmas. Mostly I hoped he'd tell me what was on his mind, what kinds of things he worried about, what he wished for. I had said these things to him before; mostly he gave me a vague brush-off for an answer. I needed to be able to understand it all better. Even more, maybe Mike would understand a little better and be more patient with him.

The medium with whom I had spoken several months ago called me the day I was making cookies. She said I'd popped into her mind again, so she thought she should call and see if things were going OK. I told her that today was a very nice, quiet day and that I was in the kitchen, baking, one of my favorite things to do. I now believe she knew or sensed something I wasn't yet aware of.

Matt kept calling me that day, asking when Mike would be coming home to the house in Little Silver. He said there was no reason for his asking; he was just wondering. It always worried me—did he want Mike home as soon as possible because he needed money, or because he had to clean the house before Mike's arrival? If he had said, "I can't wait for Dad to bring the cookies home," I would have felt better. Matt confirmed my suspicions a year or more later; he had wanted to ask Mike for money so he could buy more heroin.

How did we not see his addiction earlier than we did? We knew he had experimented with alcohol and pot when he was a teenager. He had seen counselors because of it through most of high school. It seemed to us that he had it under control, that it was kind of a high school phase he had gone through, and he was really over it. He had cleaned himself up and was getting a fresh start.

I was sure he smoked pot and drank in college, but I thought, probably naively, that it was more socially. He had summer jobs, and his schedule, while not necessarily to our liking (he was out late into the night but able to sleep late fairly often) was consistent and seemed to fit his lifestyle. His grades were fine; he kept a 3.0 average through all eight semesters.

He had since admitted that he had started to use heroin in November of his senior year of college; before that it was painkillers. He didn't come home much, so we didn't see him enough to notice any changes. He had a job at a Mexican restaurant during the first semester of his senior year, and he held onto that until he came home for Christmas break of that year. He never went back to that job during his second semester. He said they didn't need him anymore; business had slowed down. It wasn't until later that I realized he had found a better way to get money for his heroin without his having to work for it—us.

He ran around a lot during that winter break. I didn't notice that he kept odd hours or was up a lot at night—no more so than usual, anyway. It was, after all, vacation, and he was always playing computer games late at night, or talking on the phone, and he was seeing Daniella. Apparently he was still able to withdraw money from his bank accounts and take cash advances on his credit cards, so it wasn't until the end of January when I guess it all got too much for him, financially anyway, when he came to us about his "gambling problem." That must have been when his money supply ran out. And that was when Mike and I started to notice the changes in his behaviors, sleep patterns, and eating habits. He explained it away by saying he was worried about the gambling debts and the bookie, and we believed that. At that time we knew of no reason not to believe it.

Once Matt went back to school, he always needed $300 for more books or computer repairs, or to fix a friend's car he had dented. We were angry and frustrated, but we never seriously gave any thought to the possibility that it could be drugs. Why the hell didn't we? Other people had told me that it sounded like he was using drugs. I guess we just didn't want to hear it. Years later, Matt admitted that it was all for drugs. How would we have found out anyway? He never would have agreed to a drug test. And what could we have done about it? Not given him money, I suppose. And just after graduation, he started stealing it. So we weren't necessarily giving it to him, but he was getting it from us, and from Mike's softball team, by stealing their entire treasury, and by forging checks from our account and Tim and Laura's.

And there were so many unexplained absences. Why did we always believe his cell phone wasn't working or the battery was dead? We truly were in the dark about all of this until his arrest in November 2009. I suppose a parent is blind to anything negative about their child. By the time a year had passed since his arrest, we didn't trust anything he said, and he'd get so mad at us for questioning him.

And when *could* we start to trust again? After he was clean for six months? Six years? Ever? Maybe if he'd gone to meetings and counseling, and taken and passed drug tests, I would have trusted him a little. Maybe if he had talked more, opened up more, I would have trusted him a little.

CHAPTER SEVENTY-EIGHT

Matt started his job as a driver's helper on Monday December 20. He didn't go to work the next day, however, on December 21; he said his car wouldn't start. He left his phone on vibrate and fell back asleep, so he missed two calls from his boss (Mike's friend), who was offering to give him a ride, and from us, wondering what was going on, because Mike's friend, as well as our former neighbor, had called Mike. Yet while he was supposedly asleep, he sent a text to a friend, which he sent to Mike by mistake, talking about concert tickets or skateboards or something like that. Did Matt just need to chill after one hard day of manual labor? Or did he take the $100 Mike had given him (he said he wanted to do some Christmas shopping after work, and the gift he had in mind for us would cost $60 to $70) and play all day—using drugs, relaxing, and snacking? I could only guess. For some reason, probably because Mike was friends with the people who had hired Matt, they gave him another chance.

Matt got mad when we doubted him, but I wished he would look at himself from our perspective.

He and I had a small a text/e-mail fight a couple of days before Christmas. Lately I never saw him in person or talked to him on the phone. He'd communicate with me only via text or e-mail. I had texted him about something (work, money—who knows?), and he sent me the following reply—"I can't take any more from you guys. I'm going to lose my mind, and I'm really not in a good place because of the way you guys batter and batter and batter me."

So I replied, this time by e-mail, "How do we get out of your life? Why don't you tell me what boundaries you want to put up for us? What you want and don't want from us. We'll see if they sound fair. We don't want to be the cause of your being in a place that's not good."

Matt replied, "That was selfish. It's not just because of you guys that I'm in a bad place. But no matter what, you guys will always have a million questions and suspicions, no matter how good I'm doing. I don't know—it just seems like something so small could happen or be said, and you guys will turn it into something that isn't what happened. But you have your reasons, and I'm sorry I don't cope with that well."

I replied, "I won't sleep much tonight. I hate when we fight. It seems like Dad and I never say or do the right thing."

His final reply was "I feel like I never say or do the right thing either. Like I always make it worse when we disagree or fight."

If he'd been able to think rationally, he would have seen why we couldn't trust him. He knew from rehab and counseling that an addict never can be trusted. More likely it was that he knew there was reason for us not to trust him, and he was instinctively overprotesting in an attempt to prove us wrong.

It wasn't a great way to start off the Christmas season.

CHAPTER SEVENTY-NINE

Merry Christmas. Matt was with us for twenty-four hours; he joined us Saturday after dinner (after meeting up first with a friend in Atlantic City), so he was with us for the Laverty gathering on Christmas Eve and spent Christmas Day and dinner with us. The gift Matt had ordered for us hadn't arrived yet, he said. As if we cared about that. As if there really was a gift. For Christmas we decided to give him a laptop, as well as the silly stocking stuffers. We were supposed to have another Laverty gathering on December 26, but with snow in the forecast—and in fact flurries already starting on Christmas night— we agreed Matt he should go home Saturday night. We didn't want him to get stuck in Ocean City and miss his probation appointment, or work, when he had just received a second chance.

Good call. We got about eighteen inches of snow in Ocean City, and Little Silver got around twenty-five inches. Matt's work and probation were both canceled Monday and Tuesday. But amazingly enough, Matt was able to get into New York City for a concert Monday night. The ticket was free, he said, and a "female friend" had given him two round-trip train tickets to the city for Christmas because she knew he wanted to go. Things always seemed to work out the way Matt wanted them to.

Before the storm got really bad, he went to the A&P to stock up on some groceries (we had given him a gift card in his stocking), but when he got in the car, it wouldn't start. So many times he used the excuse that the car wouldn't start because the battery was dead. It was true that the car died, but this time it wasn't the battery. We'd just given Matt money to have a new battery installed due to all the times he'd said the car wouldn't start. The police called a tow truck (even though we were AAA members) to have it towed to our house because all the local auto repair shops were closed due to the storm. On Christmas Eve I'd noticed that his car had been damaged and that the side mirror had been torn off. I hoped the car would already be at the repair shop when Mike got home, because Matt would be at work, and Mike would call me to vent about the car. And so, again, I would be in the middle of it. Matt told me it had happened in a parking lot in Red Bank, which was probably a lie. I was so afraid he was back to his old, lying ways. I hoped he would be strong enough to resist going back to drugs.

I wished the programs Matt had attended as an inpatient had dealt with not just the addiction but also physical issues such as hygiene, healthy habits, and exercise. I know these things aren't the main issues for heroin addicts, but neglect in these areas often is a by-product of addiction. My opinion, however, was that once addicts were clean and sober they'd feel so much better about themselves if they were eating healthy meals regularly, sleeping on a normal schedule, and getting exercise. I felt these habits had been lost, due to the damage that heroin had done to Matt's brain, and he had relearn them, much in the way that a person who's suffered a traumatic brain injury often must relearn skills previously taken for granted, such as walking, talking, and eating.

I also wished the program would have worked on skills Matt needed to get back into the community, such as learning how to be considerate of other people, finding a job and taking responsibility for getting there on time, and developing a good work ethic.

Matt had lost or forgotten a lot during his drug years, so much so that he had to relearn these things. Even so he looked at our reminders as nagging. I suppose we were nagging him, enabling him, but we didn't want to support him financially forever. Tim and Laura were a different story. They never would challenge or question our actions. They always would be completely dependent on us; they had no idea there was a choice regarding most things and had no ability to make that choice. Having Matt live with us as a dependent adult would be a horrible arrangement, one that permanently would ruin our relationships. He never would abide by our requests or house rules. I didn't even know if he was concerned about what would happen once we stopped paying his bills. Maybe he assumed we were bluffing and would continue to pay. Maybe we *were* bluffing. I don't think, though, that he had put even that much thought into it. He was living the AA motto "One day at a time" in everything he did. I was sure that some of this was due to what he was keeping bottled up inside, and I wished he would follow up and find a professional to help him organize his thoughts and actions. He told me he wanted to talk to someone and actually made—but then cancelled—a couple of appointments. One appointment he just forgot about.

Matt didn't want to think of himself as an addict, which wasn't a good way of thinking. He was—and always would be—an addict; hopefully from this point forward, he'd be a recovering addict.

CHAPTER EIGHTY

Happy New Year. January 2, 2011, marked eight months of drug-free living for Matt, as far as I knew. In thinking about that statement, I realized that in the last two years I'd had only four months of relaxing and worry-free days—the days Matt had spent safely in rehab.

I couldn't help it. I couldn't stop thinking, Is he OK? *Will he get up on time and get to work?* When he didn't answer his phone, I'd worry and wonder. My therapist was always telling me I needed to try to do things to take my mind off Matt for just a little while. Work helped, of course, as I usually was immersed in one project or another.

I could see how addiction happened. I'd occasionally taken a sleeping pill (prescribed by my doctor) for those nights when I couldn't fall asleep. More recently there had been days when I wished I could take several of them, just so I could sleep through the day and forget for a while. But of course I couldn't do that. I had too much responsibility, too much to do.

I tried to walk three or more miles a day, four or five times a week (although I seemed to go in fits and spurts, walking daily for a couple of months and then stopping for a few months). I spent a lot of my time praying, thanking God for giving me the strength to get through this mess one day at a time.

Mostly it was just "me" time. My counselor wholeheartedly approved of this and reminded me, whenever I saw her, to keep it up. Although I had this opportunity to be living (kind of) on my own for a few months, the time wasn't my own. I'd always have to think and do things for Tim and Laura, and I found myself doing the same for Mike and Matt more than I should. Therefore my walks were my only totally "me" time. Mike realized how important this was to me. Did Matt? Did he even know about my daily walks? Probably not, and why should he have? He was in his own world. Whether or not he was using again, he was exhibiting self-centered behavior and wasn't always using good judgment.

Mike knew a couple of people with connections in the music business who had told him to have Matt give them a call. Mike had passed along the names and numbers to Matt, who had yet to call either of them. Another friend of Mike's looked at Matt's Myspace page and said he never would hire a candidate if he or she had a Myspace page that looked like Matt's, which apparently was full of filthy language. Mike told Matt he should immediately clean it up or delete it, but he hadn't done either, so Mike couldn't give Matt's résumé to contacts. I wondered why he wouldn't clean it up, or for that matter, do anything that would improve his chances in the job market. Did he not have the confidence that he could do whatever job he was hired for? Any of these contacts could lead to his big break.

Something was locked up inside him. He needed to find someone to talk to, not just at NA/AA meetings, although that would be a start. I couldn't help him. He had to do it on his own, and he had to *want* to do it.

It made me so sad.

CHAPTER EIGHTY-ONE

I read about studies of drug addicts in the early 1970s that show that more than half of addicts relapse within three months after treatment, with most relapsing within six months after treatment. Relapse-prevention programs were strengthened as a result of these findings, but relapse remains a constant risk for addicts. The causes for relapse are many and varied, including psychological stress, depression, interpersonal problems, lack of social support, poor coping skills, and decreased commitment to abstinence. More recent studies do not show a significant difference in the statistics.

After reading about these studies, I did not feel one bit better.

CHAPTER EIGHTY-TWO

I had a lot on my mind and wanted to get it out. Matt wouldn't listen when I talked to him; texting or e-mailing were still our primary means of communication.

The following is what I sent to him on Tuesday, January 11, 2011, via e-mail.

Dear Matt,

This is what I want to say to you but haven't because it might cause you to shut down and/or tell me that you're "in a bad place right now because of the pressure" that I put on you. I suspect that you're using drugs again. There are too many things that don't add up: missing family events, missing work, being late for work, falling asleep at work. And you have no ambition or drive to find permanent work, even with potential connections in the music industry. I can't believe your boss is giving you another chance; I'm sure it's only because he's a good friend of Dad's. And it makes us feel incredibly embarrassed. If you were left to your own devices, it seems like you wouldn't even try to keep the job. You haven't felt well for the last week or so, yet you won't go to a doctor. Are you going through withdrawal, trying to detox on your own?

You're still asking for money. Just now you called looking for money because you're "in a bind," and you didn't want to go to Dad. You pleaded; you begged. That screams of a desperate person if ever I heard one. You said that you owe money to two people who helped you out with some bills, and you eventually told Dad it was just one person (Josh). Which is it? Of course, it was the magic number—$300. Bills? That's a joke. We pay your bills—bills we should not have to touch. I wonder if you've sold your computer yet.

I asked if you were using again. You said no, and you passed a drug test yesterday. To me that just seems like good timing on your part, except that you won't be able to get away with that for long. You'll want more and more drugs, and you'll keep taking your chances until you get caught. You said you would take another test today and would pass it. Funny, though, that we don't have any more tests, because you helped yourself to them. Why did you take them? And who said you could? Go ahead and say that my accusations are triggering you to use. I told you, during your last year of college, that it seemed like I was supporting a $300-a-day drug habit and that if it turned out I was, I would never forgive myself. So if you tell me you used again, and it was because of me, go ahead. I'll already be punishing myself for the rest of my life for feeding your habit.

I pray that I'm wrong. I pray every day for you, your health, your strength, and your sobriety.

I've watched friends lose people that were important to them because of substance abuse, and I can't fathom how they could choose their substance of choice over their family and loved ones. I can't imagine how you made that choice so many times over the last few years. Even more I can't fathom how either you or my friends would be willing to risk giving up your futures, maybe even your lives.

We always had a good relationship. You said, in one of the family groups, that you felt like you could talk to me like you would talk to a friend. I'm sure you don't think that right now. Friendship is based on truth and trust. Right now you have broken both of those tenets.

I hope we can salvage our relationship. It will take work on both of our parts, but I think more on your part. After all I'm not the one lying. My refusal to give you money without involving Dad was only an act of "tough love," maybe the only one I've performed to date. I'll have to learn to be strong and do more of that. You have tried to pit Dad and me against each other and have done so several times. That's not fair. I'm trying not to enable you anymore. You've put us both in very tough situations.

Your counselor called yesterday, just to check in and see how everything was going. Dad will return his call. Maybe your counselor knows something concrete that we don't know.

You need help. I hope you reach out for it before it's too late. I am sick. I know in my heart that you are using again, and I am powerless to do anything about it.

I love you more than you can understand.

—Mom

CHAPTER EIGHTY-THREE

We knew something was going on with Matt and we had to confront him in mid-January, and I wondered when this nightmare would be over. I immediately wished I could take back the thought because I feared that the only way it would end would be with Matt in jail or dead.

I knew. I knew that he had relapsed.

In rehab Matt had met someone who was supposedly in the music field who later was sleeping at his apartment for a little while. Matt was shadowing him and the band he was promoting to finally break into the field himself. However, Music Man also knew where to get drugs. At one point he had gotten drugs for Matt before Matt had given him the money, which was how the latest big press for money had come about. Originally Matt told us the guy had given him $1,000 to book a band or a venue or something, but Matt had used the money for other things. We did give Matt money a couple of times to pay the guy back, but Matt just took the money and bought more drugs. This individual wanted his money and also a ride from Matt back to New York. I prayed Matt would be safe and come back alive. The guy had nerve; he picked up Matt's cell phone and called

Mike, looking for the money, and actually threatened Mike with talk of not wanting to "hurt Matt" but needing the money he was owed.

I told Matt to call Bayview House that night and set himself up to start IOP immediately. I hoped he did. My gut told me he needed inpatient treatment, but then he wouldn't be able to keep his job. It also would interfere with his probation. Even so he clearly needed intense help. He told me once that he was too chicken to ever use needles; that changed, however, as he had switched to needles as his method of use. He said he'd been using again since the beginning of January. He had gone through a lot of money, and therefore a lot of heroin, in that time period. Mike found all of his syringes in his backpack. (I was stunned to learn that, in many states, a person can just walk into a pharmacy and buy needles!) Mike also found some of his own cholesterol medicine in the backpack. Was he dealing? And using Mike's medication to stretch the amount of heroin? He was getting sneakier every day.

He had been coming to our house on the weekends, which I couldn't understand, because a few months ago he couldn't wait to have his own apartment. One weekend he broke in through a window, because he had locked the door that led from the garage to the kitchen. Mike discovered a broken decoration in the kitchen. Matt said he had no idea how it had happened. These were little things that didn't really matter—just more stories, lies to unravel, as Matt himself was becoming unraveled.

It occurred to me that we had only scratched the surface.

Initially Matt wasn't willing to go to inpatient rehab because he wanted to keep his job, as well as his appointments with his probation officer. Eventually, however, he went to Bayview House to reenroll in the IOP program. Alas, drugs were still in his system, so he couldn't begin treatment right away.

I suspected this as soon as he had started asking for money again. When would this end? He stepped up his use a notch, by moving to needles. What would be next?

It turned out that he had been using all week, while we were waiting for the drugs to get out of his system. We were at our wit's end. Mike was really falling apart and didn't know what to do next. How could I take control when I was in Ocean City? Mike talked to Matt's lawyer to find out how to handle the probation piece of the puzzle. Next we needed to find a new program for Matt, preferably long term and preferably not near us but still in New Jersey. There wasn't much anyone could tell us on a Sunday. I had names of places within a hundred-mile radius of Little Silver and Ocean City that accepted our insurance, but they were all just shots in the dark. We had nothing, and no one to recommend any of them.

I felt like I had known this was coming and should have had a plan in place already, but Mike would have said, "It sounds like you want him to relapse." I'm pretty sure that he did, in fact, say that on more than one occasion. I sent e-mails to any contact I could think of who might have recommendations for places, or who could get some recommendations for us. Unfortunately, again, because we were doing all of this on a weekend, we wouldn't make much headway until Monday.

I wanted Matt to be far away from us, and I wanted him in an inpatient facility for as long as possible. Twelve weeks seemed to be the longest I could find. We needed to be away from him so we could heal. He needed to be away from us so he could learn to think for himself again and not fall back on Mom and Dad, the ultimate enablers.

Mike finally got a recommendation for a rehab facility through the brother of a friend. Matt seemed willing to go and said he was packing his stuff up. But what if he took off? I didn't think he would, because Music Man had taken up residence at Matt's apartment, still waiting for his money. Any money we had given Matt to pay this man back was used to buy drugs for himself. Were he and Matt dealing together?

Mike was a wreck: scared, upset, mad, and nervous—I guess all the same things I'd been feeling for a long time. Originally Mike planned to be the one to take him, alone this time, to rehab. Mike was concerned about Music Man, afraid that Matt ultimately wouldn't cooperate regarding rehab. Mike and Matt would go to a City of Angels meeting together, a group Mike had been trying to get Matt to attend with him for a while, as it was founded by the brother of one of Mike's friends. After the meeting a van from Malvern Institute, in Malvern, Pennsylvania, would come pick him up. The last time he had used drugs was the day prior to this, so he still had drugs in his system. He would detox over the next several days, and then his healing would start.

Matt called me when he and Mike were on their way to the City of Angels meeting, after which he would go to rehab. He sounded subdued—not scared, not apprehensive. I asked him whether he had gotten all of his important stuff out of the apartment, such as his computer. He informed us that the computer was at a pawn shop. He only had pawned it for a small amount, because he had intended to buy it back.

He had sold or pawned a valuable gift he'd received with a sentiment behind it (the Tag Heuer watch at graduation) once—shame on him.

He did it a second time—shame on us for giving him the second watch.

Then he did it a third time, with the computer. We were fools for giving him anything of value in the first place. But we wanted so badly to believe in him and wanted him to see tangible proof of our faith in him.

I suspected there would be another batch of secrets and lies to unravel. People to whom he owed money would start calling. Mike already had seen a phone number on Matt's phone that turned out to be a collection agency. I believed we'd find out that he had been using longer than just since the beginning of January. Apparently he had gotten paid by the building-supply company, cashed the checks, and bought drugs. The cable and electric bills at the apartment were in his name, and apparently the unpaid bills were still in his backpack. Did his roommate give him money for his portion, and did Matt use the money for drugs?

As we learned, the brain of an addict is affected, not just while he or she is on drugs, but for a long time afterward. Matt couldn't prioritize or multitask; he had no coping skills and didn't seem to have the motivation to want to try to regain them. What would it take to get him to turn himself around before it was too late?

Mike talked to probation, as Matt was apparently supposed to meet with his PO shortly after he was admitted to Malvern. The glitch, which we didn't even think of but should have, was that Matt wasn't supposed to leave the state while he was still on probation. Whoops. We hoped that probation would let him stay put, since he was already there. He would still have to come back to live in New Jersey for the duration of his probation so they could keep track of him. From a rehab perspective, he could be at Malvern Institute for as long as ninety days. That's what I was hoping for. After that the plan was that he would live at a halfway house for several months, something with more accountability and structure than an Oxford House, someplace where he would be monitored and tested regularly.

CHAPTER EIGHTY-FOUR

Matt called us within a few days of his admission to Malvern Institute. Basically he called to ask for money. Mike had given Matt $20 and a roll of quarters before Matt had left, and he said he used the quarters on laundry (even though he had a lot of clean clothes with him) and the phone call to us, on a pay phone.

I felt I was still talking to drug-addict Matt: no pleasantries just getting right down to what he wanted-money. If I remembered correctly from the last time, it would be another week or so before remorse would hit—if it did at all.

I spoke to Matt's counselor, Jake, who agreed that Matt was apathetic at the beginning of his stay but that he soon became more receptive and responsive. We still hadn't heard any words of apology, but we knew by this point that his apologies meant nothing. He may not have even realized all the havoc he had wreaked over the last few months, let alone the past two years. We were scheduled to visit him after her had been there for ten days. The impending visit filled us with mixed emotions.

Some of my anger was fading. My knowing he was safely at Malvern until February 23 and after that would be at a halfway house or some other sober-living place—hopefully for a few months, maybe as long as nine months—where he would be tested regularly gave me some sense of calm. I was sorry he had to lose the delivery job with the building-supply company, because it was manual work, kept him busy, gave him exercise, and left him physically tired at the end of the day. Maybe he would be able to find someplace else like that. Maybe the next place he went, the sober-living place, would help him get placed in a job.

Maybe, maybe, maybe.

He sounded good, positive, upbeat. He also said he would talk to one of the doctors about his anxiety, depression, or whatever it was.

We did visit Matt on the planned day, mostly because it was what we were supposed to do after he had been there a week or more. We had a good visit with him, I think. Mike said that I did better than he did and that he had a hard time making small talk. I told him that maybe if he had gotten his big issue off his chest early in the visit it might have been better. Mike told Matt that in the two weeks he had been gone, during which we had received several phone calls from him, he had yet to hear two things—"I'm sorry" and "Thank you." Matt said he thought he did say "Thank you" the night he left and that he was sorry but realized that those words, coming from him, didn't mean much to us. I told him I was angry because I didn't think he had tried; I said he had given up. He had given up talking to counselors and sponsors. He had given up going to meetings. And he didn't even try to ask for help.

Matt said he knew he needed to talk more about what he was feeling. He knew he needed another month of inpatient treatment after this stay, and then another three to six months in a halfway house or some other type of sober-living arrangement. I asked him where he saw himself in five years, what he thought he would be doing, where he would be living. He said he would be working for a music production company, maybe even running his own production company, and he would have his own apartment.

I told him never to give up on those dreams. I hoped that he would keep those dreams alive and that they were well within reach.

He already had admitted to us that he had pawned his computer, but only partially, so that he could buy it back when he got his paychecks. (I suppose he thought he would be able to pay Music Man with those paychecks as well.) He also admitted he had pawned the electric saw that Mike had noticed was missing. He said that was all. I didn't know why I felt compelled to hear every detail or why I needed to know exactly when he relapsed, or why. He said it was about a month before he told us, which put it around Christmastime. I knew in my gut it was earlier than that.

Then there was the subject of the apartment. The one roommate had left, but there was still one other person there. Matt hadn't asked what was happening with it or apologized for bailing out on it, which left us (Mike really) to pick up the pieces and move his furniture out. If I were the landlord, I would expect to see all of February's rent. There were two people living there, as far as the landlord knew; between the two of them, they should have been able to come up with the money. Although, when I spoke to Matt's roommate, he'd said he thought he wouldn't be too far behind Matt (in terms of rehab.), so I guessed things weren't going well for him either.

I'd been making calls to our insurance carrier as well as residential treatment programs in New Jersey. Probation wanted him back in New Jersey after he completed his thirty-day stay. I was hoping they'd agree to let him stay in Pennsylvania for another thirty days.

A couple of long-term places accepted our insurance, and a couple of others said they'd take it if we had out-of-network benefits. A representative at one of the facilities I called asked where else I was researching and actually told me which ones she wouldn't recommend.

I thought it was nice that she took that extra step, because for the most part, I haven't found our insurance carrier to be much help, or any of the rehab places to be much help for that matter either. It seemed to me that it should be about the health of the individual, but instead it was all about money for the facilities (how much money they can get out of the insurance carrier) and for the insurance carrier (how little they can get away with paying). I would love to know, if money were no object, what would be considered the best facility in the country? Who would even be qualified to decide that rating? On what would it be based? Success rate, I suppose. How would I find out that information? It didn't matter. We didn't have the means to send him there, unless it accepted our insurance, and at that point, if it was located in New Jersey.

It seemed like the short-term places we could use were all in Southern New Jersey. For long-term aftercare, there were places in Northern New Jersey, which might be good, for accessibility to New York City and career connections for Matt. Probation told him he could go to New York City for work, if that was where he found a job. His counselor was involved and would help with the selection.

CHAPTER EIGHTY-FIVE

My tears flowed when I remembered small things. He didn't show up for family events, he had taken all of my state quarters; he had lied for six months about working on his second internship.

My therapist encouraged me to feel these things, work through them, and let the tears fall. She constantly reminded me what a wonderful person I was—not just a wonderful mom—and that I was doing so much for so many people and that I was entitled to feel overwhelmed.

Even though Matt was safely at Malvern Institute, I was scared for him. He couldn't shake loose the incredible hold heroin had on him. When he'd gotten out of rehab in August, he had an apartment, a car, and a cell phone and said he spent his time job-hunting, but he also went to the beach, hung out with friends, and spent a lot of time at our house (when we weren't there). This new cycle of his behavior all started around mid-September.

How would he survive if we cut him off? Realistically he would have to have a couple of months' rent saved up to be able to get an apartment, before he even looked at finances to see what he could afford on a monthly basis. If he couldn't keep up, he'd get evicted.

Sure, he could sleep in his car, depending on the weather, but how long could that last? Where would he take a shower? How would he get a job if he couldn't make himself look presentable? It was a vicious cycle.

Matt could stop that cycle, though. If he could turn himself around, look for any and as many jobs as he could get, and save every penny he made, he could afford a place and pay his bills. At the point where we were then, I didn't see that happening. I prayed that Malvern Institute would be the miracle he desperately needed.

Thinking about his future was so upsetting. Knowing that Tim and Laura would be dependent on us forever was overwhelming enough, but we pretty much had always known that. I was so afraid that Matt would always be dependent on us as well, but he would want it on his terms. We couldn't support a drug addict, although we had apparently been doing that for quite a while—two years to be exact. He needed to support himself, but the person he needed to support had to be a clean, clear-thinking, levelheaded adult. I hadn't seen even a glimpse of that person in at least two years, maybe longer. I believed he had a couple of good years at the beginning of college, but we were blind to so much, so who knows what all we missed?

CHAPTER EIGHTY-SIX

Finally I was angry.

I was so tired of all the lies. Matt was still saying he had relapsed around Christmastime, but I didn't believe that; I knew it had to have been earlier.

It was around Thanksgiving of 2010 when he was having car problems and when we gave him money for a new battery. After Matt left for rehab, in January 2011, Mike retrieved Matt's car from the apartment, and it broke down for Mike as well. So there really was a car problem. This time, though, AAA came and looked at the battery and could tell that it hadn't been replaced recently. All the things Matt had said he needed were really just scams so he could get money for drugs. And shame on us—again—for thinking maybe we could finally start trusting him again. He asked for money so he could buy Christmas gifts. He explained that someone was going to hook him up with cheap concert tickets, so that he, Tim, Mike, and I could all go to a concert at Madison Square Garden. I felt kind of bad when Mike asked him if he really thought Tim and I would drive up from South Jersey into New York City. And what were we suppose to do with Laura? Mike told him to take the tickets back and said later that Matt looked a little hurt. But that was just an act. If there ever were tickets, he wouldn't be able to return them. More than likely the money only left Matt's hands to buy drugs.

I felt kind of bad for Matt's roommate and their landlord. Matt really had left them in a bind. Getting rid of the third roommate left the remaining two with more rent to pay, but they were trying to hold on and make things work—in terms of both the apartment and staying clean.

If Matt was going to continue to destroy his life, he would have to cut loose from us, and we'd have to do the same with him. We had to stop building up our hopes that this time would be different. But why didn't he try? I could imagine (but I never could begin to understand) that heroin must be a very hard demon to conquer, but when he felt tempted, he was supposed to call his sponsor or someone in his support system. Instead he had rebelled against all of it—no meetings, no counselors, no sponsors, no support team. He just kept telling lies, after so many people had given him chances. Since he had gotten out of round one of rehab, he'd had a job (he got fired for low sales), taken bartending classes (he failed the final test a couple of times and then never went back), and received the names and phone numbers of contacts in the music industry but never called them. He might have known, as soon as he got out of rehab, that he was going to use again.

Matt told me later that he hardly ever had urges after the second rehab stay and that when he did, he would call someone. I prayed he would continue to call someone. He had said he had gone to NA/AA meetings during this last relapse, but he never said anything during those meetings, because when an addict is using, they can't talk at a meeting. And although he timed his use or his attendance at IOP so that he would be able to produce some clean urine tests, eventually he stopped going. There was always something interfering with his getting there, whether it was internship, community service, job-hunting, whatever. Then he stopped going to meetings, stopped caring about anything but the drugs. The disease once had again taken over his every thought and action. It had cost him his job, as well as his newly repaired relationship with his parents. But he didn't care, because when he was on drugs, he had no conscience. He excused any crankiness or lateness by saying he wasn't sleeping well. And Mike and I *wanted* to believe the lies. We wanted to believe that it would take a while for his sleep habits to regulate, take a while for his appetite to return. We never would understand how heroin had turned him into someone who was unrecognizable and powerless to help himself.

CHAPTER EIGHTY-SEVEN

With Matt once again safely in round three of rehab, I felt I could take some time to relax in the evenings. I opened a novel and began to read it. After the acknowledgments was a quote from Shakespeare's *Macbeth,* Act Four, Scene Three.

Give sorrow words: the grief that does not speak
Whispers the o'er-fraught heart and bids it break.

So if I didn't talk about this, my heart would break. I did talk about it—out loud, to myself mostly, but also to Mike, to my extended family, to my friends, to my therapist.

I wanted this to go away. I didn't want this to be happening. I wanted Matt to have a job, to live in his own little place, and to come and visit us once in a while, maybe stop in on weekends or whenever. At that point, though, I had a very hard time thinking of his future without seeing anything but more of the same nightmares.

I felt very alone at that point. I had sent e-mails to my friends and family, telling them of Matt's recent events. I guessed it was getting old—the same story, the same ending. I supposed this was when

I should have been going to a meeting, and I planned on getting to one that weekend. My mom would have been at my house in a minute, just to sit with me. She would have changed the subject—talked about what to make for dinner—and pretended it wasn't happening, but she would be there. My sister, Beth, would be there as well, talking about something to make me smile and laugh. But they were both gone. All they could do was give me strength from the other side.

There were those couple of seconds, the brief reprieve, when I first woke up, before my brain started working, when I felt peace. Then my brain would wake up, and reality would slam into me like a freight train. And I would remember.

My son is an addict.

It didn't matter whether or not he was in a rehabilitation facility. It always would be with me, just as it always would be with him. But he was in recovery. I didn't think it would have the same "freight train" effect on Matt, because he was in control of his own destiny. He could wake up every morning and feel the sense of accomplishment that came with getting through the previous day, and look forward to the coming day, another day as a clean and sober recovering addict.

I, on the other hand, was helpless. I was in limbo, just waiting. Always waiting. Waiting for a relapse, or if he was in rehab, waiting for news. A phone call. Word of how things were going with him and for him.

But I was so angry as well. If he'd been standing in front of me at that moment, I would have wanted to slap him as hard as possible.

CHAPTER EIGHTY-EIGHT

Matt ended up staying at Malvern Institute just until the middle of February, when he transferred to Stonebridge, in Southern New Jersey, for another month of inpatient rehab. Probation wanted him in New Jersey, and Malvern found an opening at Stonebridge. After that the plan was for him to go to a transitional living place of some sort, but not an Oxford House. The people at Malvern didn't think he was ready for an Oxford House yet; they said he needed more structure than an Oxford House could offer.

I felt good knowing there were people who were really looking at *Matt's* case, not just another case that came through their door. They understood our concerns about his going to a halfway house they had mentioned, since it was in North Jersey, not far from the area where he used to get his drugs. While Matt was at Malvern, I felt there were people who were helping him follow the right path. Once he transferred to Stonebridge, I hoped there would be someone who took this much of an interest in his case. His counselor, Jake, had told me some of what they talked about. Jake knew Matt was a liar; whether Matt told him that or Jake figured it out, I didn't know.

The question remained about what to do after Stonebridge. I was going to leave it up to the professionals to figure it out. One step at a time.

We—his parents—and the professionals involved with him did have a plan. But Matt had his own set of plans. He called just one day after the counselors and I had discussed our plan. It sounded to me like Matt was in a hurry to move along, ready to leave Malvern for Stonebridge. He wanted to go to an Oxford House after that; he didn't want to go to a halfway house or anything that structured. He wanted the freedom to work odd hours, into the night, which was likely what a job in the music industry would require. He wanted to earn the trust of his probation officer so that he would be able to leave the state occasionally for something like a three-day music festival, or maybe even go out to California to find work. (*What?*) He was thinking his MTV internship might help open some doors out there.

All of a sudden, he was too ready. I felt he should still be working on recovery. I didn't think he had even started to work on the Twelve Steps, and already he was looking far down the road.

He also suggested that maybe Mike or I could pick him up when it was time for him to leave Malvern and drive him to Stonebridge. Why? I doubted it was because he wanted to spend quality time with either of us during the car ride. I had no idea what that request was all about.

Then he came up with a modified request. He asked Jake if he could get dropped off at the apartment where we were staying in Ocean City on the day he would be transported by van from Malvern to Stonebridge; then I could take him to Stonebridge. Jake said he didn't think it was a good idea. Matt said he thought that he and I could grab some lunch. Oh, really? He just wanted some of the junk food he'd been missing? Or was it something else? What was he up to?

More than a year later, Matt told me yes, all he really wanted was to hang out with one or both of us for a bit and go out to lunch.

How sad that I couldn't believe him at the time.

CHAPTER EIGHTY-NINE

I caught the tail end of a television talk show one day in early February 2011. A doctor was saying the same thing a psychologist had told me a couple of months earlier. The psychologist I had spoken to was a friend of someone at work. My coworker had suggested I call him, just to talk about what the next steps should be when Matt got out. The doctor on TV and the psychologist with whom I'd spoken both said there had to be a consequence, or several, if an addict relapses. They didn't mean I should send Matt to rehab. That wasn't punishment; rehab was a fact, something he needed to do in order to help him get better. But what would hurt him a lot to be without, besides drugs? What would he miss? If it was the car, I should take the car away. If it was stopping in to see us, we should tell him he couldn't be in our house as long as he was using.

That was easier said than done. No, not really, it was just easier on us not to lay down consequences, especially regarding the car. Without a car, Matt would have to rely on us for rides, or take public transportation, but he would have no money for that. I was making excuses—excuses as to why we continued to enable him.

CHAPTER NINETY

The transition from Malvern went smoothly. Just a few days after his arrival, I came to Stonebridge, which wasn't far from where we lived, to make sure they had all the correct insurance information. I also dropped off some things for Matt (envelopes, stamps, and a book), and as it happened, he was outside smoking. I was able to get inside without his seeing me and asked how to get out without my seeing him again (because he was still technically in the "blackout period"). The receptionist said it would be OK to say hi, and just then Matt came back inside from his cigarette break. He was surprised and seemed happy to see me; he gave me a hug. He asked about getting gift cards from Wawa and Pathmark, as the clients had to pack their lunches for days when they were in sessions all day. So it was a nice little bonus visit. He said he would call me on Thursday because he was allowed to make calls.

Later that day I saw my therapist, and she said I seemed happy and cheerful and, whatever I was doing, to keep it up!

Mike came down that evening and was leaving again the next morning, but he was there when Matt called. I had the phone on speaker, but Mike barely said a word. I guessed he wasn't ready to let up on the anger yet. As soon as he got back to Little Silver the next morning, he sent me an e-mail saying he realized that Matt had taken *his* state quarters. He must have done this a couple of months prior, and my first reaction was that if it had happened a while ago, it would do no good to bring it up now and would serve no real purpose. Then I remembered how I had felt when I realized he had stolen all of my state quarters and realized my initial reaction toward Mike was unfair. The whole thing put me in a bad mood. I went down to our house in Ocean City to check on the renovation progress and wasn't happy with the color of the stain on the stairs. I didn't like the way some of the custom-made backsplash tiles looked either; in general nothing pleased me. I went to Stonebridge to drop off the gift cards, and the receptionist said Matt had been asking if I'd been there. I handed the envelopes to the receptionist, said that I didn't need to see Matt, and left.

I remembered something a man in our Al-Anon group had shared with us, something he had said to his alcoholic loved one— "You're getting in the way of my recovery." That's how I felt and what I needed to say to Mike. Certainly Matt was getting in the way of our recovery, but Mike and the anger he couldn't let go of—and his using me to vent to—was also getting in the way of my recovery. I knew he certainly should have been able to talk to me, his spouse, and expect that I would listen, but he couldn't let go of the anger over something that happened a year or more ago, let alone yesterday. He could barely be civil when he talked to Matt. It ruined my mood, and yes, it was getting in the way of my recovery.

CHAPTER NINETY-ONE

Matt's few weeks at Stonebridge went by quickly. At the end of the first week of March, he had an interview at an Oxford House in Ventnor, just a few towns over from our house. There were two vacancies and four people applying for them. His best friend from Stonebridge, Chris, was one of the other applicants, and he was really hoping that the two of them would be selected. Was it wrong for me, or at least a part of me, to hope he wouldn't get in? I didn't even know what they based their decision on—if the person seemed rehabilitated enough? If he was sloppy or neat? How many times he had relapsed? If Matt didn't get in, he would stay at Stonebridge until another opening became available, either there or at another Oxford House. I knew he wanted to get in, because he said he wanted the freedom to look for a job. I felt that he wanted freedom, period.

Matt and I hadn't discussed the car, and I was thinking it would be better to have him take the bus or jitney. That's what the psychologist I spoke to would recommend. That meant we would be handing over money for bus fare. Matt also asked if, once he was in Oxford House, he could use my computer to look for work via Craigslist and the Internet. It was a good idea, but I didn't want him to get into the habit of hanging out at our house every day.

The Oxford House accepted both Matt and Chris. We had a meeting at Stonebridge just a couple of days before he moved out, first with just his counselor (Ben) and Mike and me; then with all the inpatients, with Mike, Matt, and me in the middle of the circle.

Ben said Matt needed to be busy right away, all the time, either working at a job or going back to school. He'd start job-hunting right away but wouldn't have the car right away. It would have been easier for him to have it, but this wasn't about "easy." He had to be more resourceful and ask for rides, look for a bus schedule, etc. Apparently there was a computer at the Oxford House that he could use, and the public library wasn't far. Mike and I needed to be firmer and not continue to enable him. I was probably more at fault than Mike. I didn't know how all of this would play out. It wasn't rehab. Oxford Houses were self-governed. The residents looked out for one another and could call for a drug test if anyone seemed suspicious. They had a curfew during the probation period; there were assigned chores; and they had to pay their rent on time.

Matt had said he was learning to be more open and honest. He admitted that he had lied to everyone—family, friends, and counselors—in the past, but now he was opening up and being truthful. It was true, at least, when he was clean and sober. I prayed it would continue.

I felt, at that point, that I was over my anger. Mike, however, could still barely be civil to him, yet he continued to say that he didn't feel the need to talk to a therapist or counselor. He said that the Al-Anon meetings we attended were all he needed.

I was scared—and worried and happy and apprehensive. I told myself to take a deep breath and to think positive thoughts.

Getting ready for the move to Oxford House felt, in a way, like sending him off to college. He needed sheets and towels; he said he needed some new clothes because he had gained twenty-five pounds while he was at Malvern and Stonebridge. It was very much like college, except there was no student loan to cover all expenses. Instead we had to pay the money upfront. There was a nonrefundable deposit and two weeks' rent. Rent was $130 a week, which wasn't bad, but it was still money that we were putting out. He also still had bills that we, of course, had been covering, until he could land a job that would pay him about a $1,000 a week. Hmm. Plus he needed money for food, as well as gas, once he got the car back. We planned to give him grocery gift cards to last for two weeks, and then we (I) would have to learn to say no when he asked if we could help him out. He would have to learn to shop smartly and eat frugally. He couldn't just order pizza a few times a week. Ramen noodles and peanut butter sandwiches would have to tide him over sometimes. He had to start preparing his own meals, rather than buy ready-made frozen stuff. At the Oxford House, he had use of the kitchen and a couple of shelves on which to keep his things, and of course a refrigerator.

Mostly, though, he needed to find a job. It wouldn't be easy, however, since he wouldn't have use of the car right away.

I had to let go. He had to worry about those things, not I. I was using up too much energy when I did the worrying for him. I had told him I didn't expect another relapse, but if there was one, he would have to go to a shelter. I said he was welcome to come over for dinner, or stop by to say hello, but he wouldn't be sleeping in our house again anytime soon. He hoped to find a job and work forty hours a week, but he and Ben agreed that he needed to keep busy, so he also would take classes at the community college. He planned to take business classes and hoped to get an associate degree in business. After that he thought he might take courses in counseling.

Ben had said that by now he could run all of the meetings. He knew what to say and what to do. I asked both Matt and Ben if Matt believed in the twelve-step program, because at one point Matt had called a rehab facility in Florida that was supposedly very good and took a holistic approach rather than the 12-step approach. He said he believed in the steps, even though he had never gotten past the first step. Stonebridge incorporated both the holistic approach as well as the 12 steps in their program, so I was comfortable that Matt got as much out of Stonebridge as he would have from any other program.

He settled into the Oxford House, which was an old shore house, not in great shape but had character. In its day, I am sure it was gorgeous, one of the grand houses. It was four houses from the beach. He stood on the front porch and said he didn't even have to walk to the beach to check out the waves because he had a great view right on the porch. That alone should have been incentive for him to stay clean and sober.

Again, it felt a bit like moving him in to college for the first time, carrying everything up three flights of stairs, lugging so much stuff in from the car. Mike and Matt did most of it; I was content to stand on the porch.

Then shopping for things he needed: clothes, toiletries, etc. were all purchased during a Target shopping spree. Also some groceries, but he had a gift card from Pathmark and Wawa, so he would shop more on his own later.

We had lunch with him. It was nice to sit down with him for 45 minutes and catch up with his latest news. He told us that he had been to a couple of NA/AA meetings. He told us he might meet up with a buddy from Little Silver who now lives down here

The gentleman who was the house supervisor at the Oxford House, Alvin, met us at the house at the appointed move-in time. He had one of those looks about him, like he had seen a lot over the years. His face appeared weathered and tired; I supposed a lot of years of using had taken their toll physically, yet he also looked happy. He could have been thirty-five years old or fifty-five years old. He and Matt shook hands. I was behind Matt and held out my hand to shake his and said I was Ann. He opened his arms wide and said, "I need to give you a big Oxford House hug."

It was exactly what I needed.

CHAPTER NINETY-TWO

Sometimes several hours would pass without my thinking about Matt and whether he was doing all right. Then I seemed to make up for the time by worrying too much. I knew he was "safe" right now and that if he used he would get caught, and I didn't think he had money to buy drugs at that point anyway. But one morning he called to say that he and a few of his new friends were driving to North Jersey to the home of one of his friends to pick up some of his things. That sounded fine, but I also thought they might really have been going to Elizabeth to buy drugs. I had no reason to think that, as Matt had been sounding and acting fine. I just couldn't relax yet. It was way too soon. March 17 was his sixty-day clean mark. He sounded so proud when he told me. Then again how could he not be clean? He had been in rehab for all but two weeks of that time.

CHAPTER NINETY-THREE

Matt told me that one of his friends from Little Silver, who had moved to Oregon, was apparently due to come into some money from a dying relative and wanted to open a music venue. Matt said he would move to Portland and work for him. Well, he would have to hold that thought for fourteen more months, when probation would say he could leave the state. If he were out West, though, he couldn't just drop in and ask for money. He could always ask us to wire it via Western Union, which he had done before, but if that happened, the answer would have to be no.

He seemed to be looking for work; he said he had left messages and résumés with potential employers and had contacted the band people he had dealt with before rehab, but I didn't know how hard he really was trying. He also called his Uncle Dan, as Dan had said a buddy of his who owned an electrical business might need a right-hand man. I knew Matt would feel better about getting around when he had his car back, but it was still being fixed, and we were working on getting it down to the shore. We didn't particularly want him to go back to Little Silver to get it. I wanted to keep him away from the negative people, places, and things that had influenced him there.

Matt and I saw each other every few days and had lunch in Atlantic City one day. He told me again he had made some calls and sent out résumés. I suggested he apply to Kmart, Sam's Club, and nursing homes. I had seen ads in the newspaper for jobs that involved working with disabled people. Certainly Matt had life experience doing that, if not formal education in that field. I'd rather have seen him do that than randomly walk in off the street and ask places whether they needed help. He said he had asked in a skateboard store. They weren't hiring but were opening another store in Atlantic City. That would be fine, if it paid more than $8 an hour. Maybe it would. Didn't it take a certain skill level to put a skateboard together and talk skateboard lingo? I realized Matt had been out of rehab only for a week, but he needed to find a job.

I had stayed in touch with Shannon, one of Matt's counselors from Bayview House. She wanted him to come back as an alumnus, when he had been clean for nine months, and talk to the inpatient group. I thought it would be kind of neat for him to go back in November, on the anniversary of his arrest, or the anniversary of his admission to Bayview House. November 2011 would mark two years since this journey through hell had begun for us.

Matt talked about things he wanted to do, places he wanted to go. I wanted him to have his dreams and goals, but it always bothered me to hear him talk about things like overnight concert trips. He said he probably would be working the sober booth at some upcoming concerts. I reminded him that his only payment for that was the free ticket for the show, and he wouldn't get reimbursed for gas and food.

I just wanted him to keep the idea of budgeting his money always on his mind, and even more important, the fact that he needed to get a job—and still more important, the fact that he needed to work hard on staying clean.

CHAPTER NINETY-FOUR

Matt found a job the last week of March of 2011, at the restaurant at a small local airport. He started the last week of March, as a waiter. It apparently got very busy in the summer, so he'd have the opportunity to make good money with the tips. That worried me. I knew I'd have to talk with him about that, because I was afraid that when he had money in his hand, he'd be tempted to buy drugs. If he could resist the drugs, he'd spend his money on concert tickets or other things he wanted first, instead of his bills.

He worked fairly steadily until the end of April before he treated himself and went into the city, after which he did his disappearing act. He was supposed to work, but he wasn't at the restaurant and wasn't answering calls or texts. Eventually I got a convoluted story out of him. His phone was charging overnight, and the alarm was set for 7:00 a.m. Somehow, during the night, the phone turned off. His boss called at 9:00 a.m., but since the phone was turned off, Matt didn't get the boss's call or mine. He woke up around 1:00 p.m. and saw that his phone was off. When he turned it on—voilà!—there were the voice mails and text messages. Did I believe him? I wanted to. He seemed worried about the job but also said he didn't think he'd ever get put on the schedule for more than three days a week, even during the summer. He said he was going to look for something else and had a buddy who worked at a pizzeria and would see if they were still hiring. Meanwhile he had to go to the restaurant and face the music.

I considered the scenario. He had been in New York City for two days and then missed work the next day. As I thought back over the past year, I knew I had reason to be worried.

He did lose his job. His boss said he understood what had happened but that he would be replacing Matt with someone more dependable. The boss's wife said she liked Matt and would have given him a second chance, but she had to abide by what her husband decided.

Matt told me all of this over the phone and then a short time later appeared at the house, needing $20, which he said couldn't wait until I gave him the weekly grocery gift card the next day. I was remaining calm because I told myself he would get tested at IOP. To be sure that would happen, I called Stonebridge and asked them to test him. Maybe Matt was feeling pretty low at that point, but maybe not. He had put his social calendar ahead of his obligations. He had to go to the restaurant to get his final paycheck and had said he would turn it over to us. If he gave us some reason for not turning it over to us (he owed money to a friend, or the restaurant withheld it for taxes), I would know there was a problem.

Soon after, he came over to get gas money so he could go to another show, this time in Philadelphia. No, he was not to leave the state unless it was for work. But you see, it wasn't just a show. He said he might be introduced to someone who dealt with the show's production, so it would actually be networking, which might lead to a potential job. I wanted to be positive, both for me and for him, but it was so hard when he was always asking for money.

I felt like Matt was disappearing again. Again I placed a call to Ben. The counselors were always my only lifelines when Matt closed up.

Matt asked if a friend could join us for Easter dinner. "Of course," I told him. His question had taken me by surprise, though, because we never said anything about even expecting Matt for Easter dinner, especially because we had been burned a few times recently. So many times he had disappointed us by not joining us at family gatherings—and then telling lies to cover up his drug use. Did he think the truth would hurt more than the lies? We'd already been hurt by hundreds of his lies. Did he really think it would devastate us to hear the truth, even if the truth was that he was high at the time and couldn't get himself together to come? That actually would have explained things more. It still would have shown me that he was prioritizing drugs over his family, but I already knew that, so why not just admit it?

Matt did join us for the family gathering on the day before Easter and brought his friends Anthony and Chris. He also came to Easter dinner at Mike's father's house. Easter marked Matt's ninety-day clean mark. He told me he would help me organize the boxes in the garage that weekend and probably would bring a couple of friends to help. I hoped he would follow through. He eventually did come over and help with the garage, but not until a few weekends later.

CHAPTER NINETY-FIVE

April 11, 2011 was the one-year anniversary of Matt's grandfather's death. Matt had been on heroin during the funeral. He had driven me from the church to the cemetery and was falling asleep at the wheel.

Matt had said he was going to go to the cemetery to mark the anniversary; that was between him and his conscience. Cemeteries aren't for everyone. Several of my relatives had said that they didn't like to go and that their loved one wasn't there. For me the cemetery was a quiet place for meditation. I didn't know Matt's reasons for wanting to go, but I could guess he wanted to apologize.

I didn't really want to talk about it with him; I wasn't in a mood to be chatty with him. He was chatty when I saw him, talking about concerts he wanted to go to. I wanted to hear him talk about how many job applications he had filled out, or openings he had heard about, before he thought about being able to go to concerts. I wanted to hear about his plans for earning money and paying his bills. Was I supposed to let him set the pace and start paying when he was ready? I didn't think so. But I didn't want him to accuse me of stressing him out and badgering him. Was this my fault and Mike's for laying out our expectations and not following through? Of course it was.

CHAPTER NINETY-SIX

Matt was starting to bring his friends with him when he stopped by to see us in the newly renovated Ocean City house,, and I was starting to get to know a couple of them somewhat. I hadn't known who his friends were since he was in eighth grade. Matt and a couple of his friends from Stonebridge stopped in after we had only been in the house for a couple of days. I was going through a box of baby books and keepsakes. Matt was very excited to see his baby book and asked, "Is the splinter still in the book?" I had forgotten, but he remembered having a huge splinter removed from his foot (he had been in the emergency room and had x-rays and stitches) and thought it was neat that I had saved the splinter. He explained that he had jumped off a deck at the beach and landed on a splinter that ended up getting hammered into his foot, right down to the bone. I suppose it made a good war story. He wanted to show the splinter to his friends and ended up showing them a lot of things in his baby book.

Every so often I saw glimpses like that of the old Matt.

Still he only came to see us when he wanted something, like new shoes, or money to go to an NA convention in Ocean City, Maryland. He visited for more than an hour one day, chatting and also using my computer. He never walked upstairs to say hi to Mike, who was in his office, working. Of course Mike noticed and said something about it to me. What could I do? I did give Matt little reminders that Mike was there too, but it was almost worse when Matt would say hello only because I had told him to. I couldn't always say, "Oh, Matt, go say hi to Dad," nor should I have had to. I shouldn't be the go-between for them. We had raised Matt to be, at the very least, polite, but he shouldn't be "polite" with his father. I knew it hurt Mike that Matt talked to me more than he talked to him. Part of that was, as Matt once said, that he felt comfortable with me, as if he were talking to a friend. But part of that was also because Matt knew he was more likely to get money from me than from Mike. I gave him lectures too, but they didn't come off sounding as much like lectures as they did coming from Mike.

I believed Matt was staying clean and so far wanted to stay clean and make a fresh start. Why, then, would he not talk to us about his debts and ask for help in cleaning them up, or at least ask for suggestions regarding how to deal with them? I don't mean the fines the judge had given him. I'm referring to Matt's credit card bills, parking tickets, and phone bill. If they were my bills, I would have felt better if they weren't hanging over my head. He could have approached it in one of two ways—either by asking us for help or by stepping up the pace of his job search.

Where was the motivation? The drive? The ambition? Did the drugs stunt his emotional growth so much that he had gone back to acting like a fourteen-year-old? Or maybe he never got past that stage. He wanted to make just enough money to buy cigarettes and gas and didn't seem to have any desire to save any money. I supposed he thought the bills would magically get taken care of. And they would, of course, by ever-enabling Mom and Dad.

CHAPTER NINETY-SEVEN

"Hooray, hooray, the first of May!" That phrase once conjured up memories of my carefree college life. Now, though, May brought back some not-so-pleasant memories. Bad things seemed to happen at the beginning of May, at least regarding Matt and his recent past. Just a year ago, Matt had gone back to inpatient rehab, round two. Two years ago was his "graduation," followed by the party the next day. Mike and I had known for a while about his "gambling problem," but around his graduation was when things really started to spin out of control, when Matt was starting to unravel, and the stealing, lying, and forging had started. We wouldn't know the whole story until his arrest months later. We probably still don't know the whole story.

How could we have been so blind? It was partly because we didn't know the signs of drug abuse. Maybe we saw signs but didn't want to believe them—not our son! We should have seen a change in him, but what could we have done? He wouldn't have gone to a doctor; Matt wouldn't have done anything positive until he was ready to admit he had a problem and needed help.

This May brought even more problems. I'd said I felt like Matt was disappearing again, and a mother's intuition is usually right. I hoped he would figure out why he felt the need to use again. He had last used on a Sunday and had played out the charade by letting me give him the rent money and a grocery card on Monday, knowing they were useless, because he wouldn't be in Oxford House more than another couple of days. And he continued the charade—or maybe it was just an out-and-out lie—by taking the $60 Mike had given him for gas and a haircut. Maybe he got the gas; he definitely didn't get a haircut. Maybe he bought fast food with the rest of the money; maybe he bought just enough heroin to tide him over. They tested him at the house, and he failed and was evicted. Mike and I had hoped he would stay clean and continue outpatient treatment. He could apply at other Oxford houses and hope that one would accept him.

So he was sleeping upstairs, in our home, something we had vowed after round two would not happen. Ben actually thought his staying with us was the best choice, the other choices being a shelter or inpatient rehab. Ben also felt that the other two options were too easy for Matt and that he would learn quickly that he could relapse and still have a place to go until he got back into an Oxford house. So, against our better judgment, Matt slept in our home. Sending him to a homeless shelter wasn't something I was ready to do. I believed we had secured our valuables and bank information so that he couldn't get to anything. He wasn't sleeping in the room originally dubbed "Matt's room," as that was where Mike's office was, and Mike would need to get in there early to work.

Ben said that Matt was depressed and felt like a failure. Ben told him he wasn't a failure; he'd just had a slip-up. Matt told him he wasn't sure he could detox and stay clean on his own, as an outpatient. He told Ben he had called a facility in Florida to see about availability as well as insurance matters. Ben reminded him that his probation officer had said he had to stay in New Jersey. Matt wondered aloud what would happen if he just went to Florida anyway and called his PO once he got there and got settled. Fortunately Ben convinced him it would be a really bad idea.

I knew I wouldn't be sleeping well while he was under our roof.

Matt was really restless, up and watching TV until after 3:00 a.m., and up at 6:00 a.m. and 8:00 a.m. to go outside for a cigarette. He finally got up at 10:00 a.m. for good, saying he was going to look into the job in Atlantic City again. Then he called me around 11:30 a.m., saying he was driving up to Toms River to see some friends from rehab who were at an Oxford House there. After that he stopped answering his calls or texts—another disappearing act? Mike had given him $30; did he use it to buy drugs again, just enough to tide him over? Was he asleep in his car somewhere? Or worse?

I prayed that he was OK, safe, not in a police station or jail, not in a hospital or a morgue. Time would tell. I took a sleeping pill that night, so maybe I would sleep, despite this new development. I had been up since 3:00 a.m., when I had first heard him up, at the kitchen counter, using my computer. Maybe Mike could be the one to take the call from him this time.

CHAPTER NINETY-EIGHT

On May 11, 2011, Matt admitted at IOP that he was still using. He had failed a drug test and then called us to say he would be going back to inpatient treatment at Stonebridge. Rehab round four.

Was this what it felt like to be in shock? I mostly felt numb. But I also felt sad, hurt, and violated. My gut had been telling me something was wrong, but I thought I'd secured all the checkbooks. I asked him if he had taken anything from us, and that's when he told us, on speakerphone so Mike also could hear everything, that he had taken, forged, and cashed a few more checks. Mike was yelling—no, roaring—with anger.

Matt had made fools of us too many times. The next time he got kicked out of someplace for using, he could damn well go to a rescue mission.

He said he had found a packet of checks in a file drawer upstairs. Maybe I had left them there, but I didn't think so, which meant he had rooted through other drawers at some point, taken a packet of checks, and moved them upstairs so he could have easier access to them.

But when did he do this? He was never alone in the house; we had told him he had to leave if we were both going to be out. Mike had caught Matt walking around in his office one night when he had he slept here. Matt had said he was looking for some paper—not a good excuse, since he was sleeping in the room I used as my office, which had paper in it. So that may have been when he actually had retrieved the packet of checks from where *he* had put them, but when did he get them in the first place? I had, or thought I had, moved everything into the night table by my bed. Surely either Mike or I would have woken up if Matt had come into our room and opened a drawer that was inches away my head.

There was, however, one time when he and Chris had come over to help me move boxes in the garage. At one point Matt went inside and was in there for ten or fifteen minutes, longer than I thought it would take to go to the bathroom. When I went in, I found him upstairs. He said he was using the upstairs bathroom. I guess that mystery unraveled, and I knew he was exploring. He recently has said that he may have poked around that night but didn't take anything and didn't remember how he had managed to find and procure the checks.

I uncovered a couple more lies, things he really had no reason to lie about. A woman from our insurance carrier had called and left a message for Matt so she could tell him about outpatient services available to him. He told me he called the woman back and explained that he was all set up with outpatient counseling. The same woman called again more recently. As it turns out, he never called her. OK, it was rude for him not to return the call, and it was a service that could only help him, but why would he lie? Just to prevent us from nagging him about something else?

I also found out that on April 25, the day he said he had paid his own rent because his tips at the airport restaurant had been good that week—guess what? He didn't pay the rent. I imagine that's when he started to buy heroin again. But again, why lie? He already had told us his tips weren't good at all and probably wouldn't get better until the middle of May, so we were planning on having to pay his rent until the restaurant got busy and stayed busy—at least until the middle of June. So why did he tell us he had paid it? So we would ease up a little because it looked like he was starting to show some maturity and responsibility? Instead, while we were dealing with Matt's relapse and getting his things out of the Oxford House, the house manager, sweet Alvin who had given me a hug that first day, had to go back over Matt's account and explain to me why he stilled owed money.

Matt told me he had looked into the facility in Florida; he said it was covered by our insurance and that our insurance would even pay for his airfare to get there. I reminded him that he had to stay in New Jersey for another year. There are facilities in New Jersey that take a holistic recovery approach, which I don't really know anything about. If that's what Matt wanted, he could transfer to a different facility, as long as it was in New Jersey. Much later I asked him what had made him look into that place or any other place in Florida. He said all he could think about was "getting the hell out of Jersey."

I wished there was a rehab facility, covered by our insurance, where he could have stayed for a year, though Matt never would have agreed to that.

CHAPTER NINETY-NINE

I saw a commercial for a convenience store's frozen cappuccino. It reminded me of a time only a couple of years ago when Matt and I were out running errands and stopped at Dunkin' Donuts for coffee, and he talked me into trying one of their new flavors—caramel mocha or something—because he liked the sound of it and thought I would like it as well.

That commercial made me miss the clean and sober Matt. We did have a nice relationship when he wasn't using, when he wasn't asking for money. When he was using, he would disappear. And lie. And steal. I hoped we would get that clean and sober Matt back. He was fun to be around and a really nice kid. But he wasn't a kid; he was an adult—a really nice, personable, polite adult. He and I both liked music, so we talked about that a lot. His years working at PNC Bank Arts Center had exposed him to music that I liked but that he never would have chosen to listen to, and he developed an appreciation for some of it. More recently, when he talked about music, I'd just roll my eyes and brace myself, because I knew he was only fishing for money to go to a concert.

CHAPTER ONE HUNDRED

Matt stayed at Stonebridge for twenty-eight days. I wasn't particularly friendly toward him during the first couple of weeks he was there. He had told me he had a good support system in South Jersey, but it didn't seem that way, and I told him so. I said he had made fools of Mike and me too many times. I said we loved him and would look forward to his dropping in for dinner with us, but that if he relapsed again he could go to a shelter and soup kitchens or sleep in his car, because he wouldn't stay in our home. He said he knew that and understood the reasons for it.

One afternoon I dropped off some items Matt had said he wanted, and the receptionist was sort of—but not really—teasing me a bit about enabling (because I had brought the things Matt wanted, I suppose). I guess I would have to find the strength to say no when he asked me to bring him things. He could live without Wawa coffee and snacks, but he would find a way to get them anyway, by begging and borrowing from fellow inpatients, and would probably be known as the one who always mooched off everyone else—especially when it came to cigarettes. He truly was addicted to cigarettes. Every facility he had been in had told us not to worry about getting him to quit smoking; the said it was hard enough to kick the drug habit. Deal with one habit at a time, they all said. Good point, but I didn't want my son to get clean once and for all, only for us to lose him to lung cancer.

Would I have the strength not to give in? After dropping off the items at Stonebridge, I came home and sobbed; I didn't know why. I was so sad about the loss of my little boy and the path he was taking. What if he couldn't turn everything around? So far it didn't seem he had the strength to do it. As soon as he got money, he'd buy drugs. We couldn't control his money, and he always lied about why he hadn't gotten paid so that we'd think he didn't have any. When he ran out of money, he'd steal it from us. Maybe, down the road, he'd find a job that would last long enough for him to set up direct deposit into an account managed by us (yeah, right). First, though, he'd have to admit that money was one of his downfalls, but up until this point, he hadn't done that.

Oxford House interviews were set up during his last week at Stonebridge, and we also had a family session that week. During that same week, we had a second family session at Stonebridge that included counselors, a facilitator, and other inpatients. The counselors knew Matt had attended these sessions numerous times and probably could lead the groups. I thought this session might help Mike say what was on his mind and also allow the counselors and Matt's peers to give him feedback.

Matt's former roommate in the apartment after Bayview House was at Stonebridge as an inpatient. He gave me a hug and seemed happy to see us—as happy as he could be, given the situation. He looked like hell. He had been in and out of rehabs and detoxes since Matt had left the apartment and also had done a brief stint in jail. His mother wasn't speaking to him, because he had stolen her jewelry, so maybe a hug from me gave him a small bit of comfort.

The discussion with Matt and the group was no better or worse than any of the other times. The counselor who facilitated the meeting was tough on Matt. She told him his "game was getting old." He said he wanted to stay clean and reach his goals, and he knew he had to take baby steps. I told him that if he ended up in the grave I probably would end up there as well. Matt seemed not to react.

Afterward the counselors told us he was ours for the day. This came as a surprise, but Mike and I rearranged our schedules. We went out to lunch, and he came back to our house for a while, to do some stuff on the computer for his enrollment at the community college. He was on Facebook for a while and found out that a girl he knew from Bayview House had died recently of an overdose. He mentioned it almost nonchalantly, and I told him that, with every drug-related death of someone he knew, the odds would get greater that the same thing would happen to him. He just nodded; he knew that was the reality of addicts and their circles of friends.

There was no understanding the mind of an addict. All I could think was that his brain was badly traumatized, diseased, bruised, infected, and damaged by the drugs, and it would take a long time for it to heal. I also knew the healing wouldn't start until he stopped using drugs, and he might not ever heal completely. I could only hope and pray that his brain would heal enough for him to finally listen to voices of reason and take the help he'd been offered so many times. He was far too young to waste the rest of his life.

Matt told me he had never touched my jewelry. He said he didn't know what might be family heirlooms so he didn't want to take a chance of taking something important. It puzzled me that he would even think of that or consider that it might upset me to lose family heirlooms. Yet it didn't bother him to sell not one but two expensive watches he had received that had sentimental value.

More stories were unraveled, stories I didn't even know were out there.

Matt had slept in his car for two nights prior to Round Four of rehab before telling us he had relapsed and had been kicked out of Oxford House. He had parked his car near Longport Bridge one night, until a policeman asked him what he was doing. He said he wanted to watch the sunrise, but the policeman said that he had seen him there for quite a while and that he couldn't stay parked there. Matt drove away. One of the tenants at Mike's father's house told Mike's brother that there was someone sleeping in a car in the driveway the first day she was there. It was Matt. He had moved from the parking spot near the bridge and parked in his grandfather's driveway for a while. He finally pulled away when he saw someone walk up the steps to the main house.

CHAPTER ONE HUNDRED ONE

As Mike and I settled into our newly renovated seashore house, which was now our permanent home, we pretty much had gone through all the boxes. The only ones left were filled with family photographs. Every so often Mike would pull out a picture and show it to me, saying, "Here's one of happier times." I only looked at a couple of them—one of Laura, walking through the sprinkler, and one of Matt on his boogie board. I told Mike I couldn't deal with those pictures yet. Why? Did looking at the happy memories make our current circumstances all the more painful for me? That was certainly part of it. Did I feel like I shouldn't allow myself to be happy at that moment, even if it was just feeling the happiness of the past? Perhaps, but the past hadn't always been happy. There was a lot of pain, not just with regard to Matt. The pain from Matt didn't start until he entered ninth grade. A lot of painful times had to do with Laura. I'd never forget those dark days when we were told that she was dying, and I'd never be able to restore those horrible days in my life.

There also were some terrible times regarding Matt that couldn't be erased. They were part of our family's history—hopefully just a small part that had thus far lasted for more than two years but that I hoped would soon pass.

Maybe looking through the photos would be cleansing for me, help me remember that there was hope. But I wasn't ready yet. I needed a long block of alone time to do that.

CHAPTER ONE HUNDRED TWO

One of my niece's sons, Will, who was almost six years old, overheard me talking about Matt to his mom one day during the summer of 2011 and said, "I thought Matt was in jail." There were a couple of awkward laughs, but I was surprised, because the one time that Matt was in jail, for just six days, Will had been only about four years old; I was amazed he would remember that. Mike and I are very close to our siblings, their spouses, and their children, especially since our parents are deceased. I spent a lot of time wondering what our relatives thought of the situation and what they would say to us if we asked for their opinions. I knew they all felt bad for us and what we were going through—not just with Matt, but also with Matt's issues on top of Tim and Laura being totally dependent on us. I felt kind of paranoid, thinking that some family members were avoiding us because of Matt.

Finally I asked for their thoughts. Their answers were candid and sincere and ran the gamut from anger to embarrassment, to sorrow.

Will's mom, Jen, wrote the following to me.

Both Wes and Will heard a lot about Matt over that first initial summer. It was something I never thought I would have to explain to my four- and six-year-olds. They knew at four and six what drugs were and what being arrested and put in jail meant and that it was one of their cousins to whom this happened, not a fictional character on a TV show.

The reason I no longer ask about Matt is because I am pretty sure I will have already heard his tale of woe. For the last three years, he has given you and Mike the same list of lies and stories, the same excuses, and the same apologies. It kills me every time he lies to you, because I see the hope in your heart and know that it will be just a few weeks or even days until your hopes are dashed, because Matt has gotten the money, a warm bed, or food that he needed for the moment, but not the need to stop destroying his life and pulling his whole family along for the ride. I have seen your health decline in leaps and bounds since you discovered Matt's problem. If he cannot see the damage he has done (which I can't imagine) and he does not care, then the thousands of dollars of therapy you have provided for him and the thousands of dollars for rehab, places to live, food, two cars, a computer, watches, and shoes have all been for what?

I watched my mother die. I knew she was not feeling well, and I did everything to try and help her. Matt is doing the opposite. He is slowly killing both you and Mike. Drugs or no drugs, that upsets me beyond words. We all have our demons; we all make choices. I sat in your living room and watched Matt look me in the eye, tell me he was doing OK, he was tired from watching TV all night, and he was getting ready to go to a meeting. As he drove away in your car, I knew everything that came out of his mouth was a lie.

He is my cousin, my family, and blood. But that does not mean I like him right now, respect him, feel sorry for him, or can trust him. I know you say you never can give up on him, but it kills me to see the hope you have each time Matt goes into rehab. And, almost immediately after his admission, he starts telling the same series of lies and tales that he has been spinning for years and uses your love and kindness for his own selfish reasons again.

I can't imagine what it is like to be in your shoes. You and Mike have definitely been dealt an extreme hand. I cannot judge you for the decisions and choices you have made for Matt, but as your niece and friend, I want to wring Matt's neck for what he has done.

I will always be here to listen and help. I hope this book has helped you in some way and in turn can help others. I do hope and pray that Matthew one day is clean and can function on his own as an adult and that you and Mike can have peace of mind. I truly wish this for you.

I know you said that you would not be offended, and my intent was not to hurt you in any way. I guess, as you have seen, people/family don't know what to say, or how to say what they are feeling. Well, I hope you can tell I'm madder than hell at Matt, and my heart is breaking for you and Mike.

It was so good for me to hear this from Jen, as we always had been close, but I felt that we had drifted apart, and in my heart, I knew the reason was Matt. Would I have listened if had she told me this earlier? Probably not. Maybe I wasn't ready to accept the truth of Matt's problems; more likely I didn't yet have the courage to change myself and let him fall.

I wondered aloud to my brother, Steve, why other family members never mentioned Matt and his problems to me. He wrote me the following.

We all feel very bad for you and Mike, and for Matt, for the situation he is in. My guess is that some people just do not feel comfortable dealing with it. I have given you my honest opinions all along. You and Mike have given him too much money all along, but I understand why. I am afraid to imagine how he would have gotten the money and drugs otherwise.

I also have told you that he needs a change in his environment once he gets out. He wants to work with the rock culture and live and socialize with other addicts (even though they are trying to stay clean). That is a formula for failure.

Being angry with Matt is a natural reaction, but it does more harm than good. Enabling him, as a reaction of love, also does more harm than good. Matt needs everyone's unending love (as tough as it has to be sometimes), kindness, and positive support to pick himself up every day, one day at time, and beat this disease. Our prayers need to be for him to hear these words and gather the strength to do this, for it is his life, and only he can manage it.

Another niece, Liz, had a different take when I asked her what her thoughts were.

I hate to see the tight hold heroin has over Matt and others. It's terrifying to see the lack of power people have over conquering their addictions. A small part of us wants to judge and swear that would never happen to us or our family. That's really fear talking, once you realize that heroin doesn't discriminate. It touches all corners of all societies, all classes, and all races. All it takes is one weak moment or even just curiosity to try it, and then you're caught in a web that's so difficult to escape.

I feel sorry for Matt and about the sadness, frustration, and curiosity he first felt when he started smoking pot and drinking back in high school. I wish I could have stopped the pattern then. I wonder what was really bothering him. I remember the look in his eyes and his downward glance when I ran into him last summer at the mall and lent him money that he "owed a friend." I remember his awkward hesitation when I asked if he was staying out of trouble, and he said, "Trying to." I wish I could have kept him safe then, when I suspected his drug use but never accused him outright.

I am sad for the struggle he has to deal with now and the precious time that he has wasted. I am heartbroken for the disappointment he has caused you and Mike. I am sad for the times that Matt promises recovery and then steals from those who love him most. I am scared for all of the times ahead that he will be tempted and will struggle to resist relapse. I am impressed by the strength of you and Mike as a team and that you have persevered through so many struggles. I hope that I could weather the storms as you have. Given your circumstances, I doubt I could stay strong like you have.

We hold no grudges against Matt. Drugs are bad shit.

My parents have expressed sheer sadness, rather than judgment. I don't think they put anyone at fault, but they are very sad that you and Mike have been dragged through this after having struggles with Timmy and Laura. My mom always says she thinks of you all the time. I think she really just doesn't know what to say; this particular struggle is sort of foreign to her. My dad has surprised me with the sadness he feels.

Mike's sibling Joe and his wife Helen know a little too closely what we are going through. Helen wrote the following.

When we first heard about Matt's problem, I got worried right away because I went through this with my younger brother when our kids were babies. My parents were both gone, and I was the closest family member living in the same town. He stole from us all the time and worried me whenever he was around the girls. I will never forget the day he came by and I ran upstairs with the girls because he was high and upset with me because I didn't want him near the girls. He stood at the bottom of my steps (inside the house) with a huge kitchen knife, waving it at me and screaming that he wanted to hold the girls. I really believed he could have hurt us, and I kept telling him to leave and he wasn't welcome at our house anymore. He left, and we went through years of his dealing with the drugs and alcohol. Joe will tell you about the call we got one day from his wife to come over because she came home to find him locked in the garage with the car running. We flew over to find him passed out under the back of the car. He was trying to kill himself.

All I know is it is such a powerful addiction, and there is nothing you can do for the person other than tough love. The hardest thing ever to do to someone you love that is hurting—but you have to do it—is to cut them off for their own good so they can hit their bottom. You have to be strong and not help, other than getting them to rehab if they are willing. They have to want to get better for themselves, and it's so hard. I felt it was better that my brother moved away for a couple years, but then he moved back to Ocean City. I was so worried it would bring back the old habits due to people, places, and things, and it did in a way, but he thought it was OK, because they were prescription drugs for his back this time, and not heroin. I kept my distance for a while, and he was upset with me because he thought I turned my girls against him, but I told him they could figure things out for themselves.

Joe and I told our girls about Matt, and they were so shocked and just couldn't believe it. We talked with them about it and shared our feelings and experiences with drugs. Our girls always seem to take to heart our conversations, and we are so lucky. We know the drugs are out there, and we can't be with them twenty-four/seven anymore. This can happen to anyone, so we just try to keep in touch as much as possible, checking that everything is OK. Lots of prayers.

We have mixed feelings for Matt. First we feel angry and want to smack him for all the damage and pain he has caused you and himself. He looks good, and you can't imagine why he can't make better choices after the first time, but that just goes to show how addictive heroin is. Second, we love him too and just want to hug him and say it's OK.

I wish we had a better answer. I think you and Mike have done all you can and being a parent makes it so hard to cut them off (the tough love). He is your son, and you want to help, him but you can't. He has to do it himself and will only realize this when he hits his rock bottom. You cannot enable him in any way, or he won't realize how bad his situation is, and he has to want to change it himself. He has to feel he has nowhere to go before he will change. I remember hearing this over and over and how hard it was. The feeling of not knowing if my brother was alive or not. He was really bad, but he made it through and now it is taking a toll on him physically.

I so understand what you are going through. You have to remember all the bad things Matt has done to you and hold on to that anger to help you give the tough-love message to Matt. You got Matt to rehab, so he is in good hands. He knows what he needs to do but has to get to that rock bottom and not want to feel the pain anymore from the drugs (physically and emotionally). Only he can do this, and he has to want better for himself. Unfortunately we can't do it for him.

I asked my brother John for his thoughts regarding the situation with Matt. He wrote the following.

Over the years we have seen your son Matt progress from a happy, smiling, young boy to a confused, mixed-up young adult. And why—or I should say, how—did that happen? We, meaning my family, all know that you and Mike are model parents to all of your children. You have always been there to help guide Matt through life, as well as to provide him with support when he finds himself in trouble. So how did this happen and where does he go now? I know you have told me he has been to many rehab locations, and most of them he gets discharged from only to get more drugs. My thoughts here are that he has to find a facility where he can rehabilitate himself in a more rewarding manner. There may be classroom requirements, but he should also have physical exercise, team sports, and hobbies (e.g., music, games, etc.) to keep him interested. Maybe even a boot camp experience. But first he must start something, and he must finish it. If he figures out how to finish something, anything, maybe he will start moving forward again. Don't give up.

And as for you and Mike, don't come down hard on yourselves. It has been very difficult on both of you, and we all don't know how you can do it.

Yes we do. It is called love.

I did know that several of our siblings had a very hard time even making conversation with Matt. Mike's brother Dan explained it this way.

There were many times when I thought about grabbing Matt by the throat but realized that it would not do any good. We have such a trust in our family that it is hard to imagine that someone could be so deceitful and dishonest. As much as I love Mike and Ann, it is difficult to watch what they go through without reacting. I have a very difficult time making small talk with Matt at family gatherings because I have a hard time talking to someone I can't trust.

His wife Diane added the following.

Honestly, at first I was a little bit embarrassed to have a nephew who is a drug addict. I was never comfortable talking about it, as if it would somehow reflect on my immediate family or me. I was also not overly comfortable talking to my own kids about the situation. Later I realized that drug addiction is a sickness. And I am no longer embarrassed by it. It led to frequent and open conversations with my own kids. We are honest about Matt's situation. I have watched them go through a grieving process of sorts. Anger that Matt is being so "stupid." Shock that he was in jail. Hope that maybe this time in rehab will work. Ambivalence that he "messed up" yet again. Sadness that the story hasn't had a happy ending yet.

At times I am furious at the stress and strain Matt puts on his parents both emotionally and financially. I am appalled that he could be so self-centered as to not see or even care what he is doing to the people who love him the most. Every time I let myself be hopeful for him and his parents that this stint in rehab will be the turning point, I am disappointed. But most of the time, I just feel sad—sad for Mike and Ann, sad for Matt, sad for the horrible situation that seems so hopeless. Sad that I am unable to do anything to change the situation for them.

There is not a day that goes by that I don't think about them all, saying a silent prayer that Matt will somehow have an epiphany and find the strength to overcome this disease and that Mike and Ann can find the strength to also get through this horrible nightmare. As Dan so bluntly puts it, "They can't even buy a break." At the end of each day, I also feel so grateful and relieved that we didn't get the phone call to tell us that Matt is dead somewhere.

But even after everything Matt has done and put his parents through, he is still family. The bottom line is that I still hang on to the idea that deep down Matt is still a good kid who made one really bad choice that will follow him the rest of his life.

Another relative put it quite simply yet powerfully.

An addict cannot practice his/her addiction unless enabled in some way.

I guess that statement says what I already knew yet couldn't stop—we enabled him all the time.

The opinions of our relatives were mixed, but most of them felt strong anger toward Matt for what he had done to himself and to us, as well as sadness for us and what our lives have become. Most felt we weren't tough enough on him but probably wouldn't have done any differently themselves. Most felt that Matt needed to hit rock bottom and that prison might have been what he needed. At the very least, he needed a new course of direction, a new start. They felt that he was a compulsive liar and that we had been fooled by his lies every time and that our babying him only enabled him and prolonged the situation. They felt Matt was lost and without a compass, or maybe never had a compass to begin with. Some felt that his struggle would be long term or that he would end up dead, either from an overdose or from being with the wrong people at the wrong time.

Most weren't too optimistic. Most couldn't imagine what we were going through, and of course everyone felt extremely bad for both Mike and me. No one would have wished this burden on us. One relative even said he wished he was younger and could have taken Matt under his wing in order to help him.

It sounded like the consensus was that we had not handled the situation appropriately—that we should have let him to go jail and should have said no to him more often, more loudly, and more forcefully. Some of our relatives implied that Matt was a loser and maybe even a lost cause. I had asked for honesty, and I wasn't hurt by the comments.

They were right.

When Timmy was just a few days old, he had surgery to correct the spinal fluid that was pressing on his brain. We stayed at my mother's for several weeks afterward, as Mike and I were house-hunting in upstate New York. We took Timmy to Children's Hospital for his neurosurgery six-week checkup, and the doctors immediately knew that his shunt wasn't working properly and that he would need more surgery. My mother told me she had known something wasn't right after the first surgery. I replied that I wished she had said something earlier. I wanted to say the same thing when all our relatives gave me their true thoughts about Matt—that I wished they had said something to me sooner—but I know it wouldn't have mattered. Back then I wasn't ready to hear what they might say and certainly wasn't ready to act on it.

CHAPTER ONE HUNDRED THREE

Our friends were great. Most of my friends just listened and offered words of comfort but always asked how things were going with Matt and how I was doing. None of them had ill feelings toward Matt. A dear friend, Carole, checked in with me weekly. She always had been attuned to my emotions and was supportive and comforting, yet she worried about Matt and about me. She always wanted to know what was going on with Matt, the good and the bad, every step of the way. She listened and commented, understood my fears and worries, and gave me words of comfort and reassurance. She did not pass judgment; she only gave me support for whatever I was feeling.

Another good friend, Anne, who has known us since Matt was three years old, checked in with me a couple of times a week, if not more often. She always tried to reassure me, telling me what a nice kid he was, what a good person he was, and that he would be fine. After a while I had to tell her to stop saying it, because it only made the pain worse. She said she didn't know what else to do or say. When her youngest child was a very sick, very premature newborn, the people she remembered most from that time were the ones who had said positive things to her, so she was just going from her experience. And

Anne really did believe Matt would get well. She told me she could understand how much I hurt when I knew who he used to be and what he had turned into, and how it pained me that my hands were tied and I felt totally helpless to do anything. But she also understood that I was—and always had been—there for him, 100 percent and then some. She knew I was hurt by his behavior, but his behavior was fueled by a medical disorder called addiction, and she was certain he didn't want to be where he was at that point. She said that although she was a nurse by trade, she wasn't a professional in this particular field, so she could only go on what she wanted to see for Matt, the family, and me—and that was peace.

Yet another good friend, also named Anne, expressed only sadness for me and what I was going through. I asked her, though, what she really thought, and in contrast to my other friend Anne, this is what she said.

To be fair, when Matt's issues started, I was already involved in Al-Anon and was going to an alcohol counselor, so my opinion was then—and is now—tempered by knowledge that you as a parent didn't have at that time.

I think it would have been better for you and Mike to have been on the same page in addressing Matt's issues from the beginning. I think Matt's disease took advantage of the divide in your own opinions.

In the past two years, I think you've taken a stronger stance, but Matt (the disease) seems to have stepped up his game also. It is so hard to know what to do, especially with someone so young. I know, with my own experience, that I had to completely reject any contact and detach. Detaching with love is what I wish both you and Mike had done a long time ago and wish you would do now, but I recognize that it is so difficult to do with your child.

I pray for you whenever I pray, and I don't think I could handle your situation any better than you do.

Would it have made a difference if Anne had said anything sooner? I don't think so. I was too busy justifying Matt's actions and making excuses for him to really have listened to her thoughts and suggestions.

A good friend from college, Val, with whom I e-mail on a daily basis, and who lives in Maryland and never has even met Matt, said what she sensed and felt, from talking to me, was the following.

He piles on the lies. I have no leg to stand on, as I have no kids. I see him leeching the life out of you and pretty much telling you what you want to hear, day by day by day. I empathize wholeheartedly with his chemical imbalance, and believe he has one, and that is a bitch to fight. Does he need more meds? I don't know. But he has bled you dry in more than one way and continues to do so, not being mean-spirited but not straightening out either. The tales are endless and the lies are endless, and what will possibly turn it around? Yet I see you and Mike clinging to the hope that something will turn it around, and then he cashes forged checks and lies again. If I were around him, certainly I would be cordial as hell, because I totally understand about the brain/chemical imbalance.

Another good friend from college, Wendy, now living in Washington State, had read my book proposal and asked for permission to read portions of it to her classes at the high school where she works. Wendy is the campus supervisor, also known to the kids as "security." She interacts with the students a lot, runs a club called "Open up and to the Point" for kids to confidentially talk, and goes into the classrooms as well, so this topic is very personal for her. She said the excerpts that she read had quite an impact on her students, and they were waiting anxiously to hear more. Wendy had only met Matt when he was four years old, so she didn't know him or comment on him as a person. She only knew what a terrible disease addiction is and said, "In hearing your story, I learned of your heartache and anguish and strength and courage."

Mike and I a few friends who, sadly, were in a select "club" with us—a club no one wanted to be a part of, comprised of families who have had their lives upended by addiction and who could wholeheartedly relate to our struggles, our pain, and our frustration. It was so helpful for us to use one another as sounding boards, to ask one another other "Why?" and to generally compare notes. And we were grateful to be able to talk to people who said, "I know how you feel" and meant it.

Finally we had been fortunate to meet the brother of one of our friends. Kevin had lost his son to a heroin overdose in June 2008. He and Mike corresponded frequently, and Mike recently signed off on an e-mail to him with just the word "Peace," to which Kevin replied, "I have been looking for that since June 30, 2008. Some days I actually find it for brief periods." He had told us that he had found, through personal experience, that "there is a very fine line between hitting bottom and death." Those are powerful words to think about. After his son's death, Kevin started an organization called City of Angels. The organization describes its goals as follows.

The road to recovery is a difficult one to travel. City of Angels envisions this road with fewer obstacles for those seeking freedom from their addiction. It is our hope that the journey will begin at the City of Angels Recovery Assistance Center. It is here that those struggling with addiction, those in recovery, and their family members can find the map to a healthy lifestyle. City of Angels

*will offer assistance in navigating the treatment system but re-
alizes that successful completion of a treatment program is not
the end of the road. Upon reentry into their daily lives, City of
Angels will be available for those in recovery by providing emotional support, sponsors, a safe and drug-free meeting place, help
finding employment, psychoeducational programs, and daily living assistance.*

*City of Angels NJ, Inc., realizes that addiction is a devastat-
ing disease that destroys too many lives, and seeks to foster strong
relationships with the community, schools, the criminal justice
system, and various treatment centers in order to bridge the gap
between addiction and a healthy lifestyle.*

City of Angels was instrumental in getting Matt situated in rehabs a
couple of times. More than that, though, the people there had been
wonderful about talking us through some tough days, like those
nightmarish couple of days prior to Matt's actually going to rehab.
At times they had been our only lifeline.

CHAPTER ONE HUNDRED FOUR

In June 2011, as his clean life started, Matt had been out of round four of rehab and in an Oxford House for ten days, with no job yet and no real signs that he was looking very hard. Mike gave him some leads—"Help Wanted" signs we had seen, places that handled a lot of banquets and might need help. It seemed as if Matt was waiting for his buddies to see if their employers needed any more help. I wondered what was going on in his mind. Was he timid? Was he afraid of being told no? We he afraid of being hired and failing at the job? Did he lack self-esteem? Was he afraid of what he would do when he got a paycheck? Or did he just not want to work and want us to support him forever?

He did officially sign up for classes, bought books, and started to attend classes. He said that he enjoyed them and that they seemed interesting. I prayed that they would hold his interest and that he would stick with it. More important I hoped he could get through the summer without any relapses. He definitely would have to learn how to multitask. We gave him his laptop back, the one he had pawned before round three of rehab. Mike had gone to the shop and retrieved it and had held on to it until the appropriate time.

Matt eventually landed a job at a local year-round market that had been an Ocean City establishment for many years. Initially he would do prep work with the food but could move up to being a cook. I was hopeful, and Matt sounded happy and proud. Would this be a new start? Finally?

On his second or third day on the job, Matt received a message from the mother of a college friend, asking him to call her back. The boy's father was one of Matt's music professors. It turned out that the boy had hanged himself earlier that week. He had been in trouble with drugs off and on and in jail for a time. I had met him once or twice at our house in Little Silver.

Matt wanted to go to Vermont that Friday for the service. His probation office would likely allow it, because it was a funeral. We, however, didn't want him around the group of kids from that scene. Additionally it wasn't a good idea for him to ask for time off when he had only been working at the market for a week. He would have to think long and hard, and I prayed he would make the right decision. He did not go to the funeral.

He worked at the market for barely three weeks and then decided not to show up. I happened to be in the market that Monday and asked for him so could say hi. When the owner told me that he had not shown up for two days, I felt betrayed and embarrassed. What happened to the manners we had taught him? He apparently didn't show up one Sunday, but they were willing to overlook that. They assumed there was a mix-up with the schedule and were going to let him work the next day—except he didn't show up.

Matt told me he couldn't work there anymore, because he had been moved up to cook and was working too hard for too little pay. Additionally all the other kids who worked there spent their whole shift talking about where they were going out drinking after work, and he had seen some pot being sold in the parking area as well. He said he couldn't work in that environment. Poor Matt. He had so much bad luck. Yeah, right. He really just decided that he couldn't work fifty hours a week as a cook for only $8 an hour.

My gut was telling me he was using again. I could have called and asked his house manager if he had paid his rent. If he didn't, I could assume that he had spent the money on drugs. Why didn't I? Maybe I didn't want to hear that he hadn't paid the rent. Maybe I wanted him to confess it on his own rather than be cornered into it.

I'd had high hopes for him with that job. The job wasn't the greatest, but he would move up there. He was cooking; he was busy; he could be busy all year. This wasn't just a summer job. Someone had given him a chance, but he had bailed on them during their busiest weekend of the summer.

But what if Matt wasn't using? What if this was just his way of getting out of an uncomfortable situation? In my heart I didn't believe that. I had to unravel the lies that were entwined in these latest actions.

What did it take to give an addict the drive to get clean and stay clean? On January 12, 2012 NPR's health blog discussed an article titled "What Vietnam Taught us about Breaking Bad Habits."

In May 1971 two congressmen discovered that 15 percent of US servicemen in Vietnam were actively addicted to heroin. President Richard Nixon took action. In June of that year he created the Special Action Office of Drug Abuse Prevention, dedicated to fighting the evil of drugs. In addition to the department laying out a program of prevention and rehabilitation, Nixon also wanted to see research performed regarding what had happened to the addicted servicemen once they returned home.

The addicted soldiers were kept in Vietnam until they detoxed. Once they were back in the United States, research showed, the number of soldiers who continued their heroin addiction was shockingly low—only about 5 percent.

In this way, says David Neal, a psychologist at Duke University, our environments come to unconsciously direct our behavior—even behaviors that we don't want, such as smoking.

> *"For a smoker, the view of the entrance to their office building—which is a place that they go to smoke all the time—becomes a powerful mental cue to go and perform that behavior," Neal says. "And over time those cues become so deeply ingrained that they are very hard to resist. And so we smoke at the entrance to work when we don't want to. We sit on the couch and eat ice cream when we don't need to, despite our resolutions."*

According to Neal, one way to battle bad behaviors, then, is to disrupt the environment in some way.

It's important not to overstate this, says NPR's blog, because a variety of factors are probably at play. But one theory about why the rates of heroin relapse were so low upon the servicemen's return to the United States has to do with the fact that the soldiers, after being treated for their *physical* addiction in Vietnam, returned to a place that was radically different from the environment where their addiction had taken hold of them.

So this study proved what has long been taught in AA and NA—that the recovering addict must change the people, places, and things with whom he or she was previously associated. My question was, "Is it really that easy?" Would moving Matt to Florida or some other place lessen his odds of a relapse? I was still thinking Matt could find drugs even when he was alone in the middle of a desert, or on a beach in the middle of winter.

CHAPTER ONE HUNDRED FIVE

We received a back-to-school ad in the mail from a linen and home store. I had a memory flash of when we had taken Matt to buy all of his stuff for college.

Matt was so not into it. He put the shopping trip off until about a week before he left for college, which meant there weren't too many choices, especially when it came to selecting those twin sheets that were specified as needing to be "extra long." Mike and I were the ones holding the list of suggested items to bring and checking things off as we put them in our shopping carts; Matt just pretty much said "OK" to everything we showed him.

I guess it didn't matter to him what he brought with him. A stereo, a computer, a refrigerator—they were his necessities; he could take or leave anything else. He just wanted to get there and be on his own.

Each time he got out of rehab, we would go on a similar, but scaled-down, shopping trip. Mike looked at it as our buying Matt things he probably already had (new underwear and socks, etc.); I preferred to look at it as a fresh start, a new chapter in his life.

CHAPTER ONE HUNDRED SIX

Matt seemed to have taken the month of July 2011 off, as he was only halfheartedly looking for work.

He asked me to purchase two tickets online for him for a concert and said he would stop by to give me the money. He did stop in, to print out the confirmation for the tickets, but wanted to wait and give me the money after the concert, because he wanted to be sure he had enough money for food, gas, and parking. And off he went.

He had conned me yet again. I know...I know... Why did I buy the tickets for him? Did subconsciously I want to be the favored parent, or was I simply being a mom who wanted to make her kid happy? Did I just always fall for his line? Yes. Yes. And yes.

I sent him a text message telling him that I was pissed and that he shouldn't come here again unless he came with the money he owed me. I felt like crying. I told him I had unconditional love for him and couldn't love him only when he was the "good" Matt, but this was BS. I told him it was yet another example of how he couldn't plan ahead by putting money aside.

I was mad at him for doing this to me and mad at myself for falling for it. He did come by and give me the money, and he apologized.

He said he understood how it looked bad and why we were suspicious. I thought I had turned a corner this time. I hoped I had.

At the end of July, Matt finally got a job at a local restaurant. It was right on the water, at a marina, and pretty upscale, so I hoped it would produce good tips, which hopefully Matt would start saving. I felt I had reached the end of my tolerance for being conned by him. I wanted the best for him, and the best was a clean and sober life. And if he didn't have the funds to get to a concert, poor baby. It was time he learned to grow up and plan ahead. I'd been telling myself and others that his brain was still scrambled from the drugs; he thought his brain was working just fine. That may have been true, but I no longer could use it as an excuse for his actions. I should have told Matt that, but would he have listened?

Mid-August 2011 marked his ninety-day clean mark, as far as I knew, although later I found out that he had relapsed, starting in July. I felt like he was getting cocky. When he wasn't working, he was running around, borrowing my car to help people move. I had to wonder whether something had happened to his car. Of course he said no.

One day around this time, two things came in the mail for him. One was a hospital bill from the night when he had gone to a concert on a boat in New York City. He said he had fallen and scraped his knees as he had gotten off the boat, and it was the boat's policy to take him to the hospital. Fine. But why would he not bother to tell me that after it had happened, especially since I specifically had asked how the concert was? The other was a ticket from Ocean City for his failing to wear a seatbelt. He said he would pay it the following day. He had been working a lot and paying for his Oxford House rent as well as his food and gas. He just never had any money left over. Things weren't adding up. After I pressed Matt for answers regarding his recent behavior, a few more lies unraveled.

He told me he recently had lost his phone.

He also had lost his wallet the night of the concert in New York City and therefore his license.

He was borrowing my car a lot because he had crashed his car into a pole in the parking lot at work, rushing to get there on time, and he had left it at the restaurant, totaled.

Next he told me he hadn't paid his Oxford House rent for a month. He had spent all his earnings at the casinos but had hoped to eventually win it all back.

Because he hadn't paid his rent, Oxford House had asked him to leave, and he had been sleeping on the floors of random acquaintances for about a month.

Finally he told me that he had withdrawn from one of his two classes because the timing of work and class didn't coincide.

By the end of August, I believed all of this was spinning out control. I predicted that he would use until he went to his scheduled probation meeting and that he would then tell his PO he thought he needed to go away to inpatient rehab; ideally he would say that he needed to go to a long-term facility.

I had started looking (again!) at potential places for round five. A few sounded good, but I wasn't sure they would work with our insurance. One that sounded good wasn't in New Jersey, but so far his probation officer wouldn't budge on the requirement that he stay in New Jersey until he was finished with probation.

Matt was out of control. Every time he opened his mouth, he lied. I thought he could be helped; his counselor had faith in him. At one point Ben said, "I have more faith in Matt than he has in himself." Why couldn't Matt make it work? Was he afraid of what was out there in the "real world"? He talked about wanting to get a job in music, at a venue, working with the production of shows…but did he really? Or was he afraid of failure? He seemed definite about that being his career choice and confident that he had the skills to do it, but maybe he wasn't.

At that point it seemed like we couldn't do any more. Likely we had done too much already. I was sure we had made things worse by helping him out, and I was so sorry for that, but I thought at the time that any parent would do the same things we had done.

I needed to find a way to get through that week, in anticipation of what might happen at the end of it. I assumed Matt would use drugs all week and continue to sleep on the floors of acquaintances or coworkers. He probably would shower there as well, although most of his clothes were in the back of my car.

I had to let this happen. Even Ben asked me why I was doing all the legwork. His point, plainly and simply, was that I was enabling him yet again. My logic was that, in the case of the traffic ticket, if I didn't pay it, he would go before a judge, who would look at his record and...what? Take away his license? (That wouldn't have been a big deal, since he had no car at that point anyway.) Send him to jail for ten days? Or sixty? I knew I wasn't ready for that; it seemed, though, that Matt was ready and willing to take that risk. Part of the reason I wanted to pay for the ticket was because the car was in my name, even though I really was trying hard to stop enabling him.

Matt needed to pay the ticket by August 23 or go to court. He also had been badgering me about needing money to pay back money he had borrowed from someone at work. Since I recently had found out that he just stopped doing the work for his second class, the on-line class, I told him to sell his laptop. I even drove him to the pawn shop, negotiated with the owner, and got just $200 for it. That was all Matt really needed anyway. Then we drove directly to the restau-rant, where Matt handed over $100 to a fellow employee—whether to purchase drugs or as payment for drugs already given to him, I didn't know. I didn't care. Then we went to the Ocean City traffic court and paid the ticket. From there I drove him to the Department of Motor Vehicles to get his license replaced. I wonder what they would have said if they had known, based on information I learned later, that Matt was high at the time.

Matt's life was spinning out of control. Everything about him was unraveling, more so than ever. It was almost as if this journey had made a complete circle. In January 2009, he had told us he had a gambling problem. That turned out to be a lie—I suppose because he wasn't ready to tell us he was addicted to heroin. Now he was back to gambling, if we could believe that, but said he didn't have a gambling problem; he just went to win some money to pay some bills, and then he got behind on his rent and wanted to win enough to pay the $560 he owed in rent, all at once. Of course, as he later told me, that wasn't true. But why, then, were advertisements from the casino coming to our address, addressed to Matt? As far as I knew at the time, he wasn't using drugs, but I never seemed to know when he was. The things I had learned over the past few days had astounded me, and I was sure there were more than a few lies entangled in his stories.

Matt was able to replace his phone, since the one he had lost was insured. He also had changed his phone number a few weeks prior to that; he said he was getting calls from people he didn't want to talk to. Bookies? Dealers? Collection agencies? It had, of course, crossed my mind that maybe he was doing his disappearing act again.

All I could do about that was shrug my shoulders and tell myself that if he acted or looked funny, IOP would test him.

I could never stop loving, worrying about, or wanting to protect and save Matt. At some point, though, I knew I had to push him out of the nest and let him fly or fall. He would have to learn his lessons the hard way.

But for me, that would be like tearing my own heart out.

CHAPTER ONE HUNDRED SEVEN

At the end of August, we had to evacuate Ocean City, due to the hurricane, so we went inland to Mike's sister's house. We didn't invite Matt to go along with us, and he chose not to go to one of the shelters set up in town. Instead he got a ride to a friend's house in Toms River, where he rode out the hurricane. The friend was having surgery the following Monday, so Matt had to get out of their house by Sunday, and the friend couldn't give him a ride back to Ocean City. Mike drove up to Toms River to get him at the end of the weekend, even after doing a lot of back-and-forth driving because of the hurricane, not to mention that the weather was still terrible. In Ocean City Matt had been sleeping on a friend's floor. The friend lived in a rooming house and had allowed Matt to sleep on his floor, in exchange for half the rent. The friend's parents, however, had picked him up and taken him home, because of the hurricane, and he wouldn't be back until after the weekend. Matt had no place to stay, and unless he could make some calls and find another floor to sleep on, Mike was going to drop him off at a rescue mission in Atlantic City. Better Mike than me—I didn't think I could do it. As it turned out, the rescue mission was closed. It seemed he had to have set up a reservation to stay there. So we let him sleep in our car, in our driveway.

Matt had to see that this was what his life had become. He could afford to live off of his tips, as long as he didn't also have to pay for rent and gas. Summer was coming to an end, and the restaurant would be closing for the season. He would have no income then and therefore no money to pay his friend for the privilege of sleeping on his floor. Would that force him to go to rehab? Or could he stay clean for a couple of weeks and get accepted back into an Oxford House? When I asked when he had used drugs last, the answer was always "a couple of days ago." We had no idea if he was still using, or how frequently.

I felt he was one step away from becoming a homeless person. I wanted him to be optimistic, but I also wanted him to see what the reality of this was. Even if he could stay clean, he would have this job only for another couple of weeks, maybe a month at best, maybe making enough money to buy food and give his friend some rent money.

I was finding it hard to be with him or even talk about him, but not because I was very angry. I actually wasn't that angry, but I wished I were. I was back to being sad, although I still felt used enough not to let him sleep inside our home, and used enough not to fall for his tricks. I told myself that if he had conned us yet again (by asking for the money for his friend's "rent") it would catch up with him. He would screw up at work, or maybe not even show up for work, and then they would fire him. Then he would have nowhere to go because he wouldn't even have enough money to make a donation at the rescue mission in exchange for sleeping there.

I tried not to let myself think about all of this, because I feared I would start crying and not be able to stop. My child should have had more than this. He *could* have had more than this. He had done this to himself. How could a mother stand by and watch her son destroy himself? Part of me wanted to rent him a small apartment so he would feel like he had something, but I knew that wouldn't change a thing. Maybe it would win us an award as the ultimate enablers. So many dreams had fallen apart, had become unraveled, all because of this horrible disease called addiction, this horrible disease that had taken our Matt.

This wasn't the life I wanted for him, nor was it the life he should have wanted for himself.

I didn't understand why he wasn't actively looking for work for the fall, someplace where he could make enough money to afford a place to live. Maybe he thought he ultimately would be back in rehab and was just letting it all play out. Maybe he thought it was too overwhelming to even try. I wondered how he really felt about it all.

Above all I knew it was slowly killing me.

He said he needed rent money for his friend *right away*. We argued and yelled; there were lots of hang-ups and callbacks, but eventually, ultimately, Mike gave him the $70. Time would tell if it was for rent or another fix; I could only guess. The only way I couldn't beat myself up over the fact that we were potentially giving him money for drugs was by thinking that maybe he would get caught sooner and therefore get help sooner.

CHAPTER ONE HUNDRED EIGHT

Twenty two years ago, when my youngest child was a very sick eight-month-old baby girl, there were so many days and nights that I spent crying my eyes out, because her doctors had told us that her brain was deteriorating and that she likely would live for only another few weeks, maybe a couple of months.

One night during that time, as I lay in bed—maybe I was in that state between waking and sleeping—an angel appeared to me. She looked a little like one that would be on top of a Christmas tree, and she actually looked like a china angel figurine my mom always had on the mantle in our living room. The angel was smiling at me, and her arms were open wide, as if to embrace me, or welcome me into her arms. Initially I was alarmed, because I thought she was taking me, and I thought, *No, it's not my time to go!* She kept smiling, and holding her arms open, and nodding at me. I knew then that there was an angel watching over Laura and me, and that gave me strength.

Later, as I spent many days and nights crying my eyes out over Matt's destiny, I was waiting for that angel, or another one, to give me reassurance. It didn't work that way, though, and I was reminded of something I'd heard, or maybe read, that said God always answers our prayers, but he does it in his own time, and he doesn't always give the answers we want to hear. So maybe there would be no reassurances about Matt. Laura had been a helpless baby; Matt was a grown man, a very mixed-up and confused man, held in the grips of a terrible disease. Only he could help himself, and he wasn't choosing to do so. I still didn't even know what all of his problems were: drinking, drugs, lying, gambling, depression, and who knew what else. I don't think he even knew.

CHAPTER ONE HUNDRED NINE

On September 11, 2011, the tenth anniversary of the most horrific event Americans alive today have ever known, I couldn't stop thinking about the people who had lost their lives and could do nothing about it. Obviously the terrorists knew how their lives would end, and the passengers of Flight 93 knew how theirs ultimately would end. The thousands of people in the Twin Towers were unsuspecting, just starting their day, and then soon realized what had happened, what *was* happening, and that they wouldn't get out alive. Some made the choice to jump and get it over with, knowing the inevitable outcome but choosing to end it their way; others stayed and tried to find a way out, also knowing the inevitable outcome.

I watched Matt, not knowing if he was on a good path or just lying to me once again. He was in control of his outcome; his life was in his own hands. How could he choose, especially after 9/11, anything but a good life?

CHAPTER ONE HUNDRED TEN

Matt's job at the restaurant ended rather abruptly in the middle of September. One day he was working, and the next he got a call saying they didn't need him for the rest of the season. I actually called the restaurant, under the guise of seeing whether Matt was scheduled to work that night, and they told me he was no longer working there. I asked whether something had happened, and they said no; it was just the end of the summer season, and they weren't busy enough to need so many people. Matt was really pissed that I had called, which I didn't understand. He said that the manager had her moments, and he didn't want to stir up anything.

Right away he got another job with a landscaper from an ad he saw on Craigslist. It was hard, dirty work, and he'd be out in the sun all day. I thought it was just what he needed. Additionally he and a couple of friends had found a cheap apartment in the rooming house where Matt had been sleeping. It wasn't really an apartment, just one big room with two sets of bunk beds in it, plus a small bathroom. Were things starting to look up? Was he starting to take proactive steps?

He needed money, money, money, left and right, including his portion of the first and last months' rent and security deposit. He also had to buy five T-shirts and a sweatshirt, all with the landscaping company's name and logo on it, plus a pair of heavy-duty pants. I don't recall discussing any of this with Mike or Matt, but Mike gave him the money, so he and Matt must have talked about it.

Matt started work on a Tuesday. He picked up his paycheck three days later and quit. He told the owner, manager, or whoever, that it wasn't for him. We found that out through Mike's brother, who knew the owner. Much later Matt told me he was going through withdrawal (again) that week and was too sick to do the work.

Once again we were getting no answers to our calls or texts. After collecting his paycheck, he had crawled back into his shell. To make matters more unsettling, Mike and I would both be out that Friday night—me just for four hours, Mike overnight.

It was the middle of September. As far as we knew, Matt had a place to sleep, and his rent was paid for until October 15. But he had no money coming in for food.

The begging and pleading throughout the weekend after he quit his job was really quite incredible. And so were the stories!

Of course he swore his needing money had nothing to do with drugs. He said he owed his friend money for the times he had slept on his floor, and the friend needed to buy a bus ticket so he could get home and be with his dog, because his family was putting him to sleep. Matt's probation was that afternoon. He said he would ask for help then, regarding to whom he could talk about his issues—specifically spending more money than he had, which was none, apparently. I wasn't sure, but I didn't think he felt he had any other issues.

By the end of the following Monday, I knew more. I knew he hadn't gone to probation since July. He was now in violation, and a bench warrant had been issued for him.

I'd been asking God to help him, even if the help wasn't pretty. I'd been praying for him to hit bottom so he finally would get the wake-up call he needed and then get the help he so desperately needed. I always kept in mind, though, what our friend Kevin had told us— "There is a very fine line between rock bottom and death." Things seemed to be moving quickly, and Matt's lifestyle was getting in the way of reality. Maybe this was how God was answering me.

I made arrangements for Matt to see his probation officer in Cape May Courthouse on the following day. His PO didn't know what would happen, as the outcome was up to Middlesex County. At least Matt was now back in the computer system as having attended meetings with his probation officer. He still owed fines, but the PO kept saying he was looking into getting the rest of the fines reduced or waived, since we had paid, at that point, more than $3,000 out of pocket for Matt's inpatient stays alone. Then, finally, Matt admitted to us that he knew he needed help, but he wanted to get high "one last time." He actually asked if I would give him some money to help with this last request. I was stunned, astonished, and told him, "Sorry, but no."

Why couldn't I feel anger?

CHAPTER ONE HUNDRED ELEVEN

Round five of rehab started at Timberwood on September 25, 2011. I had been up in Red Bank at work all day, training someone to cover for me while I took a much-needed week off. While I was gone, Matt finally had called Mike and asked to be picked up and taken somewhere. "I can't live like this anymore," he'd said. Mike picked him up, and he slept on the couch at our house that night (I was on the love seat in the same room, not sleeping), while we scrambled to figure out where to take him. Bayview House and Stonebridge both said he needed more help than they could give him. I called several emergency rooms, only to be told they had no detox units. I called a couple that did have detox units, only to be told they had no available beds that night. And I really wanted him to go immediately, for a few reasons: 1) I wanted him to go while he was willing to go; 2) I didn't want him looking for that last high, which might kill him; and 3) I didn't want him staying at our house. I called several facilities, some of which had detox units, but again there were no rooms at the inn that night. A couple of facilities offered to set up an intake appointment for Matt several days down the road.

Kevin and the City of Angels team were working on this as well and gave us the names of two facilities that would give us appointments the following day, thanks to Kevin's assistance. We took the appointment at 9:00 a.m. on a Saturday, at a facility about an hour west of where we lived.

When we dropped Matt off for his fifth rehab stay, he would stay for about a month, as was the norm, and then our hope was that he would agree to go to a long-term facility, because clearly he couldn't live independently. He needed to answer to someone, like a gatekeeper or a watchdog. He needed someone who would check on him and see that he got to work, managed his money appropriately and accurately, did his chores, and got back to the facility at curfew. He also needed to answer to a higher power, and hopefully he finally would find that.

The weekend after he left, I spent a good part of a day sorting through Matt's "stuff" that was stored in our garage, looking for a few specific things he wanted to have: warmer clothing, books, and a baseball hat. It was so sad for me to think that this was what his life had come down to—nothing but plastic containers marked "shirts," "linens," and "pants," plus boxes of knickknacks and wires to his various electronics. There was also his bedroom set and a couple of large chairs in our garage, waiting for him to someday move them again into his own real apartment. I wondered whether that day would ever come. He had tried it for three months and ended up in round three of rehab. He had tried it just the previous month, but he wasn't there more than two weeks before leaving for round five.

The bench warrant that came in the mail the day he left would dictate what the next step would be after Timberwood. Matt didn't know about it yet, but I supposed he would be told at the end of the week, when we would meet with him and his counselor. Would he be able to stay down here, or would he have to go back to Middlesex County? Would it be better for him if he did? He would be totally on his own, with no car, and without us to fall back on. He would have to get a job immediately and report to someone more diligently than he had in the past.

If he did have to return to Middlesex County to live, he would need a lot. At that point, he had nothing: no money, no car, no phone—just those plastic containers full of his stuff. Half of it could probably have been thrown out, although he did have two complete sets of clothes, one size for healthy Matt and a smaller size for drug-addict Matt.

When Mike and I talked with Matt and a counselor, it certainly wasn't the conversation we were expecting. He had been there less than two weeks and felt ready to leave. He said he knew what he had to do and thought he had the drive to do it this time. So it looked like there would be no long-term stay anywhere in the near future. We set up an appointment to meet with the rehab's family therapist at the end of the following week, after which Matt would come back with us to go to an Oxford House interview and then get driven back to rehab. At the beginning of the following week, he would be picked up for another interview at an Oxford House, which meant lots of driving for Mike.

Matt later told me that Timberwood was his least favorite rehab of all the ones he had been to. He said there wasn't enough structure, and most of the time, the groups were run by the inpatients themselves, sometimes without counselors there. I thought he would have liked having less structure. At Bayview House he and his friends always complained that they just sat in a room all day, listening to counselors talk about the same things. Timberwood also gave inpatients one-time sessions of reflexology, acupuncture, massage, and equine therapy. They certainly took a different approach than the other facilities he had been to. Again I thought a different approach would be good for him, although the acupuncture and reflexology had absolutely no bearing on why we had taken him there. The main reason he had gone to Timberwood was because it was the one facility that could take him right away and because it had a detox unit.

Matt recently told us that, on his second day into round five, he had found one of his syringes in the pocket of a pair of his jeans. That's what helped him form his negative opinion of the place. It also planted the seed in his mind about getting high, and that's what he thought about, day and night, while he was there, and why he was determined to be discharged as soon as he possible. Once he told us that, it explained a lot.

I felt like we should start researching other places at that point, just in case. That was a terrible way to think; we had no faith in him or in "the drive" he said he had this time. We had no reason to have faith in him; after all he was in his fifth round of rehab. But I felt we should give him support and encouragement. Outwardly I did, but not in my heart. Mike and I always had been so frantic, looking for a place that would take him. I felt it couldn't hurt to have some places in mind. We were desperately looking for a place to bring him, even just for one night, then deal with the next day later. He needed a place to detox safely, and while he was doing that, I thought we could try to find a longer-term facility. Do these thoughts show that I had little faith in him? No. It's just my nature to be prepared.

I should have been a Boy Scout.

CHAPTER ONE HUNDRED TWELVE

Matt was discharged from Timberwood on Wednesday, October 11, after just eighteen days in rehab. He moved right into an Oxford House a few towns from where we lived. So much for long term. He felt the light bulb never had gone on before, but this time it did, and he knew what he needed to do and what he needed to avoid. Matt asked if we could help him out again with the money Oxford House required upfront (the first two weeks' rent and a nonrefundable security deposit), as well as grocery money. The counselor had asked, "What if your parents had said no to that?" I'd said that I wasn't going to blackmail him into going to a long-term facility. She suggested that he agree to long-term help if he not come through with a job (and paying his own way) after two weeks. Matt never responded to that suggestion.

I knew Matt never would agree to go. After the initial two weeks—when we would help him out—were up, however, he would be on his own and suffer the consequences. If he didn't get a job, he couldn't pay his rent. If he didn't pay his rent, Oxford House would ask him to leave. After Oxford House had kicked him out the last time, we'd thought he'd had a place to live. Sleeping on someone's floor wasn't an ideal situation, but at least he'd had somewhere to go. Soon after he got out of rehab, he told us there were a couple of nights when he had slept on benches on the boardwalk because there were no available floors those nights. He told us he had stolen dough-nuts from the grocery store so he would have at least a little food in his stomach. He said he had picked up cigarette butts from the street in order to satisfy his nicotine cravings.

Was that his rock bottom? Did he know what to do to make sure that didn't happen again? Really, we couldn't stop him. He was an adult. We told him, for probably the hundredth time, that we always would help him get help, that we always would love him uncondi-tionally, and that we would never give up on him. We also told him, though, that while he was always welcome at our house—to hang out for the day or have lunch or dinner with us—he no longer could sleep here, and certainly not live here.

Once he was out of round five of rehab and living in an Oxford House, he seemed very calm about getting around to all of his vari-ous meetings, IOP, the library, job-hunting, and doctor's appoint-ments. He had no car and hadn't dropped any hints about needing one. He seemed content to rely on public transportation. If he could get around New York City using public transportation, he could cer-tainly do it in New Jersey.

He was very anxious to find an old cell phone so he could get it set up with his phone number and make calls. I knew he would fig-ure it out. When it came to a phone, he was never too long without one. He was still getting settled into his new room and wanted to get to meetings.

I hoped that was it. A twenty-eight-day stay didn't work. A three-month stay didn't work. So maybe a shortened stay was the answer.

He seemed ready to get out of the gate and get moving on a getting job, finding a career, staying clean, and having a real life. I prayed that he would see that a life free from drugs could be a very good one.

After he had been out of rehab for just a week, I had the feeling that he had gotten out too early. We were kind of worried. He had IOP set up, but he had overslept and missed his first appointment. He said he had gone to Atlantic City in the morning and applied for jobs at a couple of places but didn't feel very well and had lain around for the rest of the day. He did get a replacement phone, but he wasn't replying to our texts.

I called one of Matt's counselors at Timberwood to see why he had been discharged so early, when we originally had discussed a twenty-eight-day stay and then a long-term facility, and I got the impression that he agreed. What had changed from Matt's first week there? At first the counselor said it had to do with insurance. I knew that wasn't the case and told him so. I could hear him shuffling some papers (Matt's files, I would hope), and then he told me that Matt had made it clear to anyone and everyone that he had been through the process of rehab so many times that he knew the lectures, knew what he had to do, and wanted to get out and do it. I asked whether he signed out AMA (against medical advice). The counselor replied that in rehab lingo, it was actually called signing out ACA (against clinical advice), and that, yes, that is what Matt had done. Matt insisted that he hadn't and that he had a certificate of completion.

It was a rough few days, as Matt sort of dropped off the face of the earth for a while. He said he didn't know why he had no motivation and didn't want to communicate. I knew depression after rehab was fairly common. He had court scheduled for the end of the week, so I knew he likely would say that he had a lot on his mind.

I told him he should be talking to someone at IOP, which he had yet to attend since he had been discharged. He was supposed to see his probation officer, but I didn't know if he had gone. He also was supposed to go with one of his friends to the restaurant where his friend worked so he could be introduced to the manager, in the hopes that they were hiring. I didn't know whether that had happened.

I agreed with the counselors at Stonebridge, who told us that Matt couldn't live independently, at least not yet. He needed a keeper, a babysitter, a drill sergeant who would make him get up and go.

Is this what the rest of his life would be like? Even if he could stay away from drugs, had his mind been so damaged that he just couldn't be organized, motivated, and responsible? And if he couldn't be these things, where would he go?

CHAPTER ONE HUNDRED THIRTEEN

In October I knew something was wrong. Matt had disappeared. I found out that he was no longer living at the Oxford House. I didn't know exactly when he had left or where he had gone. In the midst of calling him, his friends, and his counselors in an attempt to track him down, I also was receiving several calls on my cell phone that were listed as "private caller." Most were just silence followed by a hang-up, but when I got the last call, and I asked who it was, the male caller whispered, "You have to guess." It didn't sound like Matt, or anyone I knew, and it wasn't it anyone in my phone directory. Maybe it was just a coincidence, but it was scary.

At that point I was even more worried than before.

When I finally got a call from Matt, he admitted that Oxford House had kicked him out for using the previous weekend. He relapsed just eight days after being discharged (prematurely, in everyone's opinion) from round five. I had texted a couple of his friends in an attempt to locate him. I got no reply from his newest friend, and Chris said he hadn't spoken to Matt in a while.

Once Matt told me where he had been, I texted his new friend, said I knew Matt was staying with him, and thanked him for letting him do so. He actually called me back to apologize for not answering my texts and said he felt bad for not reassuring me. He said he knew that Matt was OK and that if he were sick or in trouble, he would have called me right away. Chris and another friend of Matt's, Ryan, also had been texting me, concerned for Matt. Matt might have associated with a lot of unsavory people, but he did have a few good friends. I hoped he realized just how good they were.

He finally got himself set up with IOP and had an appointment scheduled with his probation officer. Matt said that this was a one-time slip-up and that he could get through this and stay clean on his own. Why did I conveniently forget about all the other "one-time slip-ups" he'd had?" He said he would wait another week or so and reapply for living arrangements at another Oxford House. He was due in court at the end of the week, so we knew he may not have had a choice.

CHAPTER ONE HUNDRED FOURTEEN

Matt's court date was at 9:00 a.m. in Middlesex County. Because he needed to leave Ocean City by 6:00 a.m., he slept at our house the night before. I, however, didn't sleep at all. Since the previous weekend, when he had used, and over the following few days, when he was MIA, he either had straightened himself out and was really working hard to get it together, or he had turned on his acting skills again. I knew I had every reason to question his actions and his motives.

When something good happened (something simple, such as his making calls to set up appointments or filling out job applications), I always questioned it. Did he really do these things, or was he just saying he had so I would stop nagging him?

And why couldn't I sleep? I knew he couldn't access our important papers. Matt was safe, and we were safe. So why was I wide awake at two o'clock in the morning?

During this time, Chris had been trying to reach Matt, but Matt wasn't returning his calls or texts. After I really pressed Matt, it came to light that he had borrowed money from Chris over the summer

($140, when Matt was working and supposedly paying his own rent to Oxford House) and again in September, just before he had gone to round five of rehab. Chris had wired him $60 at Matt's request, saying he had to pay someone back and didn't want to ask us. Matt had been saying he wanted to get high one last time before going to rehab. I guess that's how he had gotten the money. Chris didn't know that was what it was for and felt terrible once he found out.

I wondered whether there was anyone else out there to whom Matt owed money. I also wondered how many friendships he had lost along the way, over the past three years, because of it. Early in this mess he had "borrowed" from college buddies or people in Little Silver, all of whom he probably wouldn't see again. There were a few good people, though, whom he really conned. His friend from Little Silver, Nate, had given him money for a baseball ticket that never existed. Daniella was certainly an innocent party in all of this. A couple of his Little Silver friends were good guys. I wasn't sure, again, if he really ever owed them money or if Matt just threw their names in as part of the story. I couldn't think of any other meaningful, good friends in his life he had screwed over financially, but I was sure there were more. I was amazed at how readily people I never knew to be "friends" of his had given him money. Or maybe they hadn't. Maybe every one of the stories was a lie, told just so Matt could get money from us in order to buy heroin. As far as we knew, all of these friends were paid back, by us, if he really owed them money at all.

But I believe Chris did lend him money, and I would make sure he got it back. Yes, it was Matt's responsibility to pay him back, but he didn't have any money (nor any conscience, it would seem), and it wasn't fair to Chris, who wasn't working either and who was struggling to stay clean, just like Matt. I would make sure that Chris got his money.

My guess was that when the drugs messed with Matt's brain cells, they also messed with his conscience. I wondered whether he even knew wrong from right anymore.

I read a February 2012 article on NPR's weekly blog that discussed a study of brains among siblings—some of whom were and some of whom weren't drug addicts. The study mostly focused on cocaine, but I believe that any drug could be substituted. The article stated the following.

> *A study in Science finds that cocaine addicts have abnormalities in areas of the brain involved in self-control. And these abnormalities appear to predate any drug abuse.*
>
> *The study, done by a team at the University of Cambridge in the U.K., looked at fifty pairs of siblings. One member of each pair was a cocaine addict. The other had no history of drug abuse.*
>
> *But brain scans showed that both siblings had brains unlike those of typical people, says Karen Ersche, the study's lead author.*
>
> *"The fibers that connect the different parts of the brain were less efficient in both," she says.*
>
> *These fibers connect areas involved in emotion with areas that tell us when to stop doing something, Ersche says. When the fibers aren't working efficiently, she says, it takes longer for a "stop" message to get through.*
>
> *And sure enough, another experiment done by Ersche's team showed that both siblings took longer than a typical person to respond to a signal telling them to stop performing a task. In other words, they had less self-control.*
>
> *That's what you'd expect to find in addicts, Ersche says.*
>
> *"We know that in people who are addicted to drugs like cocaine, that self-control is completely impaired," she says. "These people use drugs and lose control on how much they use. They put everything at risk, even their lives."*

But the fact that siblings without drug problems also had impaired self-control offers strong evidence that these brain abnormalities are inherited, Ersche says.

And she says the finding also raises a big question about the siblings who aren't addicts: "How do they manage with an abnormal brain without taking drugs?"

The findings about self-control have implications that go far beyond drug addiction, says Nora Volkow, director of the National Institute on Drug Abuse.

"Self-control and the ability to regulate your emotions really is an indispensable aspect of the function of the brain that allows us to succeed," she says.

That's because the part of the brain that decides whether to take a drug is also the part that helps us decide whether to speed through a yellow light or drop out of school, she says.

And this brain circuit seems to be involved in a lot of common disorders, she says.

"One of the ones that attracts the most attention is ADHD (attention deficit hyperactivity disorder), where kids are unable to control their response to stimuli that distract them," Volkow says.

Impulse control is also central to behaviors like compulsive gambling and compulsive eating, she says.

The new study shows it's possible to identify people who have inherited a susceptibility to these sorts of problems, Volkow says. And it should help researchers figure out how to help susceptible people strengthen their self-control, she says.

"Predetermination is not predestination," Volkow says.

So maybe drugs didn't totally cause Matt's brain to be scrambled; maybe it was scrambled from the start.

CHAPTER ONE HUNDRED FIFTEEN

Six weeks after Matt left round five of rehab, he still hadn't found a job. He came to our house on a Saturday to use the computer to look for jobs. He finally left around 3:00 p.m., after asking for money so he could buy a bus pass and get a haircut. He said he was going to fill out applications at a few places, get the haircut, and go to a meeting. We agreed that he would have my car back by 9:00 p.m. He called around that time to see if he could keep the car overnight; he said one of the places he wanted to apply to was only open for breakfast and lunch, so he wanted to go back there first thing in the morning and then go to a meeting. Reluctantly we agreed.

We didn't hear from him the next day, so we called and texted him around noon. He finally returned one of our texts a little after one o'clock, saying that the owner of the restaurant was busy (what a surprise—a restaurant busy at mealtime!) and had asked him to come back in a bit when they weren't so busy. So could he call us back in a few minutes? He didn't call.

We called and texted him for three more hours. We said we were considering calling the police to report that our car had been stolen. No replies. We finally drove to the rooming house where his newest friend was staying and on whose floor Matt had been sleeping. My car was parked on the side street next to the building, so we just took it. I wondered how long it would take Matt to wake up, come down, and realize the car was no longer there.

Mike was beyond furious. He kept saying that if he had a heart attack, maybe Matt might finally get the message that this was what he was doing to us. I told him he couldn't have a heart attack and leave me alone to deal with all of this.

So what would Matt's story be? Would he lie? Of course he would. Would he say his phone was on vibrate and he had fallen asleep? Would he say that he had used again? Or would it be some new and creative story?

And how long would it take for us to unravel it?

CHAPTER ONE HUNDRED SIXTEEN

More stories unraveled.

Matt hinted that the new friend, on whose floor he was sleeping, was struggling to make ends meet because work was slow, and that, since Matt had been staying with him for a couple of weeks, maybe we should give him half the rent money. I gave him $200 and thought it was generous, but then I thought about it and realized that Matt actually had been staying with him for three weeks, so I said I would give him a little more. As Matt and I were figuring it out, though, it came out that Matt actually had stayed with him for a couple of weeks before he had gone into round five, and he wondered whether I could give him the rest of the money so his friend could pay his landlord. I said no; before he had left for round five, we regularly had given him $70 to give to a different friend for rent (for sleeping on his floor).

Matt admitted that he actually had stayed with that friend only for one week, and the other times when we had given him rent money, he was really sleeping on the new friend's floor, rent free, and using the money for drugs. Surprise, surprise. He didn't understand my logic that we did pay out money for the privilege of his sleeping on a floor prior to Timberwood. It was unfortunate that some of it should have gone to his new friend, but instead he had spent it on drugs, but I said I couldn't give his friend any more money at that point. Whether he gave the money to this friend or that friend, whether he put it up his nose or in his arm, we still put out the money.

That being said, Matt was fine, pleasant, understanding, and seemed to be in a good frame of mind, even though the end result of the conversation wasn't what he wanted. But that could change in a heartbeat. I spoke once to George, his counselor at his most recent outpatient facility, but I wanted to talk to him again about Matt's issues of closing up. Even his newest friend had said that something was bothering Matt or that Matt was worrying about something, but he didn't know what. Guilt? Concern about not having a job? Who knew? Maybe there were more lies, big ones, that he wanted to tell us about, or thought he had to tell us about, but was afraid to.

CHAPTER ONE HUNDRED SEVENTEEN

Matt was due to move into another Oxford House on Halloween, so again we would be giving them two weeks' rent and the security deposit. At least we would give that to Oxford House directly in the form of a money order. Matt must have thought we were his personal ATM—and we were.

The weather was horrible the weekend before Halloween. There was flooding in Ocean City and snow in the Philadelphia area. Matt was bored and had nowhere else to go, and none of his friends were around, so he asked if he could hang out at our house for a while.

Mike went to pick him up, and they arrived just as chocolate chip cookies were coming out of the oven. Next I was planning to make peanut-butter-cup ice cream for him. He said he wanted to watch—and help, just like when he was little. I made chowder, and he stayed for dinner; he seemed in no rush to leave. After dinner he helped Mike download something from his brother's iPod.

He seemed good and sounded well. He talked a bit about a meeting he'd had with some people from a couple of clubs in the casinos, set up by his sponsor. He said it looked like he might get some work from both places.

Mike drove him back to the rooming house. I knew that Matt would ask if they could stop for cigarettes and that Matt would ask Mike for the money. But Mike didn't complain about it when he came home, so it was a very pleasant and peaceful day, and a lovely evening.

CHAPTER ONE HUNDRED EIGHTEEN

During the first week of November 2011, I was reading my journal entries from about a year before, a time when Matt was struggling and ultimately relapsing. My mood was down, and I wasn't sure whether I was mixing up the Matt of November 2011 with the Matt of November 2010. Or were they still the same person?

I thought he was staying clean; however, he had asked for money recently. He said he needed it to go out to dinner with his sponsor, who was one of the entertainment acts at a club in one of the casinos and who was working with his bosses to secure Matt a job there. Matt was supposed to meet with the man who would be his boss and who would set up his hours for the following week. Matt wanted money so he could take his sponsor to dinner as a thank-you. Was I wrong? This was a grown man with a steady job, who, according to Matt, ate most of his meals out, at nicer and pricier restaurants than Matt would frequent. One would think he would be in a much better position to pay for Matt's dinner than the other way around. Matt had met with his sponsor several times over meals, so he had said, when his sponsor was having a late lunch or early dinner, so Matt always asked for money so he could eat too. If this scenario was true, what was Matt trying to prove? The sponsor knew Matt's story; he knew he had been in and out of rehab and didn't have a job yet. Why would he expect that Matt could go out with him for a $30 lunch every week?

Was the story even true? Or did I doubt it because of what I was reading that day and because I was remembering events from Christmas 2010, when he was using but we were unaware of it? Was I confusing that erratic behavior with his behavior over the past couple of weeks?

CHAPTER ONE HUNDRED NINETEEN

Mike and I found out that Matt never went to Oxford House on Halloween, because he was afraid he wouldn't pass a drug test, which meant he had continued to use beyond his relapse on October 18, which we had thought was just a one-time relapse. So he told them he needed to put off his move-in for a week and would move in the following Monday, but he never showed up. He was afraid of a dirty test, I suppose, or, as he said, just embarrassed about not going the previous week.

Yet when I had handed him the money order for $560 on October 31, I'd told him he'd better be sure he was ready to move in, and he'd better not forfeit the money because of a relapse. He didn't care. He was back to sleeping on people's floors.

He conned me out of $120; he said he was going to buy an $83 bus pass he could use all month and then get a haircut and some groceries. He showed me the bus pass—proof of how he had spent that money—but what did he do with the other $37? He didn't get his hair cut. He bought…what? Food? Cigarettes? Drugs?

He said he didn't feel he needed to detox. I didn't even approach the subject of long-term inpatient treatment. He wanted to go to IOP that night, though, so I drove him there. I had talked to George several times that day, so I was hoping he would be able to pull Matt aside and talk some sense into him. Mike had had it. He said he could tell that Matt didn't want him as a father and also that Matt didn't want to be his son. Matt always went through me, usually via text message, if he had anything to say to Mike. It was so sad, and I felt horrible for Mike. I knew it was devastating to him.

Matt said he was very disappointed that he wasn't in the Oxford House and wanted badly to be there. I told him obviously he didn't want it that badly, because he couldn't stay clean. He knew he had to get clean for probation and for court.

What would happen after that? Would the cycle continue or finally end? It seemed like the more Matt needed help, the less willing he was to get it. When he was feeling good about himself and doing well was when he was most willing to go into rehab for the long haul.

I felt Matt was running out of time. For what I didn't know. Time to get himself together? Time to admit he needed help? He seemed so depressed. He had agreed to see a psychiatrist and possibly start taking antidepressants. I felt he needed to do it as soon as possible. George had told him that if he missed another IOP session and/or failed a drug test, he would send a letter to his probation officer, recommending that Matt needed long-term rehab.

I was sure Matt was feeling overwhelmed with so much going on. He had no job (although he was still saying that the job would come through at the club where his sponsor worked) and no place to live (all he had to do was call Oxford House and see if the slot was still open, unless he was still using), and he needed to talk to someone (all he had to do was call one of the psychiatrists on the list I had given him and set up an appointment).

Mike and I had invited him to come to our house for dinner on Friday. I'm not really sure why—just to talk a little, I think, about the next steps for him regarding work, counseling, and living arrangements. We didn't bother him all day; we just picked him up when it was time. It was horrible, like having an eight-hundred-pound gorilla in the room. He sat sullenly on the couch, staring at the TV. He came to the table when dinner was ready then retreated again. I don't think Matt and Mike spoke to each other at all.

On the drive back to the rooming house, I talked to him about reaching out to someone—a friend, counselor, or sponsor (although he and George decided that he needed to find a new sponsor, someone who kept hours that were more similar to Matt's)—and just talk. It wouldn't necessarily put him in a great mood, but it might take some of the weight off his chest and shoulders and help him get through the day.

Because that's what it's about—one day at a time.

Then I came home and brought in some stuff that had been in my car for a while—trash, a bottle of water, etc. I used the water to wash down my bedtime medicines and realized it wasn't just water. It tasted bitter, like it had something else in it. I called Matt, and he said he knew nothing about it. We wondered whether we should go to his counselor with it (literally give the bottle of water to him) or tell Matt first that we were going to do that. Would he suddenly have an explanation for it? If it wasn't his, would he rat out a buddy? Or would he continue to say he had no knowledge of it? If continued to deny it, we would have to take it to George.

CHAPTER ONE HUNDRED TWENTY

It boggled my mind that insurance could be so limiting when it came to drug-addiction treatment. In counseling sessions, Mike and I had learned that addiction is a disease. And who is the insurance company to say that this disease can be "cured" with twenty-eight days of inpatient treatment? In our case they said that the client had to have tried, and failed, outpatient treatment first. I sent an appeal, with documentation of Matt's prior outpatient treatment, but because it was several years prior, going back to high school, they stood by their denial.

What will it take to prove to insurance carriers that more coverage is needed? Certainly addicts die every day because they don't get help. I'm not saying their deaths are on the hands of the insurance carriers. Maybe these addicts don't want help. But what will it take to show the insurance companies how intense the treatment needs to be? I pray it's not my son who teaches them that lesson.

But it's not just the insurance carriers. The system as a whole needs an overhaul. Studies have shown that just 2 percent of addicts get clean and stay clean. It seems to me that no matter how "good" a rehab facility is, the statistics don't vary much.

Does the government need to get involved and mandate unlimited inpatient care for addicts who qualify, the qualifications being that the addict shows true desire for rehabilitation? Certainly there are addicts who know the system well and would go to rehab or detox units only if they were out of drug money, out of food, in need of a shower, and sicker than they ever have felt before, but I feel there are an equal number of addicts who really want to kick the disease but are limited by the boundaries of their insurance carriers. And if they want to get better, to get clean and stay clean, their first thought, or the thoughts of their loved ones, shouldn't be, *Can we afford it?*

I'm sure there are many people who wonder why insurance would continue to pay for treatment at all. Did we just have a really good insurance plan? I think so. Regardless of Matt's issues, we knew Tim and Laura always would have medical issues, and we needed the best coverage available. Yes, it helped that the company Mike worked for offered wonderful benefits, but he also had a lot of money taken out of his paychecks for the privilege of having those benefits.

Clearly Matt knew the system. Rehab meant nothing to him. It was just a waste of time to him, I think, but at least he got meals and a bed out of it. He knew the right things to say and do while he was there—how to be a model patient—so he could be discharged on time or ahead of schedule. He also knew how to time his drug use so he would pass a scheduled drug test (at probation meetings or one of the days he attended IOP). He knew that if he might fail a drug test at probation, all he had to do was admit it right away and not take the test (therefore there would be no official documentation that he had failed it). That way he could avoid being in violation as long as he said he wanted to go to rehab.

I was sure many addicts knew the system as well, which told me there's something wrong with the system. It seemed like rehab wasn't helping an awful lot of addicts, including Matt. Maybe they didn't really want help on a permanent basis, but there must be something else that could work. As the saying goes, "If they can put a man on the moon…" I will finish it. "…why can't they come up with a cure, a deterrent, something, to get addicts to get clean and stay that way?" The way it is now seems like a charade to me.

Matt didn't think he needed help. Yes, he said he would talk to a psychiatrist in order to get a prescription for antidepressants—which, in all likelihood, he wouldn't take. He never was good at taking medication on a regular basis, whether it was a vitamin or a course of antibiotics. He was the kind of person who would sporadically take medication, if he remembered, even if he was supposed to take it daily.

One day he seemed ready to buckle down and help himself, with the help of others, as an outpatient. By the next day, however, he was back to believing he didn't have a problem.

Mike and I tried another dinner with Matt a week or so after the disastrous dinner. There were no fights, unless they occurred while he and Mike were outside. I talked to Matt about my book and got a little information from him. He said he would answer the questions I asked and hoped his answers wouldn't make us madder, or mad all over again. I said I was asking as a writer and was just doing my research and needed to get the facts straight. So it all went well. Nothing really surprising came out, but some truths did bubble to the surface.

I asked him about the bottle of water again. He tasted it and agreed that it definitely tasted off. All he could think of was that when he was shooting he may have cleaned or flushed the needle in the bottle of water, and there may have been heroin remnants on it.

Right after he said that, he poured the water down the drain. Reflex action? Or did he want to destroy evidence? Was it a true story? Did it even matter?

We asked him about his sponsor, the lunches, and the potential jobs. He said he did go to lunch with him once, so when we gave him the money one time, it was legitimate. The other times we had given him money for lunch with his sponsor, he had spent it on drugs. He said his sponsor knew that he had relapsed and said that the job possibility would have to wait a few weeks for Matt to come down and clean up, and then maybe they would revisit the job possibility. Matt said he really did talk to someone from the music club in one of the casinos who had said he would call if something came up, but Matt said he hadn't heard from him. Matt was assuming that his sponsor had told him about the relapse. I saw an ad in the local paper several months later for someone to work at the club where his sponsor worked, in the ticket area. So apparently there really was a job that he could have had if only he had stayed clean.

Matt also talked to us about Oxford House. He said he was embarrassed to call the one in Ocean City, because of the way he had handled it when he was supposed to move in there at the end of October and again at the beginning of November. He said he had left a message at another Oxford House in Ventnor City, where he had lived when he was released from Timberwood, to see whether there were any openings.

If his stories were true, it sounded like he had relapsed on October 18 and had used drugs every few days for at least a couple of weeks.

CHAPTER ONE HUNDRED TWENTY-ONE

After having some dental work done, Matt spent an afternoon at our house. Two cavities had taken over his front teeth, one of which had led to his needing a root canal. He wasn't happy. "He only gave me one shot of Novocain," he said, "and he didn't even tell me he was doing the root canal until he was halfway finished!" We went to the grocery store with the intention of getting soup for him, but instead he found some stir-fry shrimp lo mein that he thought sounded like something he'd be able to eat.

He cooked his meal, seemingly happy to be puttering around in the kitchen, insisting that Mike and I both try some of it. Then he stretched out on the couch, watching TV and snoozing. At one point, out of the blue, he said, "I love this house. It's so comfortable and cozy." I told him I was surprised at that, because he never seemed to take an interest in it, either when we first bought it, or later, during the renovations. I said I could understand that, because he had grown up in the "big" Little Silver house, so that's where his memories were. He reminisced about that house a bit (he said it had an awesome finished basement) but reiterated that he loved the warmth and comfort here.

I almost felt like he was up to something. Was he going to ask us if he could live here if he didn't get into the Oxford House? Or was it really just a nice, genuine comment? I never could be sure.

He asked me which of us would drive him to IOP that night. I said I was pretty tired and hoped Mike would drive him. He replied that he'd had a nice time with me the previous day (when I drove him to his psychiatry appointment and then waited for AAA to come and replace my car's battery after my car wouldn't start). I had gotten him a piece of pizza and then finally dropped him off at IOP. That night, at the house, I told him I wanted him to feel that way about being out with Mike for an afternoon.

CHAPTER ONE HUNDRED TWENTY-TWO

I couldn't put my finger on it. I knew Matt was frustrated by not having a car. I knew he must be bored to tears, sitting in his friend's room all day. I wanted to tell him that he had put himself in this situation, but I didn't want to rub salt in his wounds.

I had put $150 on a Visa gift card over the last ten days, for groceries and a bus pass to get him around Ventnor City. He didn't buy the bus pass. He had convinced me that the Visa gift card was more sensible than a grocery card, because he could use the Visa card anywhere. Before that I had given him cash to get a bus pass to use between Ocean City and Atlantic City. An unlimited monthly pass costs $83, which left him $16 to buy some lunch and a pack of cigarettes. He didn't buy that ticket; instead he bought a cheaper ticket that was good for just ten trips.

He seemed clearheaded, not cranky or agitated. He smoked a lot of cigarettes; he admitted to a pack a day, but he probably smoked more than that. If he wasn't using at that point, I was afraid that his frustration and boredom might drive him to use again.

He would be seeing his psychiatrist before Thanksgiving and also would go to IOP. He was scheduled to move into Oxford House the week before Thanksgiving, although I would double-check with the house to actually confirm that.

CHAPTER ONE HUNDRED TWENTY-THREE

The day before Thanksgiving 2011, I took a break from Thanksgiving preparations (dinner for twenty-five people at our house!) to regroup and go over the events of the last day and a half. My mind was still spinning. When would this all end?

Matt was supposed to have moved into an Oxford House in Ventnor City at the beginning of the week, but with his IOP and another appointment, he could only get there at about 5:00 p.m., and the house manager called him to say that no one would be at the house at that time; could he move in on Tuesday instead? That was fine, except I had called Tuesday to double-check on the time, and the house manager had said, "Yeah, we were expecting Matt last night, but he never showed up." I said that someone named Jack had called Matt and said that the timing wouldn't work out on Monday, and Matt should come on Tuesday instead. He said that he was Jack, but he hadn't called Matt.

Mike and I played out the charade a bit, picking Matt up and bringing him to our house so he could get a few of his things out of the garage, and then we confronted him. He said he didn't want to live in the Ventnor house; he really wanted to live in the Ocean City house. OK, all he had to do was say so. But why did I get the money order he needed? He only needed one for $180, because he still had one of the money orders, for $280, from when he was supposed to move in to the Ocean City house on Halloween. At that time we had given him one money order for $300 and another for $280; he cashed the $300 one and used the money for drugs.

I asked for the two money orders back, since he wasn't moving in, but he said he didn't have them. He had cashed both of those in order to repay people he had borrowed money from a few weeks before, when he had bought drugs.

He knew, though, that he had to straighten himself out. He went to IOP and made an appointment to talk to George, one on one, prior to the next day's IOP session. Additionally he would make some calls and try to get an appointment with a psychiatrist. (We had just found out that the psychiatrist he was seeing was actually a psychologist and therefore could not prescribe medication.)

I spoke to him around 11:00 a.m. on the day before Thanksgiving to see if he needed a ride anywhere, since I'd be heading his way. He said he didn't need to go anywhere but added that he might go out later and then go right to counseling. Mike and I were busy with work that day, finishing up some projects prior to the holiday, and then starting to prepare what we could ahead of time for Thanksgiving dinner.

George called us around seven thirty to say that Matt hadn't shown up for IOP or for the private session. He told us Matt needed to do a lot of work in order to kick this, but he didn't seem willing to work. We finally got Matt on the phone, and he said that he had lain down after I had called earlier and had just woken up.

Really.

We told him to figure out his life and to call us when he had a plan.

I figured we wouldn't be seeing him for the big family dinner. Happy Thanksgiving.

CHAPTER ONE HUNDRED TWENTY-FOUR

It actually turned out to be a very happy Thanksgiving.

Matt was in much better spirits. Thanksgiving Eve was bad; maybe it was his way—once we had found out and confronted him about his latest transgressions—to have an initial reaction of withdrawing and going into his shell. Maybe…maybe…maybe what? Was he concerned or afraid of our reactions? Doubtful. We never had done more than yell. We never had forbidden him from setting foot in our house, never threatened to disown him. Was he so ashamed and embarrassed that he couldn't face us, or anyone, for a while?

Matt did come to our house for Thanksgiving. He called to ask if he could come over around noon. I picked him up around then, and his friend came as well, since he had just found out that he didn't have to work after all. They helped us get things set up—the rugs, tables, chairs, and coolers. His friend was always polite and in good spirits, and Matt was in a good mood as well. Both seemed relaxed and comfortable around all of the relatives.

They left after dessert, not unusually early, saying they wanted to go to a meeting. Prior to leaving, Mike's brother Dan had invited Matt and Mike to go fishing the next day, so Matt took my car and would bring it back in the morning.

Shortly after he left on Thanksgiving night, he texted both Mike and me, thanking us for allowing him to come to Thanksgiving dinner, even though he had let us down and had kind of screwed up the previous day. Maybe something was starting to sink in, like just how much he hurt us when he did these things.

Happy Thanksgiving.

CHAPTER ONE HUNDRED TWENTY-FIVE

Matt arrived as planned at eight thirty in the morning, and he and Mike got back from fishing around four. They'd had a nice day; there wasn't a lot of talking, as they were concentrating on fishing, but there was no arguing either. It was just a relaxing day on the water.

Matt stayed at our house that night, as his friend had company, and three people sharing a single room would be a little too tight. It was to be only for one night. We had said a while back that he would never sleep in this house again, unless it was for our convenience, like before an early court date. Except for leaving to go to a meeting, he was here for the whole night, relaxing with the family (although totally in charge of the remote control!) and seeming perfectly content to do so.

It was a very pleasant evening. However, even when he wasn't using—and I couldn't be sure that he wasn't—he was continually guilty of lying and stealing, in one form or another, along with forgery at times. I knew I never could let my guard down.

When he did these things, I don't think he realized that what he was doing was wrong. Did his mind go into an alter-ego state? And then did it flip back to the other Matt, who was devastated by what he had done?

There was no figuring him out.

Matt stayed with us a second night; his friend still had a houseguest. The three of us went to Trenton that second night, so I could meet the people from City of Angels-Kevin and a man called Red Neck. While Mike and I talked with Kevin and Red Neck, Matt sat in on a Recovery meeting and then an NA meeting. I think he was half expecting that it was a set up to get him into rehab, since the last time Matt was there, he did go right from there to rehab. (It wasn't a set up that time; he knew he was going.) After he realized Kevin and Red Neck were just going to talk to him and tell him about a long-term facility, he relaxed a bit. Mike, Matt and I stopped at a diner on the way home for a late dinner. Matt was teasing me about ordering a turkey salad wrap, when I had eaten turkey for lunch and dinner for the past several days.

All in all it was a very nice Thanksgiving weekend.

CHAPTER ONE HUNDRED TWENTY-SIX

I recently heard someone say, about addicts in general, "Are his lips moving? Then he's lying."

After staying at our house that Saturday night, Matt borrowed my car to go to a meeting Sunday morning, and Mike went poking in Matt's backpack. Mike constantly wondered what he carried around in it, if he wasn't using drugs, and ever since he found the drug paraphernalia in it a while back, he was always suspicious when he saw the backpack.

What he found were some banking slips. As I was a mom who always came to his defense when he wasn't there to defend himself, I mentioned that Matt had convinced me to get him a Visa gift card, rather than one from a grocery store, and that money could be added to it as needed. That was fine; I understood that. He could use it for whatever, rather than my making trips to the bus station or wherever to make purchases for him.

However, it looked like he had put one of the money orders I'd given him on it. Why? It wasn't as if he could buy drugs with it, or even pay back anyone to whom he owed money. Maybe it was the easiest way to take care of the money orders, since he apparently wasn't going to use them at Oxford House, and then he could withdraw money as needed. Another mystery.

Mike checked the NA/AA schedules for that day to see where Matt was. There were no meetings in the area at the time he left. Mike called him and told him to bring the car home right away. I'm sure Matt knew, at that moment, that he was busted for something—again.

If we had the story right, and Matt said we did, he had used the most recent money order (for $180) to open a bank account. He had taken our car to the ATM at Wawa after we were asleep Saturday night and withdrawn $100 of it at 1:00 a.m. on Sunday, after getting a call from someone who wanted the money he had loaned to Matt. Apparently the guy wasn't satisfied with a partial payment; he wanted everything that was owed to him, so Matt went back to the same ATM and withdrew another $100, after agreeing to the $35 overdraft fee. So, at that point, he had a brand-new bank account that was already overdrawn. He had used this trick when this whole mess first started, during his last year of college, so he knew exactly what he was doing.

We were speculating that he had used drugs the Monday or Tuesday before Thanksgiving, felt like crap on Wednesday, and would have failed a drug test, so that's why he didn't go to the meeting with George or to IOP. He felt better by Thursday and was in good spirits for the rest of the week.

The full story would reveal itself soon enough.

He never ceased to amaze me with his lying and acting abilities. No, he apparently didn't financially or physically harm us this time (except for cashing the money orders that were meant for Oxford House) and hadn't stolen anything from us recently that we were aware of, but he was driving around in a car not registered to him and without our permission. Additionally he had given out our address as his address to the bank and to his probation officer, and put it on job applications. At least (hopefully) he hadn't also given out our phone number.

Mike told him to get his things together, and he would drive him to wherever he wanted to be dropped off. I told him I would call him in the morning, once I knew what time his probation officer could see him for the weekly check-in. Most likely Matt wouldn't answer my call. I would go to the probation appointment anyway, which wouldn't help Matt, as he would still be in violation of probation if he didn't show up, but I wanted to find out where we stood on the violation of not paying his fines, since that was something we were paying, and we stood to gain from his answer, depending on what the probation officer had found out.

I guess I knew we weren't making any progress. Matt barely had looked for employment, even when we had given him specifics about signs we had seen and ads we had read in the paper. He really had done nothing productive since he had been discharged from Timberwood six weeks prior. After his initial relapse (which probably wasn't just a one-time thing), he just seemed to be more open and communicative.

He was acting, all along.

CHAPTER ONE HUNDRED TWENTY-SEVEN

I had gotten to know some of Matt's friends a little, once he started attending rehab and then was living in or around Ocean City. During the rougher times with Matt, I often gave into my fears and thought of all the "what ifs" and allowed my thoughts to go in the direction of whether or not Matt had the motivation to get clean and stay clean. I asked a few of his friends what they did or said to themselves that gave them that motivation.

Matt had met Anthony in Stonebridge during round three. He lived in an Oxford House the entire time he was in the South Jersey area and worked in a trendy bakery/restaurant in town. He was determined to beat this habit, and although he initially attended IOP, he never attended AA, NA, or CA meetings. He left in December 2011 to move back to North Jersey to be near his family and girlfriend. In February 2012 he celebrated one year of clean and sober living, and he and his girlfriend are getting married in September 2013.

During round three, Matt also met Chris. Chris was thirty years old and had a son who didn't live with him. He supported the child and saw him, but he said he didn't want to be an active part of his life until he was sure he could be a reliable part of it. Chris spent about a month at Malvern Institute and felt he wasn't ready to go home, so he went to Stonebridge, at the recommendation of Malvern, and spent another thirty days there. From there he moved into an Oxford House and became Matt's roommate there at one time. Before and after rehab, he worked as a mechanic. He had made enough money to support his heroin habit, and as such, didn't do anything illegal, unless you counted helping himself to medications he found in the glove compartments of cars he was working on, and of course, buying heroin. After rehab he found himself checking glove compartments again and was offered drugs by his coworkers; he opted to quit his job and collect unemployment instead. This had been his only inpatient rehab up until this point. He relapsed shortly after celebrating nine months clean and moved back home to straighten himself out again. He said there was no particular trigger that caused the relapse—just that he was unhappy, isolating himself and not going to meetings, which he said were key pieces to his staying clean.

Chris was seeing a doctor and being managed with Suboxone for a few weeks, then managed his recovery himself by going to a lot of meetings. After he moved back home, he sent me a nice text message, thanking Mike and me for always welcoming him into our home. I had kept in touch with Chris for a while. At times he was my only connection with Matt, especially when Matt would go into his shell. Then Matt stopped getting in touch with Chris. Out of sight, out of mind? Was he afraid Chris would recognize signs of relapse?

Chris helped me unravel a few of Matt's stories. It turned out that Chris had loaned Matt money a couple of times. Once was the time when Matt had said he had paid his own rent back in April, and another was when he had used the money to relapse. Chris didn't want to even ask for the money back, but because he wasn't working, he really needed it. I thought Chris would make it, but I heard that he had a very tough holiday season at the end of 2011 and had checked himself into a rehab facility at the beginning of January 2012. He's now at a sober-living house in Florida.

Ryan is also from round three. Ryan was Matt's roommate at his first Oxford House, although Matt also knew him from Stonebridge. Ryan tried inpatient rehab several times (once he only lasted for ten hours!). He said he had tried pretty much every drug, but his drugs of choice were drugs like Oxycontin and then cocaine. Once he started using cocaine, he was out of control, he said. He ended up at Stonebridge and credits Ben for telling him to give it a shot and that he might like how clean living felt. January 17, 2012 marked Ryan's one-year anniversary of being clean and sober, and he lived in the same Oxford House until he eventually got his own apartment. He has a sponsor with whom he talks almost every day. He prays daily and is slowly working on the twelve steps; so far he has gotten through the first three. Ryan graduated from college in May 2012. He wrote me the following.

The day after I got out of Stonebridge, I immediately felt a kind of peace. Right away I started going to IOP and daily meetings. God is a big part of my life. I pray a lot and say thank you to God daily, I go to meetings daily and live by the saying "One day at a time." The AA meetings are my church. Until an addict is honest with himself, it won't work. I want more out my life. I want to graduate, and I want to live.

Matt made another good friend during round four. They met through the circle of Oxford House people, although they didn't live at the same house at the same time. His new friend had been addicted to Xanax. He was in rehab for five months at Timberwood North. After a brief relapse after being out of rehab for a month, he had stayed clean up until this time. After Matt left later for round six, his friend sent me a nice text message, thanking Mike and me for always welcoming him into our home. I hoped he would stay in touch. He recently had his last court appearance, for a shoplifting charge. Because he had completed his community service and was attending NA and AA meetings regularly, all charges had been dropped, and he had no record. He graduated from college with a degree in accounting and was very excited that he could start applying for jobs in his field without the worry of a criminal record popping up.

This is what Matt's friend from round four said.

> I just remember how bad it was before I got clean. I'm not exactly in the position I'd like to be in life at the moment, but I actually am learning to become responsible. I think of what it was like to wake up every morning and never have any drugs and wonder how I was going to get my next fix. I've learned to appreciate how easy life is now that I don't have to do that, or lie, or do anything of the sort. My day is planned out, now that I'm clean, and as long as I follow that plan and go to my meetings, then I will remain clean. I literally take it one day at a time and try not to stress myself out.
>
> I could easily get upset at the fact that I'm twenty-five, living in a nasty room, with no car, and serving tables for a living, but I look at it in the sense that I have a roof over my head, and I'm fortunate enough to have a job. It's all a matter of perspective for me. Plus I love my family more than anything, and once I really understood what I was doing to them, even when I wasn't robbing them blind, I really wanted to get better and have my mother be proud of me one day.

I know that may not be the answer to your question, but I guess I find motivation in the fact that although I don't have everything I want, I have my family and friends back in my life now. For me to get high would be to jeopardize that, and that frightens me more than anything. I know for a fact that I have no more chances left with them, and I don't want to be alone in life, just to get high, plus the longer I have stayed clean, the longer I believe that everything will work itself out for the better, as long as I continue to stay clean and put in the work.

Matt has the potential to feel this way and I know he will eventually, because I see it at meetings all the time. It's just a matter of when he gets his priorities in order. He knows what he has to do to stay clean; it's just a matter of him not being lazy and doing it.

What a compelling and impassioned letter. What a great kid he was—so polite, always willing to help out, certainly my only connection to Matt many times. I thought he would be an excellent role model for Matt. At the end of 2011, Matt told me that most of what his friend had said was a lie. He wasn't just a Xanax user; he was also a heroin addict—an active heroin user. According to Matt, he never stopped using; in fact he continued to use immediately after he was discharged from rehab. Matt slept on his floor many times but has since told me that they weren't "friends"; they just procured and used drugs together. Matt had looked him up when he heard he was in town and using. This "friend" worked steadily as a waiter the entire time he was living in South Jersey and was able to support his habit without resorting to anything illegal. He and Matt worked as a team, getting money from me, with Matt saying we should chip in for rent this friend had to pay, and the friend telling me the sob story that he knew where the soup kitchens were and where he could get food if he didn't make enough money for groceries that week. He always told me that his mom and I would get along very well and wanted her and me to have lunch together the next time she came to visit. He only stayed in an Oxford House for a short time and was renting a room in a boardinghouse for the majority of his stay in South Jersey. (He had told me that he did so because he just wanted a place of his own, rather than sharing a house with several people. I later realized that it was because he couldn't live in an Oxford House if he was actively using.)

I tried texting and calling Matt's "friend" over the holidays but got no replies; his phone went right to voice mail. Matt heard later that he had gone back into rehab for a few months but is now out and clean.

This proves what accomplished liars and actors addicts are. This guy really had me fooled. And it showed me how low an addict will stoop to get the money for drugs— both Matt and this "friend."

CHAPTER ONE HUNDRED TWENTY-EIGHT

Another day, another lie.

After Matt's latest indiscretion, as was his pattern after every indiscretion, he opened up and talked honestly.

We talked about the apartment that had become available in the rooming house where he was sleeping shortly before he had left for round five. I remember that it happened very quickly, because there were some girls from out of the country living there for the summer, and they weren't sure when exactly they could vacate the apartment. He and his friends jumped at the opportunity, with one buddy's mother depositing the entire month's initial deposit and rent into his account; the others would pay him their share. We gave Matt the money he needed immediately, because I had always been like that, doing things on time, or ahead of time, and offering to do more than my share, because I never wanted it to look like we took advantage of anyone.

Then I learned that there was no apartment. Well, there may have been an apartment, and there may have been girls from another country living there for the summer, but Matt and his friends never put a deposit on it, moved into it, or even set foot in it. It was just another creative way to get several hundred dollars out of us.

More money for drugs.

Matt was back to being lazy and irresponsible. He was late yet again for his dentist's appointment. I believed he had been late for every one so far. This time it was because he was driving his buddy (in the buddy's car, because the buddy had lost his license) to a doctor's appointment. I had a really hard time understanding his logic. Mike called him several times because the dentist's office had called us to see where Matt was. Matt said he was on his way and would be there in five minutes. An hour or so later, I called the dentist's office to see whether he got there and what time he would be finished.

He never went. He called the office and canceled the appointment.

I asked him why he thought his buddy's appointment was more important than his. He just said that his friend's appointment was supposed to be really quick, and he thought he could do both.

I couldn't follow his logic.

Several months later Matt told me that his friend's appointment was to get a prescription for Suboxone, and he was willing to share it with Matt. So in a way, his friend's appointment was more important to Matt than his own appointment.

He pleaded with us to let him sleep here one more time, over the weekend. His back was killing him (he fell down the steps the previous weekend) and just couldn't sleep on the floor again. Reluctantly we agreed, but we put the car keys someplace where he couldn't get to them.

The next morning Matt was up early and borrowed my car to go to a meeting. Shortly after he left, we got a call from one of our credit card companies, telling us there had been suspicious activity on our card. On Thanksgiving weekend there had been a couple of charges on it for a couple of hundred dollars in purchases from a convenience store. The following weekend there was another couple of hundred dollars in charges from a different convenience store. The weekend he had stayed here after Thanksgiving, Matt apparently had taken my credit card out of my wallet while I was asleep. Then he took my car to the convenience store and purchased a Visa debit card in the amount of $100 and put it on my credit card. He could then use his newly purchased debit card and withdraw the money from it. It took a couple of steps but basically he took cash advances on my credit card. Then he came back to our house, replaced the credit card in my wallet, and went to sleep. He did the same thing the following weekend, after pleading with us to let him sleep here one more night, because of his sore back. Again he took my credit card while I was asleep. This time, though, because he couldn't access our car keys, someone picked him up and drove him to a different convenience store. Then he came back to our house and quietly returned the credit card to my wallet once again.

Of course Matt admitted everything when confronted. He also admitted to using again—no surprise there. Immediately we made lots of calls to lots of people and places. I think he knew he didn't have a choice. No, that wasn't true; we gave him a choice—rehab or jail. He chose rehab, although plans could change, since the credit card company was investigating the stolen credit card. My relatives felt he should be in jail. Mike did too. They were right, but I didn't have it in me to be the one to turn him in. However, his probation officer told me once that my enabling him (by giving him money) was slowly killing him. Either way I was doing him a disservice.

CHAPTER ONE HUNDRED TWENTY-NINE

In December 2011 Matt went back to Bayview House in North Jersey for round six, which is where he had been for rounds one and two. He had come full circle. Were we crazy for not doing something else, something different? To quote Albert Einstein, "Insanity—doing the same thing over and over again and expecting different results." Matt's most recent counselor, George, felt he had dual diagnoses that needed to be addressed, probably depression as well as the addiction. I asked George what he would do if he had a twenty-four-year-old son in Matt's situation. He replied that there was someone in his life who had been in Matt's shoes and that he finally had turned his life around after his parents had let him hit rock bottom, living on the streets after being kicked out of the house, barely scraping by while living on a welfare check, until his friends physically grabbed him by the arms and took him to a meeting, and then to church. At the time of our discussion, he had been clean for six years. Maybe that would happen to Matt.

We would have liked George to discuss the dual diagnoses, though, with Matt's counselor at Bayview House, Shannon, who was also his counselor when he was there before, so that Bayview House could explore this. The plan was for him to stay at Bayview House for twenty-eight days, and then his probation officer had agreed to allow him to leave the state for another thirty days of rehab. Matt always had talked about rehabs in Florida, and George told us about a couple of facilities there that dealt with dual diagnoses. The staff at Bayview House would help us find the right one. After that the extended plan was to have Matt come back to New Jersey and enter a long-term facility.

Plans changed, however. After Matt had been at Bayview House for two weeks, we had a meeting with Shannon and Matt. Matt knew what he wanted and didn't want. He didn't want to go to Florida; he wanted to stay with the program that Bayview House offered, although he would move to a different location once he was stepped down. He wanted to live again in phase two for several months, which was more rigid than an Oxford House. He didn't want to take antidepressants; he just didn't want to take any drugs. He felt he was only depressed when he was using. He was offered the option of taking a drug, given once a month by intramuscular injection, that would suppress his cravings and render him unable to get high if he took drugs anyway. Initially he wanted to take it, but later said he didn't want to rely on the drug to suppress his cravings; he said he had to learn on his own how to deal with them.

We learned a lot at this meeting; a few things were unraveled. He told us that the risks of going to jail, or dying, weren't deterrents for him when he was high or on the hunt for drugs; he wasn't afraid of either possibility when he was using. All he cared about was getting the high he was looking for.

CHAPTER ONE HUNDRED THIRTY

Throughout this journey, I had commented several times to Matt that it was a shame he hadn't kept a journal that held his thoughts from both the clean times and the times when he was actively using. He had written a beautiful essay on his Facebook page shortly after he had gotten out of rehab for the first time and what we had thought would be his only time. I mentioned that I would have liked to see those and other kinds of thoughts throughout the following few years.

A couple of weeks after he was admitted to rehab for round six, he did just that. He wrote down a summary of his thoughts and actions, starting from the time he had entered rehab for round five and up until the day he sat down and wrote them.

Finally I was able to see how the mind of an addict really works. And what he wrote summed up why this journey is a story of heartache and hope.

Well, I've done it again. This time I lasted a whole six hours. That's a record for me personally—the fastest I've relapsed out of treatment. It probably didn't help that I found a spike in my pants pocket twenty-four hours into treatment [at round five]. After moving into Oxford House, I had myself convinced I was going to stay clean, yet I decided I'd hold on to that pin, for what reason I didn't know, or I knew far too well. And the $50 my parents gave me at rehab, for books and hygiene items, I so conveniently held on to throughout treatment, subconsciously or consciously knowing exactly what I was saving that money for.

I remember waiting for the bus to Atlantic City and being so anxious to get high; I decided to save myself ten minutes and wasted $20 on a cab ride. My dealer kept telling me, "I'll be good in fifteen minutes. Just come out here." So I did that. Once I got there, I started calling him from the pay phone, because on my last run, I had traded my Blackberry and iPod for a measly ten bags of heroin. Well, what do you know—dope man isn't answering the phone. Not a surprise. I've already spent $10 in quarters on the fucking pay phone, and this mother fucker won't answer. Now I realize that I have an 11:00 p.m. curfew at my new sober-living house, and it's about 10:00 p.m. now. I guess I'll try him one more time, as I probably shouldn't risk getting kicked out over being late, but I'll definitely risk it for getting high.

Ring ring. The cop man answers. He's no good, but he knows someone who is. He tells me to walk down the street to a bad area of Pleasantville. Oh, well. That's the risk you're willing to take when the idea of getting high is in the near future.

After I've waited for fifteen minutes or so, a car rolls up, and the driver tells me to walk around the corner. Now the idea of being robbed crosses my mind, but again this is a risk I'm willing to take. I walk up to the window, and all goes well. I'm already high, and I haven't even stuck a needle in my arm yet. Within ten minutes, though, I do have a needle in my arm. Instant relief. My only love. My soul mate. My demise. My struggle. My enemy. The death of me.

Within minutes I'm no longer satisfied. I'm on the bus back to Atlantic City, wondering what the fuck transpired in the past six hours of my life. I just left rehab, literally. Now I'm lonely, depressed, and scared for what comes next. I know I just fed the beast I know as my addiction; what happens from this point forward most likely I won't have much, if any, control over.

Fast-forward six days. I'm homeless again. Another record for me—six days, and I'm kicked out of the sober-living house I was in. It's a shame that I know how this story plays out. I imagine I'll float from place to place, getting high, caring less and less about my life every day. And that is just what I did. Every night I would tell myself that I'd save something for the morning, so I wouldn't have to figure out how I'd get high the next day while I was already sick; that shit sucks. But I'm an addict through and through. Every day I spend as much money as I can possibly come up with on heroin, and then I do it all within that day. It doesn't matter how many people I'm using with or around; I feel alone. I feel guilty that I put everything in front of the people I care about and who care about me. I feel lost; I have no direction whatsoever.

I love drugs. I hate drugs.

It's weird that I have trust issues, yet I trust these drug dealers I don't know at all every day. I'm so ashamed of myself. Once again I can't look anyone in the eyes when I speak to them, especially my parents or myself. Each day I spiral lower and lower into depression. This depression only started once I started *abusing opiates. I was never depressed when I was younger. This depression builds with the thought that I am not good enough. I'm dumb. I'm ugly. I'm not funny. I'm not cool. I wear a mask so that nobody sees the real person I am. I'm so used to being a scumbag that I'm afraid to let people in and show them the real person I am, who is loving and caring. Failure is all I know; it's all I've done for years. I failed my parents, failed the rehabs I've gone to and the clinicians who have tried to help, failed my psychologist, failed my cousins who once looked up to me, failed myself. I don't know how to succeed anymore. I haven't been successful in anything in a few years. Failure is just easier; hope is lost most of the time.*

Surprisingly, in the midst of all this (robbing, manipulating, scamming, and dope-fiending to the max), something clicks. I keep using rehab as a crutch, and I've always known I can fail because I can just go to rehab. It's been a long time since I've wanted to learn and participate at rehab. This time it feels different. I've said that many times, but I think after being in so many facilities and jail, being homeless, being desperate and not caring about life and being accepting of death, a person should know when something clicks, and I really know what I want— to get and stay clean.

This time I feel that way. I think I'm finally ready, no longer scared to succeed. I owe it to myself, to my family, and to my friends that I've fucked over. I deserve a good life, and I intend on having that.

Matt Laverty
December 22, 2011

CHAPTER ONE HUNDRED THIRTY-ONE

Matt didn't share much at any of the family groups this time. Was that a good or bad sign? He used to talk a lot at other meetings, but as he had said, maybe he just gone through the motions before, and this time he was silent, pensive, and listening. I hoped so. He read yet another letter of apology to us after he had been there about four weeks. No, he said, he knew apologies didn't mean much, coming from him anymore, so it wasn't exactly an apology letter, but he wanted to tell us all the things that he is now aware of and what he had done to himself, to us, and to our whole family.

January 4, 2012
Dear Mom and Dad,

Over the past few years, I caused many problems for myself, for the two of you, and for pretty much anyone who has crossed my path. I have made a mess of my life and given you many sleepless nights and heartache. I have put strain between the two of you, because I know at times it is difficult for each of you to know whether to feel sorry for me, to be angry at me, to side with me, and so on. I have caused much confusion in all of our lives, because I battle with things every day that don't make much sense to anyone. I wish something I could say would put your mind at ease, the same peace of mind I feel for the first time in probably a decade. I know that is unrealistic, though. I know I need to show you with my actions, time, and love that this time means so much more than any other time.

My life has quite literally flashed before my eyes over the past few months, and the lows I've had and the desperation I've felt have done something that I can't really put into words. It feels good to no longer fantasize about the good times and more so reflect on all the negative aspects of my active addiction and the pain it has caused for you both and myself.

I hold myself accountable for the external things I have done, such as stealing your credit cards and checks, taking your car in the middle of the night, and countless other things of that nature. I know these things are a big deal, and I don't mean to minimize them at all, but the internal pain I know you both have felt is what I hold myself most accountable for. There were times when I robbed you of your happiness, made you feel helpless and hopeless, and made you wish this were all just a bad dream.

No mother or father should have to hear their son say he isn't ready to get help because he hasn't gotten high enough yet. I'm sure every phone call we had or time we spoke, you wondered if it would be the last time you ever heard from your son. You two know this disease far too well and unfortunately know the terrible outcome it can have as well as the effect it can have on the family, due to the losses of friends' children. You also know the amount of friends and acquaintances I've lost as a direct result of this disease, and family members as well.

I hold myself accountable for all the things that have occurred in the past, but, most important, I hold myself accountable for what happens from this point forward. I know I have another chance, and I know you have another chance to recover from all the pain you've felt as well. I'm so much more motivated than I have ever been before, and I intend on showing that to you by doing the next right thing moving forward. You truly are amazing parents for sticking by my side through thick and thin, and hopefully, from this point forward, I can become an amazing son you are proud of, whom you enjoy being around, and whom you know you can count on whenever the time comes that you need me for something, rather than me needing you for everything. I am truly grateful for all the love and support you have given me.

Love,
Matt

CHAPTER ONE HUNDRED THIRTY-TWO

Matt sailed through his first twenty-eight days at Bayview house, saying that it felt different this time, that *he* felt different this time, really listening to all that was said during his counseling sessions. Mike and/or I attended the group-counseling sessions on Monday nights, and on the nights when Mike went alone, he said that he and Matt had some nice conversations and that their relationship was improving. We took him out for an afternoon, for a preapproved outing, and we had a nice leisurely lunch with him and did some shopping. Mike and I were determined to stop the enabling him this time and go forward, me more than Mike. We still brought him quarters and cigarettes each time we went to see him but weren't doling out lots of money for his job hunts or other outings.

He had a trip to the emergency room shortly after he arrived for round six, repercussions from falling down our stairs over Thanksgiving weekend. He was taken by ambulance, but after his evaluation was finished, he was informed that our insurance wouldn't cover his return trip in an ambulance. The staff at Bayview House wondered whether we could give him a ride back. We said no, as we lived about two hours south of the hospital, and suggested they call a cab for him. Matt later apologized to us for the mix-up with the ambulance. He later had to see an orthopedist about his back, and someone from Bayview House did the round-trip transportation for that.

He had a somewhat spoiled attitude when he first got there. He said he needed a winter coat, so Mike picked one up that was on sale, but Matt didn't like it. Mike was really annoyed about that, and we talked to his counselor. We said that we were trying to stop the enabling, trying not to let him run the show. So on the day we went shopping with him, he said he needed a coat and new shoes. Again we were annoyed that he had the day planned, and we talked to his counselor again, who said he did need shoes and a coat but that she would talk to him about his attitude. Matt called and again apologized; he said he didn't mean to sound demanding or ungrateful. I was concerned that the four-hour visit would be very awkward, but it turned out fine. He had met a girl who had arrived at Bayview about two weeks after he did; he didn't say a lot about her but did seem interested in her.

He moved along to phase one, the first step toward some independence, and again sailed through. His peers and counselors alike were calling him the "mayor" of the house. He had earned points that allowed him the most privileges of anyone in the house. He was in phase one for about two weeks and then moved into phase two. Once in phase two, he was allowed to go out to meetings, with a sponsor or other preapproved contact, and could start looking for jobs. He also went to a few dentists' appointments during this time, as the dental work that had started before he went into this round of rehab hadn't been completed.

At the end of January 2012, Matt finally appeared in court, after having it postponed a few times. Both the prosecutor and the representative from probation were in favor of sending him to jail, and it seemed that the judge was leaning that way as well. However, he ultimately told Matt to return to court in one month, at which time Matt probably would be sentenced to drug court.

> *The mission of drug courts is to stop the abuse of alcohol and other drugs and related criminal activity. Drug courts are a highly specialized team process within the existing Superior Court structure that addresses nonviolent drug-related cases. They are unique in the criminal justice environment because they build a close collaborative relationship between criminal justice and drug treatment professionals.*
>
> *The drug court judge heads a team of court staff, attorneys, probation officers, substance abuse evaluators, and treatment professionals who work together to support and monitor a participant's recovery. They maintain a critical balance of authority, supervision, support, and encouragement.*
>
> *Drug court programs are rigorous, requiring intensive supervision based on frequent drug testing and court appearances, along with tightly structured regimens of treatment and recovery services. This level of supervision permits the program to support the recovery process, but also allows supervisors to react swiftly to impose appropriate therapeutic sanctions or to reinstate criminal proceedings when participants cannot comply with the program.*
>
> —State of New Jersey Department of Human Services, Division of Addiction Services

I hoped this would come to be. I believed it would be a good thing for Matt and for us. He would be kept on a short leash, and there would be no second chance. Any slip-up would send him to jail. Additionally the question of his living arrangements would be decided. Matt was annoyed with this decision, or rather with the lack of a permanent decision. There was another person in court that day who had his probation dropped, so Matt was hoping for that as well. However, another person was sentenced to another thirty days in jail. He didn't see that case. He moped the whole way back to Bayview House but later apologized to Mike at the next group-counseling session.

Matt said he was starting to feel stressed about all the various places he had to be: court, probation, IOP, work, doctor and dentist's appointments, etc., and all of this with no car. (Hint, hint?) He felt he would be eating up a lot of his time just by riding the bus. That was something else he would have to work out on his own. We stayed out of it.

He found a new sponsor, Ian, and we heard Ian speak one night at a group-counseling session. I hoped he would prove to be a good fit for Matt. Ian gave him a ride to an Oxford House for an interview; he was accepted into the house and due to move in on Saturday, February 18.

However, the weekend of February 12, Matt and his new female friend Megan were caught flirting, which is against the rules. On Monday they were caught again and warned that it had to stop. Matt assured us that it would. On the morning of February 15, we received a call from Bayview House saying that Matt was being kicked out because of the continued relationship (Megan was kicked out as well). His belongings were packed up for him, and he was given a list of homeless shelters, soup kitchens, and other nearby inpatient and outpatient rehab facilities, and was told he could not return to Bayview House for treatment ever again.

How stupid he was! To have come so far and realize that he felt differently this time and wanted to make a new start with a clean life, and then to get kicked out for breaking a relatively simple rule, just three days before he was supposed to move into Oxford House! Once again my reaction was astonishment—but not sadness or anger. I was actually quite calm throughout the following few days. Mike and I kept our distance from him, letting him call us. And he did check in but never asked us for anything. He stayed with sober friends until he moved into Oxford House, made calls to set up outpatient counseling at a new place, went to meetings, and went to the library to look for jobs.

What would this mean when he went to court on March 2? We had been hoping for the sentence of drug court, but if the judge saw that he couldn't follow even the simplest of rules, would he decide jail would be better for him? If so, maybe it wouldn't be such a bad thing.

CHAPTER ONE HUNDRED THIRTY-THREE

Matt went to court on March 2 for his probation violations. The judge threw him in jail and told him he would meet with him again in a week. *As it should be*, I thought. Matt had been ill-prepared for court, although he knew what he had to show the judge—proof of where he had been living and what he had been doing during the month since his last court appearance. He had a hastily thrown-together letter attesting to the fact that he was living in an Oxford House (although not on official letterhead) but nothing from the rehab facility that gave the dates of his latest admission and discharge, nothing to show that he was receiving outpatient counseling and where, nothing from his probation officer (whose voice mail stated that he was out of town and not to leave a message)—nothing but Matt's own words. And why should the judge believe him? As the judge said, Matt had been in that court too many times already.

Meanwhile Mike and I were able to gather all of this information in about an hour. Yes, some asked why we were doing this instead of Matt, and I replied, "Because he's in jail." It was a vicious cycle. He should have been doing all of this on his own, instead of our enabling him, but he was in jail, so he couldn't, and he couldn't get out of jail without this proof.

So while he sat in a jail cell, with one hour a day free to come out of that cell, we sat at home. We went back and forth about whether to set up the prepaid collect calls for him. Ultimately I did set it up, although he made his first call before I had done so. During his daily one hour out of his cell, I supposed he would call again and every day until he went to court again. He asked me to get in touch with Megan and walk her through the process of setting up the prepaid phone card. I was happy to do that, although that was actually the first time I had even spoken to Megan, so it was a little awkward. Bail wasn't an option, so our hands were tied. The last time he was in jail, he was going through withdrawal. This time he would be able to see what jail was like with a clear head and clear eyes. Maybe he would think about all the job applications he said he had filled out this week and would realize that some may be calling him back, but he wouldn't get the call and therefore might miss out on a job offer. Would this be the wakeup call he'd needed for so long?

CHAPTER ONE HUNDRED THIRTY-FOUR

Matt was declared a free man again on March 11, 2012, although the Middlesex County probation officer and the prosecutor both thought he should stay in jail. His probation officer from Cape May County felt the same way, telling me that Matt clearly could not stay away from drugs unless he was incarcerated. Oxford House had held his place for him, so he had a place to live.

He was told to return to court on May 11, 2012, and had several things to do first. He needed to see his probation officer in Cape May County for one last visit (and probably a lecture) and to have his case transferred to the Monmouth County probation department.

Part of me thought he should have stayed in jail for a while longer. He was in the holding area (for new inmates) the entire time, except the last night, when he was in with the general population. I didn't think he had much time to experience the "real" jail, but I hoped it had taught him enough of a lesson to be motivated to get a job and stay clean.

I prayed that would happen. Every day I prayed to God to watch over Matt, to help him stay away from and fight the temptations of drugs, to walk with Matt, to hold his hand, to carry him when necessary. But I knew Matt had to be the one to ask God for help. I hoped he was doing that, but if he wasn't, I hoped God would hear my prayers and help him, for my sake as well as for Matt's.

Matt celebrated his ninety-day clean mark while in jail. He told Mike that was the longest he had been clean since he had started using. That was disturbing to me. It meant that, for every relapse, he was using for a couple of months before we had found out or before he had admitted it.

There had been so much wasted time—time when he could have been getting help—and so much time had passed when we freely had given him money, thinking he was clean and that $20 here or there really had been for gas, food, or bus tickets.

He found a job fairly quickly after getting out of jail, at a restaurant in Red Bank. He seemed to have things under control, finding the appropriate clothes he needed, managing his time and various schedules, paying his rent on time—sometimes even early—buying his own groceries, and getting to IOP and probation.

CHAPTER ONE HUNDRED THIRTY-FIVE

In April 2012 Matt had to have a clinical assessment before his sentencing to drug court. They did a drug test, of course, and he tested positive for pot—twice! He was very upset and didn't know what to do. He swore he hadn't used anything except Tylenol, for a toothache. He finally went to IOP, where they did another test, which was negative. We didn't know what had happened. Were the first tests old ones that would produce false positives if Tylenol was in his system? Matt was, of course, quite relieved, although he was still in pain and was continuing to have dental work.

He was working a lot of hours and apparently making good money. He hadn't asked us for any money at all and had used his own money for groceries, rent, haircuts, cigarettes, etc. He knew that once he was in drug court, he would have very little free time, so he did go to a concert or two, but he paid his own way and figured out how to get to and from the concert.

His girlfriend, Megan, gave him a Claddagh ring, for no particular reason, maybe their "four-month anniversary." It seemed to mean a lot to him. They spent most of their free time together, and Matt seemed very happy. I was looking forward to finally meeting her.

I really didn't talk to Matt much—just a text here and there. He was busy with work and meetings. One day I had a moment of panic when I texted him, and he didn't reply; I hoped he was busy working and not pulling a disappearing act again. I think I finally knew what the disappearing act meant, but I was thinking positively and assuming he was working.

And he was.

I wonder what his turning point finally was? Was it when he had stolen my credit card? Was it when he had asked me for money so he could get high one last time? Or maybe it wasn't anything that complicated or concrete. Maybe he was just finally tired of living that way.

At the end of April, he told me he was planning to give Mike $300 and ask him to pay off his bank account debt online. He had been in touch with the bank's collection agency, and they were pretty aggressive about wanting Matt to pay it off in full by April 30. He handed Mike $301, which pretty much cleaned Matt out. Mike took care of the debt for Matt and gave Matt a loan of $40, so he'd have some money for a train ticket. His paying off his debt on his own was a proud moment for me—for Matt too, I'm sure.

EPILOGUE

Matt opened both a checking and savings account at the beginning of May. I wondered why he thought he needed a checking account, since he'd had a checking account all through college and never had written a single check. He said he might need one, perhaps if he moved out of Oxford House and into an apartment, and once he started paying his own phone bill.

He celebrated his five-month clean mark on May 7, 2012. He talked about getting his suit ironed and cleaned before court and talked about looking into used computers so he could get back into mixing music. It really sounded like he was starting to take responsibility for his life.

Mike saw him on May 10, for his court appearance, and he brought Matt's tax refund for him. Between that and his tip money, he deposited another $1,000 into the bank. And without Mike asking, Matt handed Mike the $40 he had given Matt the previous week. He also had wanted to pay some of his probation fines prior to court but didn't have enough time after work the day before court.

Matt was sentenced to three years' probation, to be served in drug court. His attorney was surprised; he had thought it would be five years. Initially he would see the judge once a week in Middlesex County and go to probation once a week, also in Middlesex County— of course not on the same day. Eventually everything probably would be moved to Monmouth County, which would make things a little easier for Matt. He would be subjected to random drug tests as well. He could still leave Oxford House and get an apartment at some point if he wanted to, but he would have to keep all parties abreast of any address changes.

A few days before Mother's Day, I received a priority mail package from Matt—a box full of my favorite chocolate goodies from a chocolate shop in Red Bank. I believe it was the first time he ever had done anything like that without help, prompting, or money from Mike.

So is there a happy ending? I think there is, for today. One day at a time.

What comes next? Mike and I have been trying to make child-care arrangements so that we can start attending weekly Al-Anon meetings on a regular basis, something we should have done ages ago. I'm still scared, still untrusting, still worried I won't have the strength to turn my back on him if he uses again. I think I'll always be waiting for the next relapse.

I've learned more than I ever wanted to know about drug addiction.

I can't say what I would do differently—anything and everything. I'm actually quite embarrassed about my naïveté throughout this whole journey, how many times I said it wouldn't happen again, how many excuses I made for him.

My first thought is to say that, as I look back on his teen and preteen years, I would have not taken a full-time job, so I could've been home more to supervise his activities. Maybe I would've insisted that the project of refinishing the basement be completed by the time

Matt was twelve years old, so our house could have become the established hangout place. I would have made it a point to get together with family more and established traditions with them that Matt had to attend with us. And when he was arrested in November 2009, maybe we should have let him stay in jail for several months, until his court date, and then continued to practice tough love. Finally, once I started to chronicle this journey, I should have read back through it several times. Maybe I would have seen how blind we were, how transparent Matt's lies were, and the pattern of Matt's disappearing act in connection with his relapses.

Would any of that have made a difference? I can't say.

Mike and I were finally able to enforce the tough-love theory. I feel strongly that we can continue to do so.

So, for this moment, there is a happy ending. Is it a final ending? No. Matt will be an addict forever. Optimistically, he will stay in recovery forever. I know the odds, however, are against him.

But there is always hope. We never will give up hope. As long as we can find the means and the places, whether insurance pays or the government pays, we never will stop giving our son the option of recovery. As long as we have breath in us, and he has it in him, we never will give up on him, even though it sometimes seems that he has given up on himself and that we have more faith in him than he has in himself at times.

At the very least, we have to hope that a higher power will help him find faith in himself again. In doing that we hope and pray that he will once again be the sweet, caring, and loving Matt who used to be here.

Acronyms and Terms

AA: Alcoholics Anonymous
Al-Anon: support group for loved ones of alcoholics
CA: Cocaine Anonymous
NA: Narcotics Anonymous
NarAnon: support group for loved ones of addicts

Timeline

Round one, November 16–December 16, 2009: Matt was in Bayview House for his first inpatient stay.

Round two, May 1, 2010–August 3, 2010: Matt was in Bayview House for his second inpatient stay.

Round three, January 10, 2011–February 17, 2011: Matt started his third inpatient stay at Malvern Institute but was transferred to Stonebridge at the request of his probation officer.

Round four, May 9, 2011–June 7, 2011: Matt was in Stonebridge for his fourth inpatient stay.

Round five, September 25, 2011–October 12, 2011: Matt was at Timberwood for just eighteen days for his fifth inpatient stay.

Round six, December 6, 2011: Matt was at Bayview House for his sixth inpatient stay.

Made in the USA
Lexington, KY
02 December 2013